North Ayrshire Libraries

**This book is to be returned on or before
the last date stamped below.**

**MOST ITEMS CAN BE RENEWED BY TELEPHONE
OR ONLINE AT www.libraries.north-ayrshire.gov.uk**

Northwest Highlands of Scotland

Alan Murphy

Credits

Footprint credits
Editor: Nicola Gibbs
Production and layout: Emma Bryers
Maps: Kevin Feeney
Cover: Pepi Bluck

Publisher: Patrick Dawson
Managing Editor: Felicity Laughton
Advertising: Elizabeth Taylor
Sales and marketing: Kirsty Holmes

Photography credits
Front cover: Shutter1970/Dreamstime.com
Back cover: Merlindo/Shutterstock.com

Printed in Great Britain by CPI Antony Rowe, Chippenham, Wiltshire

Publishing information
Footprint *Focus Northwest Highlands of Scotland*
1st edition
© Footprint Handbooks Ltd
March 2013

ISBN: 978 1 909268 24 1
CIP DATA: A catalogue record for this book is available from the British Library

® Footprint Handbooks and the Footprint mark are a registered trademark of Footprint Handbooks Ltd

Published by Footprint
6 Riverside Court
Lower Bristol Road
Bath BA2 3DZ, UK
T +44 (0)1225 469141
F +44 (0)1225 469461
footprinttravelguides.com

Distributed in the USA by Globe Pequot Press, Guilford, Connecticut

The content of Footprint *Focus Northwest Highlands of Scotland* has been taken directly from Footprint's *Scotland Highlands & Islands Handbook* which was researched and written by Alan Murphy.

Every effort has been made to ensure that the facts in this guidebook are accurate. However, travellers should still obtain advice from consulates, airlines, etc, about travel and visa requirements before travelling. The authors and publishers cannot accept responsibility for any loss, injury or inconvenience however caused.

Contains Ordnance Survey data © Crown copyright and database right 2013

Contents

The Northwest Highlands is the part of Scotland that best reflects the romantic image of the country. Wild, rugged, and sparsely populated after the infamous 17th- to 18th-century Highland Clearances, this is the Scotland of mist-shrouded glens, towering mountain peaks, windswept purple heather hillsides, brooding lochs, ghostly ancient castles and quaint coastal ports.

Inverness is the 'Capital of the Highlands'. It lies at the northeastern end of the Great Glen, which cuts diagonally across the southern Highlands to Fort William like a surgical incision, linking deep and mysterious Loch Ness with the west coast and giving access to Lochaber, the self-proclaimed 'outdoor capital of the UK'. Still further south is Glencoe, another climber's paradise and one of the Highland's most evocative Highland glens. Inverness is also ideally situated for exploring the northeast coast, dotted with charming fishing ports and archaeological sites, while the storm-battered, remote northern coastline, running west from John o'Groats to Cape Wrath, attracts surfers and those probing the history of the Clearances.

The main town on the northwest coast is Fort William, which lies in the shadow of Britain's highest mountain, Ben Nevis. Northwest from here stretches a dramatic shoreline of deep sea lochs and sheltered coves of pure white sand backed by towering mountains and looking across to numerous Hebridean islands. West of Fort William, via the lyrical Road to the Isles, is work-a-day Mallaig, the main departure point for ferries to Skye and the Small Isles. Further north is Ullapool, a key ferry port for the Outer Hebrides and the ideal base from which to explore Assynt and the wild and near-deserted far northwest.

Planning your trip

Best time to visit the Northwest Highlands of Scotland

The Northwest Highlands suffers from notoriously unpredictable weather and that ever-present travelling companion, the midge. The midge is the scourge of many a Highland holiday: a ferocious, persistent and unbelievably irritating little beast that thrives in damp, humid conditions and will drive you to the edge of sanity. For details on how best to combat this little terror, see page 22.

The only predictable thing about the weather is its unpredictability. You can have blazing sunshine in April, pouring rain in July and a blizzard in May. So, you'll need to be prepared for everything. Climbers and walkers especially must take heed of all weather warnings. It can be hot enough for bikinis in the car park at the foot of a 2000-ft mountain, and two hours later near the summit you're faced with driving, horizontal hail, rain or snow and unable to see further than the end of your nose. People die every year on the Scottish mountains simply because they are ill-prepared; it is essential to take proper precautions, see page 24.

Getting to the Northwest Highlands of Scotland

Air

Generally speaking, the cheapest and quickest way to travel to Scotland from outside the UK is by air. There are good links to Edinburgh and Glasgow, with direct flights from many European cities, and direct flights from North America to Glasgow. There are also flights from a few European cities to Aberdeen and Inverness. There are no direct flights from North America to Edinburgh; these are usually routed via London or Dublin. There are also daily flights from Ireland and regular flights to most Scottish airports from other parts of the UK. There are no direct flights to Scotland from Australia, New Zealand, South Africa or Japan; you will have to get a connection from London.

From the UK and Ireland There are direct flights to Scotland's four main airports – Glasgow, Edinburgh, Aberdeen and Inverness – almost hourly from London Heathrow, Gatwick, Stansted and Luton airports. There are also daily flights from provincial UK airports and from Dublin. To fly on to the smaller airports, you'll need to change planes; see page 10 for domestic flights. The cheapest flights leave from London Luton or Stansted, plus a few provincial airports, with **Ryanair** and **easyJet**. If you book online, fares can be as little as £5 one-way during promotions (excluding taxes), but usually you can expect to fly for under £70 return if you can be flexible with dates and times. These tickets are often subject to rigid restrictions, but the savings can make the extra effort worthwhile. Cheaper tickets usually have to be bought at least a week in advance and apply to only a few midweek flights. They are also non-refundable, or only partly refundable, and non-transferable. A standard flexible and refundable fare from London to Glasgow or Edinburgh will cost at least £150-200 return. The flight from London to Glasgow and Edinburgh is roughly one hour.

There are flights to Inverness from London, Edinburgh and Glasgow, as well as from other regional UK airports. There are also flights from Edinburgh to Wick with **Flybe** franchise partner, **Loganair** (www.flybe.com or www.loganair.co.uk). For full details of all flights to Highlands and Islands airports from the rest of the UK, visit the **Highlands and Islands Airports Ltd** website, www.hial.co.uk.

From the rest of Europe There are direct flights to **Glasgow International** from many European capitals, including Copenhagen, Amsterdam, Paris (Beauvais), Dublin, Frankfurt, Stockholm, Brussels, Milan, Oslo and Barcelona. There are flights to **Edinburgh** from Paris (CDG), Zurich, Amsterdam, Brussels, Copenhagen and Frankfurt; direct flights to **Aberdeen** from Amsterdam, Copenhagen and Stavanger; and to **Inverness** from Amsterdam and Zurich.

From North America Because of the much larger number of flights to London, it is generally cheaper to fly there first and get an onward flight, see above for the best deals. For low season Apex fares, expect to pay around US$500-700 from New York and other East Coast cities, and around US$700-900 from the West Coast. Prices rise to around US$700-1000 from New York, and up to US$1000 from the West Coast in the summer months. Low season Apex fares from Toronto and Montreal cost around CAN$700-900, and from Vancouver around CAN$800-900, rising during the summer. East Coast USA to Glasgow takes around six to seven hours direct. To London it takes seven hours. From the West Coast it takes an additional four hours.

To Glasgow International Continental Airlines and KLM fly from New York, **Aer Lingus** and **KLM** fly from Chicago, and **Air Canada** from Toronto.

Airport information **Glasgow International** ① *8 miles west of the city, at junction 28 on the M8, T0844-481 5555*, handles domestic and international flights. Terminal facilities include car hire, bank ATMs, currency exchange, left luggage, tourist information (T0141-848 4440), and shops, restaurants and bars. For all public transport information T0871-200 2233. **Edinburgh Airport** ① *T0844-4812 8989 for general enquiries*, has all facilities, including a tourist information desk, currency exchange, ATMs, restaurants and bars (first floor), shops (ground floor and first floor) and car hire desks in the terminal in the main UK arrivals area. For details of facilities and amenties at all Highlands and Islands airports, visit www.hial.co.uk.

Rail
There are fast and frequent rail services from London and other main towns and cities in England to Glasgow, Edinburgh, Aberdeen and Inverness. Journey time from London is about 4½ hours to Edinburgh, five hours to Glasgow, seven hours to Aberdeen and eight hours to Inverness. Two companies operate direct services from London to Scotland: **National Express** trains leave from King's Cross and run up the east coast to Edinburgh,

Aberdeen and Inverness, and **Virgin** trains leave from Euston and run up the west coast to Glasgow. **ScotRail** operates the *Caledonian Sleeper* service if you wish to travel overnight from London Euston to Aberdeen, Edinburgh, Glasgow, Inverness and Fort William. This runs nightly from Sunday to Friday. Fare start from £59 per person. For more information, see www.scotrail.co.uk or the excellent www.seat61.com.

Eurostar ① *T08705-186186 (+44-123-361 7575), www.eurostar.com*, operates high-speed trains through the Channel Tunnel to London St Pancras International from Paris (2½ hours), Brussels (two hours) and Lille (1½ hours). You then have to change trains, and stations, for the onward journey north to Scotland. If you're driving from continental Europe you could take *Le Shuttle*, which runs 24 hours a day, 365 days a year, and takes you and your car from Calais to Folkestone in 35 to 45 minutes. Standard return fares on *Le Shuttle* range from £98 per car load. Depending on how far in advance you book, or when you travel, cheaper fares are available, call T08705-353535 for bookings.

Enquiries and booking National Rail Enquiries ① *T08457-484950, www.nationalrail.co.uk*, are quick and courteous with information on rail services and fares but not always accurate, so double check. They can't book tickets but will provide you with the relevant telephone number. The website www.qjump.co.uk is a bit hit-and-miss but generally fast and efficient, and shows you all the various options on any selected journey, while www.thetrainline.co.uk also has its idiosyncrasies but shows prices clearly. For advance card bookings, contact **National Express**, T08457-484950, www.nationalexpresseastcoast.com; **ScotRail**, T08457-550033, www.scotrail.co.uk; and **Virgin**, T08457-222333, www.virgintrains.co.uk.

Fares To describe the system of rail ticket pricing as complicated is a huge understatement and impossible to explain here. There are many and various discounted fares, but restrictions are often prohibitive, which explains the long queues and delays at ticket counters in railway stations. The cheapest ticket is an Advance ticket or Value Advance (**Virgin**), which must be booked in advance (obviously), though this is not available on all journeys. A **GNER** London–Edinburgh Advance Single costs between £14-100. Advance Singles with **ScotRail** on this route start from £39.50 for direct trains. All discount tickets should be booked as quickly as possible as they are often sold out weeks, or even months, in advance. A *Caledonian Sleeper* 'Bargain Berth' single ticket from London to Edinburgh or Glasgow costs from £19; to book visit www.travelpass.buytickets.scotrail.co.uk.

Railcards There are a variety of railcards which give discounts on fares for certain groups. Cards are valid for one year and most are available from main stations. You need two passport photos and proof of age or status.

Young Person's Railcard ① *www.16-25railcard.co.uk*. For those aged 16-25 or full-time students aged 26+ in the UK. Costs £26 for one year and gives 33% discount on most train tickets and some other services.

Senior Citizen's Railcard ① *www.senior-railcard.co.uk*. For those aged over 60. Same price and discounts as above.

Disabled Person's Railcard ① *Disabled Person's Railcard Office, PO Box 163, Newcastle-upon-Tyne, NE12 8WX, www.disabledpersons-railcard.co.uk*. Costs £18 and gives 33% discount to a disabled person and one other. Pick up an application form from stations. It may take up to 21 days to process, so apply in advance.

Family Railcard: Costs £26 and gives 33% discount on most tickets for up to four adults travelling together, and 60% discount for up to four children.

Road

Bus/coach Road links to Scotland are excellent, and a number of companies offer express coach services day and night. This is the cheapest form of travel to Scotland. The main operator between England and Scotland is **National Express** ① *T08717-818178, www. nationalexpress.com*. There are direct buses from most British cities to Edinburgh, Glasgow, Aberdeen and Inverness. Tickets can be bought at bus stations or from a huge number of agents throughout the country. Fares from London to Glasgow and Edinburgh with **National Express** start at around £25 return for a Funfare return (online discount fare). Fares to Aberdeen and Inverness are a little higher. The London to Glasgow/Edinburgh journey takes around eight hours, while it takes around 11 to 12 hours for the trip to Aberdeen and Inverness. From Manchester to Glasgow takes around 6½ hours.

Car Inverness is linked to the south by the notorious A9 from Edinburgh and Perth, to Aberdeen by the A96 and to Fort William by the A82. There are two main routes to Scotland from the south. In the east the A1 runs to Edinburgh and in the west the M6 and A74(M) runs to Glasgow. The journey north from London to either city takes around eight to 10 hours. The A74(M) route to Glasgow is dual carriageway all the way. A slower and more scenic route is to head off the A1 and take the A68 through the Borders to Edinburgh. There's an Autoshuttle Express service to transport your car overnight between England and Scotland and vice versa while you travel by rail or air. For further information and reservations, T08705-502309. See also page 11.

Sea P&O Irish Sea ① *T0871-664 2020, www.poferries.com*, has several crossings daily from Larne to Cairnryan (one hour), and from Larne to Troon (two hours). Fares are from £79 each way for for car and driver. **Stena Line** ① *T0870-570 7070, www.stenaline.co.uk*, runs numerous ferries (three hours) and high-speed catamarans (1½ hours) from Belfast to Stranraer, fares from £79 single for car and driver.

Transport in the Northwest Highlands of Scotland

Exploring the Highlands of Scotland is undeniably easier if you have your own transport, though the main tourist centres, including Ullapool and Wick, are easily accessed by bus or train. Getting off the beaten track requires patience but is worthwhile and easily achieved with a little forward planning. Some of the time you'll need to rely on the, sadly, ever-reducing **local postbus service** ① *T08457-740740, www.royalmail.com/postbus*, which travels countless single-track roads to deliver post to villages and hamlets scattered across the Highlands. Ask local tourist offices and post offices for timetables. Excellent online sources of travel information, including timetables and operators, are www. travelinescotland.com, and www.rapsons.co.uk. Tourist offices throughout the Highlands also carry leaflets on their local and regional transport network.

By far the most scenic route to the Highlands is the spectacular **West Highland Railway**, one of the world's great rail journeys, particularly the section from Fort William to Mallaig (see box, page 72).

Public transport can also be expensive, though there's a whole raft of discount passes and tickets which can save you a lot of money. Hiring a car can work out as a more economical, and certainly more flexible, option, especially for more than two people travelling together. It will also enable you to get off the beaten track and see more of the country. Even if you're driving, however, getting around the remote Highlands and Islands can be a time-consuming business as much of the region is accessed only by a sparse network of tortuous, twisting single-track roads. Be sure to refuel regularly, allow plenty of time for getting around and book ferries in advance during the busy summer season.

Air

As well as the main airports of Glasgow, Edinburgh, Aberdeen and Inverness, there are also several small local airports. Internal flights are relatively expensive, however, and not really necessary in such a small country, unless you are short of time. There are discounted tickets available, which must be booked at least 14 days in advance, and special offers on some services. There is no departure tax on flights from Highlands and Islands airports.

The majority of flights are operated by **Flybe/Loganair** ① *T0871-700 2000, www.flybe.com, www.loganair.co.uk*. For inter-island flights in Orkney, you should book direct through **Loganair**, T01856-873457. For information on flight schedules, call the airports listed on page 7, or **British Airways**. The British Airports Authority (BAA) publishes a free *Scheduled Flight Guide*.

Rail

The rail network in Scotland is limited and train travel is comparatively expensive, but trains are a fast and effective way to get around and also provide some beautifully scenic journeys. The West Highland line to Fort William and Mallaig and the journey from Inverness to Kyle of Lochalsh are amongst the most beautiful rail journeys in the world and well worth doing. Services between Glasgow, Edinburgh, Stirling, Perth, Dundee and Aberdeen are fast and frequent, and there are frequent trains to and from Inverness.

ScotRail operates most train services within Scotland. You can buy train tickets at the stations, from major travel agents, or over the phone with a credit or debit card. For information and advance credit or debit card bookings visit www.scotrail.co.uk. Details of services are given throughout the guide. For busy long-distance routes it's best to reserve a seat. Seat reservations to Edinburgh, Glasgow, Aberdeen or Inverness are included in the price of the ticket when you book in advance. If the ticket office is closed, there's usually a machine on the platform. If this isn't working, you can buy a ticket on the train. Cyclists should note that though train companies have a more relaxed attitude to taking bikes on trains, reservations at a small fee for bikes are still required on some services. Cycles are carried free of charge on **ScotRail** services, although reservations are required on longer distance routes.

Eurorail passes are not recognized in Britain, but **ScotRail** offers a couple of worthwhile travel passes. The most flexible is the **Freedom of Scotland Travelpass**, which gives unlimited rail travel within Scotland. It is also valid on all **CalMac** ferries on the west coast, many **Citylink** bus services in the Highlands, some regional buses and offers discounts on some city centre bus tours. The **Highland Rover** and **Central Scotland Rover** tickets are more limited. The Highland Rover allows unlimited rail travel in the Highlands region, plus the West Highland line from Glasgow, and travel between Aberdeen and Aviemore. It also allows free travel on **Citylink** buses between Oban, Fort William and Inverness. Ferry travel between Oban–Mull and Mallaig–Skye is also included on this ticket. The Central Scotland Rover allows unlimited travel in the central belt of Scotland from the East Coast, Edinburgh, Stirling and Fife to Glasgow, and also covers unlimited travel on the Glasgow Underground network.

Road

Bus and coach Travelling around Scotland by bus takes longer than the train but is much cheaper. There are numerous local bus companies, but the main operator is **Scottish Citylink** ① *T08705-505050, www.citylink.co.uk*. Bus services between towns and cities are good, but far less frequent in more remote rural areas. To identify bus times and the myriad of operators in the Highlands it's worthwhile visiting www.rapsons.co.uk, and downloading the relevant timetable. Note that long-distance express buses are called coaches. There are a number of discount and flexible tickets available and details of these are given on the **Citylink** website, which is fast and easy to use.

Available to overseas passport holders, the **Brit Xplorer Pass** offers unlimited travel on all **National Express** buses. They can be bought from major airports and bus terminals. **Scottish Citylink** runs a daily bus service between Scotland's six cities and strategic ports including Oban, Uig (Skye) and Ullapool. It offers a diverse range of discount and saver cards including an Explorer Pass that offers unlimited travel on its routes for a specified number of days.

Many parts of the Highlands can only be reached by Royal Mail **postbuses**. Admittedly, in recent years many routes have disappeared to be replaced by Dial-a-Bus services, such as in Gairloch. These operate on demand and don't follow a fixed timetable, see www.highland.gov.uk or www.royalmail.com/postbus. However, in places you can still find the friendly, red postbus. These are minibuses that follow postal delivery routes and carry up to 14 fare-paying passengers. They set off early in the morning from the main post office and follow a circuitous route as they deliver and collect mail in the most far-flung places. They are often very slow on the outward morning routes but quicker on the return routes in the afternoons. It can be a slow method of getting around, but you get to see some of the country's most spectacular scenery, and it is useful for walkers and those trying to reach remote hostels or B&Bs. There's a restricted service on Saturdays and none on Sundays.

Car and campervan Travelling with your own private transport is the ideal way to explore the country, particularly the Highlands. This allows you to cover a lot of ground in a short space of time and to reach remote places. The main disadvantages are rising fuel costs (around £1.50 per litre for diesel), traffic congestion and parking, but the latter two are only a problem in the main cities and on the motorways in the Central Belt. Roads in the Highlands and Islands are a lot less busy than those in England, and driving is relatively stress-free, especially on the B-roads and minor roads. In more remote parts of the country, on the islands in particular, many roads are single track, with passing places indicated by a diamond-shaped signpost. These should also be used to allow traffic behind you to overtake. Remember that you may want to take your time to enjoy the stupendous views all around you, but the driver behind may be a local doctor in a hurry. Don't park in passing places. A major driving hazard on single track roads are the huge number of sheep wandering around, blissfully unaware of your presence. When confronted by a flock of sheep, slow down and gently edge your way past. Be particularly careful at night, as many of them sleep by the side of the road (counting cars perhaps). Also keep a sharp lookout for deer, particularly at night.

To drive in Scotland you must have a current **driving licence**. Foreign nationals also need an international **driving permit**, available from state and national motoring organizations for a small fee. Those importing their own vehicle should also have their vehicle registration or ownership document. Make sure you're adequately **insured**. In all of the UK you drive on the left. **Speed limits** are 30 miles per hour (mph) in built-up areas, 70 mph on motorways and dual carriageways, and 60 mph on most other roads.

It's advisable to join one of the main UK motoring organizations during your visit for their 24-hour breakdown assistance. The two main ones in Britain are the **Automobile Association (AA)** ① *T0800-085 2721, www.theaa.com*, and the **Royal Automobile Club (RAC)** ① *T08705-722722, www.rac.co.uk*. One year's membership of the AA starts at £30 and £28 for the RAC. They also provide many other services, including a reciprocal agreement for free assistance with many overseas motoring organizations. Check to see if your organization is included. Both companies can also extend their cover to include Europe. Their emergency numbers are: **AA**, T0800-887766; **RAC**, T0800-828282. You can call these numbers even if you're not a member, but you'll have to a pay a large fee. In remote areas you may have to wait a long time for assistance. Also note that in the Highlands and Islands you may be stranded for ages waiting for spare parts to arrive.

Car hire need not be expensive in Scotland if you shop around for the best deals. **AVIS** offers weekend rates from around £45 and £126 for the week, though whichever operator you choose be wary of high charges for additional mileage. Even without deals you should be able to hire a small car for a week from £150. Local hire companies often offer better deals than the larger multi-nationals, though **easyCar** can offer the best rates, at around £10 per day, if you book in advance and don't push up the charges with high mileage. They are based at Aberdeen, Glasgow, Edinburgh and Inverness airport. Many companies such as **Europcar** offer the flexibility of picking up in Glasgow and leaving in Edinburgh, and vice versa. Most companies prefer payment with a credit card, otherwise you'll have to leave a large deposit (£100 or more). You'll need a full driver's licence (one or two years) and be aged over 21 (23 in some cases).

Alternatively, why not hire your own transport and accommodation at the same time by renting a campervan. Campervans can be rented from a number of companies and it's best to arrange this before arriving as everything gets booked up in the high season (June-August). Inverness based **Highland Camper Vans** is a good bet with its two-berth 'Adventure Van' starting at around £385 per week and £75 per day, or £525 per week for its four-person touring van.

Hitching As in the rest of the UK, hitching is never entirely safe, and is certainly not advised for anyone travelling alone, particularly women travellers. Those prepared to take the risk should not find it too difficult to get a lift in the Highlands and Islands, where people are far more willing to stop for you. Bear in mind, though, that you will probably have to wait a while even to see a vehicle in some parts.

Where to stay in the Northwest Highlands of Scotland

Staying in the Highlands and Islands of Scotland can mean anything from being pampered to within an inch of your life in a baronial mansion to roughing it in a tiny island bothy with no electricity. If you have the money, then the sky is very much the limit in terms of sheer splendour and excess. We have listed many of the top class establishments in this book, with a bias towards those that offer that little bit extra in terms of character. Those spending less may have to forego the four-posters and Egyptian cotton sheets but there are still many good-value small hotels and guesthouses with that essential wow factor – especially when it comes to the views. At the bottom end of the scale, there are also some excellent hostels in some pretty special locations.

We have tried to give as broad a selection as possible to cater for all tastes and budgets but if you can't find what you're after, or if someone else has beaten you to the draw, then the tourist information centres (TICs) will help find accommodation for you. They can recommend a place within your particular budget and give you the number to phone up and book yourself, or will book a room for you. Some offices charge a small fee (usually £1) for booking a room, while others ask you to pay a deposit of 10% which is deducted from your first night's bill. Details of town and city TICs are given throughout the guide. There are also several websites that you can browse and book accommodation. Try www.visitscotland.com, www.scottishaccommodationindex.com, www.aboutscotland. com, www.scotland200.com and www.assc.co.uk.

Accommodation in Scotland will be your greatest expense, particularly if you are travelling on your own. Single rooms are in short supply and many places are reluctant to let a double room to one person, even when they're not busy. Single rooms are usually more than the cost per person for a double room and in some cases cost the same as two people sharing a double room.

Hotels, guesthouses and B&Bs

Area tourist boards publish accommodation lists that include campsites, hostels, self-catering accommodation and VisitScotland-approved hotels, guesthouses and bed and breakfasts (B&Bs). Places participating in the **VisitScotland** system will have a plaque displayed outside which shows their grading, determined by a number of stars ranging from one to five. These reflect the level of facilities, as well as the quality of hospitality and service. However, do not assume that a B&B, guesthouse or hotel is no good because it is not listed by the tourist board. They simply don't want to pay to be included in the system, and some of them may offer better value. If you'd like to stay in a Scottish castle as a paying guest of the owner, contact **Scotts Castle Holidays** ① *T01208-821341, www.scottscastles.com*.

Hotels At the top end of the scale there are some fabulously luxurious hotels, often in spectacular locations. Many of them are converted baronial mansions or castles, and offer a chance to enjoy a taste of aristocratic grandeur and style. At the lower end of the scale, there is often little to choose between cheaper hotels and guesthouses or B&Bs. The latter often offer higher standards of comfort and a more personal service, but many smaller hotels are really just guesthouses, and are often family-run and every bit as friendly. Note that some hotels, especially in town centres or in fishing ports, may also be rather noisy, as the bar can often be the social hub. Rooms in most mid-range to expensive hotels almost always have bathrooms en suite. Many upmarket hotels offer excellent room-only deals in the low season. An efficient last-minute hotel booking service is www.laterooms.com,

Price codes

Where to stay

££££ £160 and over   **£££** £90-160

££ £50-90   **£** under £50

Prices quoted are for a double room in high season.

Restaurants

£££ over £30   **££** £15-30   **£** under £15

Prices quoted are for a two-course meal excluding drink or service charge.

which specializes in weekend breaks. Also note that many hotels offer cheaper rates for online booking through agencies such as www.lastminute.com.

Guesthouses Guesthouses are often large, converted family homes with up to five or six rooms. They tend to be slightly more expensive than B&Bs, charging between £30 and £50 per person per night, and though they are often less personal, usually provide better facilities, such as en suite bathroom, colour TV in each room and private parking. In many instances they are more like small budget hotels. Many guesthouses offer evening meals, though this may have to be requested in advance.

Bed and breakfasts (B&Bs) B&Bs provide the cheapest private accommodation. At the bottom end of the scale you can get a bedroom in a private house, a shared bathroom and a huge cooked breakfast for around £20-25 per person per night. Small B&Bs may only have one or two rooms to let, so it's important to book in advance during the summer season and on the islands where accommodation options are more limited. More upmarket B&Bs have en suite bathrooms and TVs in each room and usually charge from £25-35 per person per night. In general, B&Bs are more hospitable, informal, friendlier and offer better value than hotels. Many B&B owners are also a great source of local knowledge and can even provide OS maps for local walks. B&Bs in the Outer Hebrides and other remote locations also offer dinner, bed and breakfast, which is useful as eating options are limited, especially on a Sunday.

Some places, especially in ferry ports, charge room-only rates, which are slightly cheaper and allow you to get up in time to catch an early morning ferry. However, this means that you miss out on a huge cooked breakfast. If you're travelling on a tight budget, you can eat as much as you can at breakfast time and save on lunch as you won't need to eat again until evening. This is particularly useful if you're heading into the hills, as you won't have to carry so much food. Many B&B owners will even make up a packed lunch for you at a small extra cost.

Hostels

For those travelling on a tight budget, there is a large network of hostels offering cheap accommodation. These are also popular centres for backpackers and provide a great opportunity for meeting fellow travellers. Hostels have kitchen facilities for self-catering, and some include a continental breakfast in the price or provide cheap breakfasts and evening meals. Advance booking is recommended at all times, particularly from May to September and on public holidays, and a credit card is often useful.

Scottish Youth Hostel Association (SYHA) The **Scottish Youth Hostel Association (SYHA)** ① *7 Glebe Cres, Stirling, T01786-891400, www.syha.org.uk*, is separate from the YHA in England and Wales. It has a network of over 60 hostels, which are often better and cheaper than those in other countries. They offer bunk-bed accommodation in single-sex dormitories or smaller rooms, kitchen and laundry facilities. The average cost is £10-20 per person per night. Though some rural hostels are still strict on discipline and impose a 2300 curfew, those in larger towns and cities tend to be more relaxed and doors are closed as late as 0200. Some larger hostels provide breakfasts for around £2.50 and three-course evening meals for £4-5. For all EU residents, adult membership costs £10, and can be obtained at the SYHA National Office, or at the first SYHA hostel you stay at. SYHA membership gives automatic membership of **Hostelling International (HI)**. The SYHA produces a handbook (free with membership) giving details of all their youth hostels, including transport links. This can be useful as some hostels are difficult to get to without your own transport. You should always phone ahead, as many hostels are closed during the day and phone numbers are listed in this guide. Many hostels are closed during the winter, details are given in the SYHA Handbook. Youth hostel members are entitled to various discounts, including 20% off Edinburgh bus tours, 20% off Scottish Citylink tickets and 33% off the Orkney Bus (Inverness–Kirkwall).

Independent hostels Details of most independent hostels (or 'bunkhouses') can be found in the annual Independent Hostel Guide, www.independenthostelguide.com. The **Independent Backpackers Hostels of Scotland** is an association of nearly 100 independent hostels/bunkhouses throughout Scotland. This association has a programme of inspection and lists members in their free '*Blue Guide*'. Independent hostels tend to be more laid-back, with fewer rules and no curfew, and no membership is required. They all have dormitories, hot showers and self-catering kitchens. Some include continental breakfast or provide cheap breakfasts. All these hostels are listed on their excellent website, www.hostel-scotland.co.uk.

Campsites and self-catering
Campsites There are hundreds of campsites around Scotland. They are mostly geared to caravans, and vary greatly in quality and level of facilities. The most expensive sites, which charge up to £15 to pitch a tent, are usually well-equipped. Sites are usually only open from April to October. If you plan to do a lot of camping, you should check out www.scottish camping.com, which is the most comprehensive service with over 500 sites, many with pictures and reviews from punters. North Americans planning on camping should invest in an international camping carnet, which is available from home motoring organizations, or from **Family Campers and RVers (FCRV)** ① *4804 Transit Rd, Building 2, Depew, NY 14043, T1-800-245 9755, www.fcrv.org*. It gives you discounts at member sites.

Self-catering One of the most cost-effective ways to holiday in the Highlands and Islands is to hire a cottage with a group of friends. There are lots of different types of accommodation to choose from, to suit all budgets, ranging from luxury lodges, castles and lighthouses to basic bothies with no electricity. The minimum stay is usually one week in the summer peak season, though many offer shorter stays of two, three or four nights, especially outside the peak season. Expect to pay at least £200-400 per week for a two-bedroom cottage in the winter, rising to £400-1000 in the high season, or more if it's a particularly nice place. A good source of self-catering accommodation is the VisitScotland's guide, which lists over 1200 properties and is available to buy from any tourist office, but

Pitch a tent on the wild side

The Land Reform (Scotland) Act 2003, which together with the Scottish Access Code came into effect in February 2005, ensures Scotland offers walkers, canoeists, cyclists and campers some of the most liberal land access laws in Europe. Technically it means you have the 'right to roam' almost anywhere, although the emphasis is on 'responsible access' (see www.outdooraccess-scotland.com).

there are also dozens of excellent websites to browse. Amongst the best websites are the following: www.cottages-and-castles.co.uk; www.scottish-country-cottages.co.uk; www.cottages4you.co.uk; www.rural retreats.co.uk; and www.assc.co.uk. If you want to tickle a trout or feed a pet lamb check out www.farmstay.co.uk, which offers over a thousand good value rural places to stay around the UK, all clearly listed on a clickable map.

The **National Trust for Scotland** ① *28 Charlotte Sq, Edinburgh, T0844-493 2100, www.nts.org.uk*, owns many historic properties which are available for self-catering holidays, sleeping between two and 15 people. Prices start at around £300 per week in high season rising to £1000 for the top of the range lodges.

Food and drink in the Northwest Highlands of Scotland

While Scotland's national drink is loved the world over, Scottish cooking hasn't exactly had good press over the years. This is perhaps not too surprising, as the national dish, haggis, consists of a stomach stuffed with diced innards and served with mashed tatties (potatoes) and *neeps* (turnips). Not a great start. And things got even worse when the Scots discovered the notorious deep-fried Mars bar.

However, Scottish cuisine has undergone a dramatic transformation in the last decade and Scotland now boasts some of the most talented chefs, creating some of the best food in Britain. The heart of Scottish cooking is local produce, which includes the finest fish, shellfish, game, lamb, beef and vegetables, and a vast selection of traditionally made cheeses. What makes Scottish cooking so special is ready access to these foods. What could be better than enjoying an aperitif whilst watching your dinner being delivered by a local fisherman, knowing that an hour later you'll be enjoying the most delicious seafood?

Modern Scottish cuisine is now a feature of many of the top restaurants in the country. This generally means the use of local ingredients with foreign-influenced culinary styles, in particular French. International cuisine is also now a major feature on menus all over the country, influenced by the rise of Indian and Chinese restaurants in recent decades. In fact, so prevalent are exotic Asian and Oriental flavours that curry has now replaced fish and chips (fish supper) as the nation's favourite food.

Food

Fish, meat and game form the base of many of the country's finest dishes. Scottish beef, particularly Aberdeen Angus, is the most famous in the world. This will, or should, usually be hung for at least four weeks and sliced thick. Game is also a regular feature of Scottish menus, though it can be expensive, especially venison (deer), but delicious and low in cholesterol. Pheasant and hare are also tasty, but grouse is, quite frankly, overrated.

Fish and seafood are fresh and plentiful, and if you're travelling around the northwest coast you must not miss the chance to savour local mussels, prawns, oysters, scallops, langoustines, lobster or crab. Salmon is, of course, the most famous of Scottish fish, but you're more likely to be served the fish-farmed variety than 'wild' salmon, which has a more delicate flavour. Trout is also farmed extensively, but the standard of both remains high. Kippers are also a favourite delicacy, the best of which come from Loch Fyne or the Achiltibuie smokery, see page 116. Proper fish and chips in Scotland are made with haddock; cod is for Sassenachs (the English) and cats.

Haggis has made something of a comeback, and small portions are often served as starters in fashionable restaurants. Haggis is traditionally eaten on Burns Night (25 January) in celebration of the great poet's birthday, when it is piped to the table and then slashed open with a sword at the end of a recital of Robert Burns' *Address to the Haggis*. Other national favourites feature names to relish: **cock-a-leekie** is a soup made from chicken, leeks and prunes; **cullen skink** is a delicious concoction of smoked haddock and potatoes; while at the other end of the scale of appeal is **hugga-muggie**, a Shetland dish using fish's stomach. There's also the delightfully named **crappit heids** (haddock heads stuffed with lobster) and **partan bree** (a soup made form giant crab's claws, cooked with rice). Rather more mundane is the ubiquitous **Scotch broth**, made with mutton stock, vegetables, barley, lentils and split peas, and **stovies**, which is a hearty mash of potato, onion and minced beef.

Waist-expanding puddings or desserts are a very important part of Scottish cooking and often smothered in butterscotch sauce or syrup. There is a huge variety, including **cranachan**, a mouth-watering mix of toasted oatmeal steeped in whisky, cream and fresh raspberries, and **Atholl brose**, a similar confection of oatmeal, whisky and cream.

Eaten before pudding, in the French style, or afterwards, are Scotland's many home-produced cheeses, which have made a successful comeback in the face of mass-produced varieties. Many of the finest cheeses are produced on the islands, especially Arran, Mull, Islay and Orkney. **Caboc** is a creamy soft cheese rolled in oatmeal and is made in the Highlands.

Anyone staying at a hotel, guesthouse or B&B will experience the hearty **Scottish breakfast**, which includes bacon, egg, sausage, 'tattie scone' and black pudding (a type of sausage made with blood), all washed down with copious quantities of tea. Coffee is readily available everywhere, with most places now offering a selection of cappuccinos and café lattes. You may also be served kippers (smoked herring) or porridge, an erstwhile Scottish staple. Made with oatmeal and with the consistency of Italian polenta, it is traditionally eaten with salt, though heretics are offered sugar instead. Oatcakes (oatmeal biscuits) may also be on offer, as well as potato scones, baps (bread rolls) or bannocks (a sort of large oatcake). After such a huge cooked breakfast you probably won't feel like eating again until dinner.

Drink
Beer Beer is the alcoholic drink of choice in Scotland. The most popular type of beer is lager, which is generally brewed in the UK, even when it bears the name of an overseas brand, and is almost always weaker in both strength and character than the lagers in mainland Europe. However, examples of the older and usually darker type of beers, known as ales, are still widely available, and connoisseurs should try some of these as they are far more rewarding. Indeed, the best of them rival Scotland's whiskies as gourmet treats.

Traditionally, Scottish ales were graded by the shilling, an old unit of currency written as /-, according to strength. This system is still widely used by the older established breweries, though many of the newer independents and 'micros' have departed from it. 70/- beers at around 3.5% ABV (alcohol by volume), known as 'heavy', and 80/- beers

Turn water into whisky

Malt whisky is made by first soaking dry barley in tanks of local water for two to three days. Then the barley is spread out on a concrete floor or placed in cylindrical drums and allowed to germinate for between eight and 12 days, after which it is dried in a kiln, heated by a peat fire. Next, the dried malt is ground and mixed with hot water in a huge circular vat called a 'mash tun'. A sugary liquid called 'wort' is then drawn from the porridge-like result and piped into huge containers where living yeast is stirred into the mix in order to convert the sugar in the wort into alcohol. After about 48 hours the 'wash' is transferred to copper pot stills and heated till the alcohol vaporizes and is then condensed by a cooling plant into distilled alcohol which is passed through a second still. Once distilled, the liquid is poured into oak casks and left to age for a minimum of three years, though a good malt will stay casked for at least eight years.

(4.5% sometimes known as 'export'), are the most popular, while 60/-, 'light' (3-3.5%) is harder to find. Very strong 90/- beers (6.5% + ABV), known as 'wee heavies', are also brewed, mainly for bottling.

The market is dominated by the giant international brewers: Scottish Courage with its McEwans and Youngers brands; Interbrew with Calders and Carslberg; and Tetley with Tennents lagers. Tennents was the first British brewery to produce a continental-style lager commercially back in the 19th century, and, despite a competitive marketplace, remains a favourite for many Scots.

Much better are the ales from smaller independent breweries. Edinburgh's Caledonian is a world-class brewer producing many excellent beers, including a popular 80/- and a renowned golden hoppy ale, Deuchars IPA. Belhaven, an old, established family brewery in Dunbar, has some superb traditional beers including a malty 80/-, once marketed as the Burgundy of Scotland. Broughton, a microbrewery in the Borders, produces the fruity Greenmantle and an oatmeal stout. Another micro, Harvieston of Clackmannanshire (once an important brewing country) offers a wide and adventurous range of specialities, including Ptarmigan 80/- and a naturally brewed cask lager, Schiehallion. The Heather Ale Company, near Glasgow, has the spicy, unusual Fraoch (pronounced 'Frooch'), which is flavoured with real heather and hops.

Draught beer in pubs and bars is served in pints, or half pints, and you'll pay between £2.50 and £3.50 for a pint (unless you discover a 'Happy Hour' offering good deals on drinks, usually for much more than one hour! Happy hours usually apply in late afternoon or early evening). In many pubs the basic ales are chilled under gas pressure like lagers, but the best ales, such as those from the independents, are 'real ales', still fermenting in the cask and served cool but not chilled (around 12°C) under natural pressure from a handpump, electric pump or air pressure fount. All Scottish beers are traditionally served with a full, creamy head.

Whisky No visit to the Scottish Highlands would be complete without availing oneself of a 'wee dram'. There is no greater pleasure on an inclement evening than enjoying a malt whisky in front of a roaring log fire whilst watching the rain outside pelt down relentlessly. The roots of Scotland's national drink (*uisge beatha*, or 'water of life' in Gaelic) go back to the late 15th century, but it wasn't until the invention of a patent still in the early

19th century that distilling began to develop from small family-run operations to the large manufacturing business it has become today. Now more than 700 million bottles a year are exported, mainly to the United States, France, Japan and Spain.

There are two types of whisky: single malt, made only from malted barley; and grain, which is made from malted barley together with unmalted barley, maize or other cereals, and is faster and cheaper to produce. Most of the popular brands are blends of both types of whisky – usually 60-70% grain to 30-40% malt. These blended whiskies account for over 90% of all sales worldwide, and most of the production of single malts is used to add flavour to a blended whisky. Amongst the best-known brands of blended whisky are Johnnie Walker, Bells, Teachers and Famous Grouse. There's not much between them in terms of flavour and they are usually drunk with a mixer, such as water or soda.

Single malts are a different matter altogether. Each is distinctive and should be drunk neat to appreciate fully its subtle flavours, though some believe that the addition of water helps free the flavours. Single malts vary enormously. Their distinctive flavours and aromas are derived from the peat used for drying, the water used for mashing, the type of oak cask used and the location of the distillery. Single malts fall into four groups: Highland, Lowland, Campbeltown and Islay. There are over 40 distilleries to choose from, most offering guided tours. The majority are located around Speyside, in the northeast. The region's many distilleries include that perennial favourite, Glenfiddich, which is sold in 185 countries. Recommended alternatives are the produce of the beautiful and peaceful Isle of Islay, whose malts are lovingly described in terms of their peaty quality and the produce of the island known as 'Scotland in Miniature', Arran, whose 10-year-old malt, distilled in Lochranza, has won international acclaim. Scots tend to favour the 10-year-old Glenmorangie, while the most popular in the USA is The Macallan.

Eating out

There are places to suit every taste and budget. In the large towns and cities you'll find a vast selection of eating places, including Indian, Chinese, Italian and French restaurants, as well as Thai, Japanese, Mexican, Spanish and, of course, Scottish, but beyond the main cities, choice is much more limited. More and more restaurants are moving away from national culinary boundaries and offering a wide range of international dishes and flavours, so you'll often find Latin American, Oriental and Pacific Rim dishes all on the same menu. This is particularly the case in the many continental-style bistros, brasseries and café-bars, which now offer a more informal alternative to traditional restaurants. Vegetarians are increasingly well catered for, especially in the large cities, where exclusively vegetarian/vegan restaurants and cafés are often the cheapest places to eat. Outside the cities, vegetarian restaurants are thin on the ground, though better-quality eating places will normally offer a reasonable vegetarian selection.

For a cheap meal, your best bet is a pub, hotel bar or café, where you can have a one-course meal for around £5-7 or less, though don't expect gourmet food. The best value is often at lunchtime, when many restaurants offer three-course set lunches or business lunches for less than £10. You'll need a pretty huge appetite to feel like eating a three-course lunch after your gigantic cooked breakfast, however. Also good value are the pre-theatre dinners offered by many restaurants in the larger towns and cities (you don't need to have a theatre ticket to take advantage). These are usually available from around 1730-1800 until 1900-1930, so you could get away with just a sandwich for lunch. At the other end of the price scale are many excellent restaurants where you can enjoy the finest of Scottish cuisine, often with a continental influence, and these are often found in hotels.

You can expect to pay from around £30 a head up to £40 or £50 (excluding drinks) in the very top establishments.

The biggest problem with eating out in Scotland, as in the rest of the UK, is the ludicrously limited serving hours in some pubs and hotels, particularly in remoter locations. These places only serve food during restricted hours, seemingly ignorant of the eating habits of foreign visitors, or those who would prefer a bit more flexibility during their holiday. In small places especially, it can be difficult finding food outside these enforced times. Places that serve food all day till 2100 or later are restaurants, fast-food outlets and the many chic bistros and café-bars, which can be found not only in the main cities but increasingly in smaller towns. The latter often offer very good value and above-average quality fare.

Essentials A-Z

Accident and emergency

For police, fire brigade, ambulance and, in certain areas, mountain rescue or coastguard, T999 or T112.

Disabled travellers

For travellers with disabilities, visiting Scotland independently can be a difficult business. While most theatres, cinemas, libraries and modern tourist attractions are accessible to wheelchairs, tours of many historic buildings and finding accommodation remains problematic. Many large, new hotels do have disabled suites, but far too many B&Bs, guesthouses and smaller hotels remain ill-equipped to accept bookings from people with disabilities. However, through the work of organizations like **Disability Scotland** the Government is being pressed to further improve the Disability Discrimination Act and access to public amenities and transport. As a result, many buses and FirstScotRail's train services now accommodate wheelchair-users whilst city taxis should carry wheelchair ramps.

Wheelchair users, and blind or partially sighted people are automatically given 30-50% discount on train fares, and those with other disabilities are eligible for the Disabled Person's Railcard, which costs £18 per year and gives a third off most tickets. If you will need assistance at a railway station, call FirstScotRail before travelling on T0800-912 2901. There are no discounts on buses.

If you are disabled you should contact the travel officer of your national support organization. They can provide literature or put you in touch with travel agents specializing in tours for the disabled. **VisitScotland** produces a guide, *Accessible Scotland*, for disabled travellers, and many local tourist offices can provide accessibility details for their area. Alternatively call its national booking hotline on T0845-225 5121. A useful website is www.atlholidays. com, which specializes in organizing holidays for disabled travellers, recommends hotels with good facilities and can also arrange rental cars and taxis.

Useful organizations include:
Capability Scotland, ASCS, 11 Ellersly Rd, Edinburgh EH12 6HY, T0131-313 5510, or Textphone 0131-346 2529, www.capability-scotland.org.uk, **The Holiday Care Service**, T0845-124 9974, www.holidaycare.org.uk, www.tourismforall.org.uk. Both websites are excellent sources of information about travel and for identifying accessible accommodation in the UK. **The Royal Association for Disability and Rehabilitation** (RADAR), Unit 12, City Forum, 250 City Rd, London EC1V 8AF, T020-7250 3222, www.radar.org.uk. A good source of advice and information. It produces an annual *National Key Scheme Guide* for gaining access to over 6000 toilet facilities across the UK (£10.70 including P&P).

Electricity

The current in Britain is 240V AC. Plugs have 3 square pins and adapters are widely available.

Embassies and consulates

The **Foreign Office** website, www.fco. gov.uk, has a directory of all British embassies overseas.

Health

No vaccinations are required for entry into Britain. Citizens of EU countries are entitled to free medical treatment at National Health Service (NHS) hospitals on production of a European Health Insurance Card (EHIC). For details, see the Department of Health website, www.dh.gov.uk/travellers. Also, Australia, New Zealand and several other non-EU European countries have reciprocal healthcare arrangements with Britain.

Once bitten, twice shy

The major problem facing visitors to the Highlands and Islands of Scotland during the summer months is *Culicoides impunctatus* – or the midge, as it's more commonly known. These tiny flying creatures are savage and merciless in the extreme and hunt in huge packs. Indeed, it is estimated that midges cost the Scottish tourist industry some £286 million in lost revenue. No sooner have you left your B&B for a pleasant evening stroll, than a cloud of these bloodthirsty little devils will descend, getting into your eyes, ears, nose and mouth – and a few places you forgot you even had. The only way to avoid them is to take refuge indoors, or to hide in the nearest loch.

Midges are at their worst in the evening and in damp, shaded or overcast conditions, and between late May and September, but they don't like direct sunlight, heavy rain, smoke and wind. Make sure you're well covered up and wear light-coloured clothing (they're attracted to dark colours). Most effective is a midge net, if you don't mind everyone pointing and laughing at you. Insect repellents have some effect, particularly those with DEET, but those who don't fancy putting chemicals on their skin can try **Mozzy Off** ⓘ *www.mozzy off. com*, which comprises 100% plant oils, while the Thurso-made **Essential Spirit** ⓘ *www.essentialspirit.co.uk*, is also made from natural ingredients. A more radical approach is the Midegeater, a trap which emits carbon dioxide to lure the little blighters within range and then sucks them in at high speed. Those who see prevention as the best form of cure can log on to www.midgeforecast.co.uk, an online midge forecast service that gives five-day predictions of midge movements.

If you do get bitten, spare a thought for the gravedigger from Rùm. According to legend, as punishment for not burying a body properly he was stripped naked, tied to a post and left outside with only the midges for company. The poor chap eventually died of the countless bites.

Citizens of other countries will have to pay for all medical services, except accident and emergency care given at Accident and Emergency (A&E) Units at most (but not all) National Health Service hospitals. Health insurance is therefore strongly advised for citizens of non-EU countries.

Pharmacists can dispense only a limited range of drugs without a doctor's prescription. Most are open during normal shop hours, though some are open late, especially in larger towns. Local newspapers will carry lists of which are open late. Doctors' surgeries are usually open from around 0830-0900 till 1730-1800, though times vary. Outside surgery hours you can go to the casualty department of the local hospital for any complaint requiring urgent attention. For the address of the nearest hospital or doctors' surgery, www.nhs24.com. See also individual town and city directories throughout the book for details local medical services.

You should encounter no major problems or irritations during your visit to Scotland. The only exceptions are the risk of hyperthermia if you're walking in the mountains in difficult conditions, and the dreaded midge, see box, above.

Money → *US$1 = £0.65, €1 = £0.86 (Feb 2013).* The British currency is the pound sterling (£), divided into 100 pence (p). Coins come in denominations of 1p, 2p, 5p, 10p, 20p, 50p, £1 and £2. Bank of England banknotes are legal tender in Scotland, in addition to those issued by the Bank of Scotland, Royal Bank of Scotland and Clydesdale Bank. These Scottish banknotes (bills) come in denominations of £5, £10, £20, £50 and £100 and regardless of what you are told by shopkeepers in England the notes are legal tender in the rest of Britain.

Banks
The larger towns and villages have a branch of at least one of the big 4 high street banks – Bank of Scotland, Royal Bank of Scotland, Clydesdale and TSB Scotland. Bank opening hours are Mon-Fri from 0930 to between 1600 and 1700. Some larger branches may also be open later on Thu and on Sat mornings. In small and remote places, and on some islands, there may be only a mobile bank which runs to a set timetable. This timetable will be available from the local post office.

Banks are usually the best places to change money and cheques. You can withdraw cash from selected banks and ATMs (or cashpoints as they are called in Britain) with your cash and credit card. Though using a debit or credit card is by far the easiest way of keeping in funds, you must check with your bank what the total charges will be; this can be as high as 4-5% in some cases. In more remote parts, and especially on the islands, ATMs are few and far between and it is important to keep a ready supply of cash on you at all times and many guesthouses in the remoter reaches of Scotland will still request payment in cash. Outside the ferry ports on most of the smaller islands, you won't find an ATM. Your bank will give you a list of locations where you can use your card. Bank of Scotland and Royal Bank take Lloyds and Barclays cash cards; Clydesdale takes HSBC and National Westminster cards. Bank of Scotland, Clydesdale and most building society cashpoints are part of the Link network and accept all affiliated cards. See also Credit cards below. In addition to ATMs, bureaux de change can be used outside banking hours. These can be found in most city centres and also at the main airports and train stations. Note that some charge high commissions

for changing cheques. Those at international airports, however, often charge less than banks and will change pound sterling cheques for free. Avoid changing money or cheques in hotels, as the rates are usually very poor.

Credit cards
Most hotels, shops and restaurants accept the major credit cards such as MasterCard and Visa and, less frequently, Amex, though some places may charge for using them. They may be less useful in more remote rural areas and smaller establishments such as B&Bs, which will often only accept cash or cheques.

Visa card holders can use the Bank of Scotland, Clydesdale Bank, Royal Bank of Scotland and TSB ATMs; Access/MasterCard holders the Royal Bank and Clydesdale; Amex card holders the Bank of Scotland.

Traveller's cheques
The safest way to carry money is in traveller's cheques. These are available for a small commission from all major banks. American Express (Amex), Visa and Thomas Cook cheques are widely accepted and are the most commonly issued by banks. You'll normally have to pay commission again when you cash each cheque. This will usually be 1%, or a flat rate. No commission is payable on Amex cheques cashed at Amex offices, www.americanexpress.co/feefree. Make sure you keep a record of the cheque numbers and the cheques you've cashed separate from the cheques themselves, so that you can get a full refund of all uncashed cheques should you lose them. It's best to bring sterling cheques to avoid changing currencies twice. Also note that in Britain traveller's cheques are rarely accepted outside banks or foreign exchange bureaux, so you'll need to cash them in advance and keep a good supply of ready cash.

Money transfers
If you need money urgently, the quickest way to have it sent to you is to have it

wired to the nearest bank via **Western Union**, T0800-833833, www.westernunion.co.uk, or **Money-gram**, T0800-8971 8971. Charges are on a sliding scale; ie it will cost proportionately less to wire out more money. Money can also be wired by **Thomas Cook**, www.thomasexchangeglobal.co.uk, or transferred via a bank draft, but this can take up to a week.

Cost of travelling
The Highlands and Islands of Scotland can be an expensive place to visit, and prices are higher in more remote parts, but there is plenty of budget accommodation available and backpackers will be able to keep their costs down. Petrol is a major expense and won't just cost an arm and a leg but also the limbs of all remaining family members. Expect to pay up to 15p per litre more than in central and southern parts of Scotland and don't pass a fuel station in the Highlands and Islands if short of fuel. Accommodation and restaurant prices also tend to be higher in more popular destinations and during the busy summer months.

The minimum daily budget required, if you're staying in hostels, very cheap B&Bs or camping, cycling or hitching (not recommended), and cooking your own meals, will be around £25-30 per person per day. If you start using public transport and eating out occasionally that will rise to around £35-40. Those staying in slightly more upmarket B&Bs or guesthouses, eating out every evening at pubs or modest restaurants and visiting tourist attractions, such as castles or museums, can expect to pay around £50-60 per day. If you also want to hire a car and use ferries to visit the islands, and eat well, then costs will rise considerably and you'll be looking at least £75-80 per person per day. Single travellers will have to pay more than ½ the cost of a double room in most places, and should budget on spending around 60-70% of what a couple would spend.

Opening hours
Businesses are usually open Mon-Sat 0900-1700. In towns and cities, as well as villages in holiday areas, many shops open on a Sun but they will open later and close earlier. For TIC opening hours, see page 25. Those visiting the Outer Hebrides need to be aware of the strict observance of the Sabbath on those islands.

Post
Most post offices are open Mon-Fri 0900 to 1730 and Sat 0900-1230 or 1300. Smaller sub-post offices are closed for an hour at lunch (1300-1400) and many of them operate out of a shop. Post offices keep the same ½-day closing times as shops.

Stamps can be bought at post offices, but also from vending machines outside, and also at many newsagents. A 1st-class letter weighing up to 100 g to anywhere in the UK costs 60p and should arrive the following day, while 2nd-class letters weighing up to 100 g cost 50p and take between 2-4 days. For more information about Royal Mail postal services, call T08457-740740, or visit www.royalmail.com.

Safety
Incidences of serious crime in Highlands and Islands tend to be the exception rather than the rule and are so rare that they always make front page news. In fact, if someone failed to say 'good morning' – heaven forfend – it would provoke such an outrage that locals would be talking about little else for weeks to come. In most island communities, even sizeable ones such as Tobermory on Mull, people don't even lock their doors at night, and will even leave their car keys still in the lock. The major safety issue when visiting the Highlands and more remote parts relates to the unpredictable weather conditions. Everyone should be aware of the need for caution and proper preparation when walking or climbing in the mountains. For more information on mountain safety, see www.mountaineering-scotland.org.uk/safety.

Telephone → *Country code +44.*
Useful numbers: operator T100; international operator T155; directory enquiries T192; overseas directory enquiries T153.

Most public payphones are operated by **British Telecom** (**BT**) and can be found in towns and cities, though less so in rural areas. Numbers of public phone booths have declined in recent years due to the advent of the mobile phone, so don't rely on being able to find a payphone wherever you go. BT payphones take either coins (20p, 50p and £1) or phonecards, which are available at newsagents and post offices displaying the BT logo. These cards come in denominations of £2, £3, £5 and £10. Some payphones also accept credit cards.

For most countries (including Europe, USA and Canada) calls are cheapest Mon-Fri between 1800 and 0800 and all day Sat-Sun. For Australia and New Zealand it's cheapest to call from 1430-1930 and from 2400-0700 every day. Area codes are not needed if calling from within the same area. Any number prefixed by 0800 or 0500 is free to the caller; 08457 numbers are charged at local rates and 08705 numbers at the national rate. To call Scotland from overseas, dial 011 from USA and Canada, 0011 from Australia and 00 from New Zealand, followed by 44, then the area code, minus the first zero, then the number. To call overseas from Scotland dial 00 followed by the country code. Country codes include: Australia 61; Ireland 353; New Zealand 64; South Africa 27; USA and Canada 1.

Time
Greenwich Mean Time (GMT) is used from late Oct to late Mar, after which time the clocks go forward an hour to British Summer Time (BST). GMT is 5 hrs ahead of US Eastern Standard Time and 10 hrs behind Australian Eastern Standard Time.

Tipping
Believe it or not, people in Scotland do leave tips. In a restaurant you should leave a tip of 10-15% if you are satisfied with the service. If the bill already includes a service charge, you needn't add a further tip. Tipping is not normal in pubs or bars. Taxi drivers will expect a tip for longer journeys, usually of around 10%; and most hairdressers will also expect a tip. As in most other countries, porters, bellboys and waiters in more up-market hotels rely on tips to supplement their meagre wages.

Tourist information
Roughly speaking, this book includes the northern half of mainland Scotland. It's covered by **VisitScotland's highland region** ⓘ *T0845-225 5121, www.visithighlands.com*, whose tourist offices can provide free information and book local accommodation (for a small fee). From Nov-Mar smaller TIC offices may be closed or have restricted opening hours.

Tourist Information Centres
Tourist offices – called tourist information centres (**TIC**s) – can be found in most Scottish towns. Their addresses, phone numbers and opening hours are listed in the relevant sections of this book. Opening hours vary depending on the time of year, and many of the smaller offices are closed during the winter months. All tourist offices provide information on accommodation, public transport, local attractions and restaurants, as well as selling books, local guides, maps and souvenirs. Many also have free street plans and leaflets describing local walks. They can also book accommodation for you, for a small fee.

Museums, galleries and historic houses
Most of Scotland's tourist attractions, apart from the large museums and art galleries in the main cities, are open only from Easter-Oct. Full details of opening hours and admission charges are given in the relevant sections of this guide.

Over 100 of the country's most prestigious sights, and 75,000 ha of beautiful countryside, are cared for by the **National Trust for Scotland (NTS)**, 26-31 Charlotte Sq, Edinburgh EH2 4ET, T0844-493 2100, www.nts.org.uk. National Trust properties are indicated in this guide as 'NTS', and entry charges and opening hours are given for each property.

Historic Scotland (HS), Longmore House, Salisbury Pl, Edinburgh EH9 1SH, T0131-668 8600, www.historic-scotland.gov.uk, manages more than 330 of Scotland's most important castles, monuments and other historic sites. Historic Scotland properties are indicated as 'HS', and admission charges and opening hours are also given in this guide. Historic Scotland offers an **Explorer Pass** which allows free entry to 70 of its properties including Edinburgh and Stirling castles. A 3-day pass (can be used over 5 consecutive days) costs £25, concessions £20, family £50, 7-day pass (valid for 14 days) £34, £27, £68. It can save a lot of money, especially in Orkney, where most of the monuments are managed by Historic Scotland.

Many other historic buildings are owned by local authorities, and admission is cheap, or in many cases free. Most fee-paying attractions give a discount or concession for senior citizens, the unemployed, full-time students and children under 16 (those under 5 are admitted free everywhere). Proof of age or status must be shown. Many of Scotland's stately homes are still owned and occupied by the landed gentry, and admission is usually between £4 and £8.

Finding out more

The best way of finding out more information for your trip to Scotland is to contact **Visit Scotland** (aka the Scottish Tourist Board), www.visitbritain.com. Alternatively, you can contact **VisitBritain**, the organization that is responsible for tourism throughout the British Isles. Both organizations can provide a wealth of free literature and information such as maps, city guides and accommodation brochures. If particularly interested in ensuring your visit coincides

with a major festival or sporting event, it's also worthwhile having a look at **EventScotland**'s website, www.eventscotland.org. Travellers with special needs should also contact Visit Scotland or their nearest VisitBritain office. If you want more detailed information on a particular area, contact the specific tourist boards, see below.

VisitScotland regional offices

Orkney Tourist Board, 6 Broad St, Kirkwall, Orkney KW15 1NX, T01856-872001, www.visitorkney.com.
Visit Shetland, Market Cross, Lerwick, Shetland ZE1 0LU, T08701-999440, www.visitshetland.com.

Visas and immigration

Visa regulations are subject to change, so it is essential to check with your local British embassy, high commission or consulate before leaving home. Citizens of all European countries – except Albania, Bosnia Herzegovina, Kosovo, Macedonia, Moldova, Turkey, Serbia and all former Soviet republics (other than the Baltic states) – require only a passport to enter Britain. Citizens of Australia, Canada, New Zealand, South Africa or the USA can stay for up to 6 months, providing they have a return ticket and sufficient funds to cover their stay. Citizens of most other countries require a visa from the commission or consular office in the country of application.

The **Foreign and Commonwealth Office (FCO)**, T0207-270 1500, www.fco.gov.uk, has an excellent website, which provides details of British immigration and visa requirements. Also the Home Office UK Border Agency is responsible for UK immigration matters and its website is a good place to start for anyone hoping visit, work, study or emigrate to the UK. Call the immigration enquiry bureau on T0870-606 7766 or visit www.bia.homeoffice.gov.uk.

For visa extensions also contact the **Home Office UK Border Agency** via the above number or its website. The agency can also be reached at Lunar House, Wellesley Rd, Croydon, London CR9. Citizens of Australia, Canada, New Zealand, South Africa or the USA wishing to stay longer than 6 months will need an Entry Clearance Certificate from the British High Commission in their country. For more details, contact your nearest British embassy, consulate or high commission, or the Foreign and Commonwealth Office in London.

Weights and measures

Imperial and metric systems are both in use. Distances on roads are measured in miles and yards, drinks poured in pints and gills, but generally, the metric system is used elsewhere.

Volunteering

See www.volunteerscotland.org.uk.

The British Trust for Conservation Volunteers, Sedum House, Mallard Way, Doncaster DN4 8DB, T01302-388883, www.btcv.org. Get fit in the 'green gym', planting hedges, creating wildlife gardens or improving footpaths.

Earthwatch, 57 Woodstock Rd, Oxford OX2 6HJ, T01865-318838. Team up with scientists studying our furry friends.

Jubilee Sailing Trust, Hazel Rd, Southampton, T023-804 9108, www.jst. org.uk. Work on deck on an adventure holiday.

National Trust for Scotland, Wemyss House, 28 Charlotte Sq, Edinburgh EH2 4ET, T0844-493 2100, www.nts.org.uk. Among a number of Scotland based charities that offer volunteering opportunities. You could find yourself helping restore buildings on St Kilda or taking part in an archaeological dig on Loch Lomondside.

Contents

Footprint features

Northwest Highlands of Scotland

At a glance

⊖ **Getting around** There are public buses and good train links but a car is necessary to explore remote areas.
🕒 **Time required** At least 1 week.
☀ **Weather** Be prepared for bad weather on the mountains.
✕ **When not to go** Oct-Mar some tourist facilities are closed.

Inverness

Inverness is the only city in the Highlands and as the busy and prosperous hub of the region, its population has trebled over the past 30 years. All main routes through the Highlands pass through here at some point, so it's a hard place to avoid. The town's position at the head of the Great Glen and on the shores of the Moray Firth have made it a firm favourite with tourists, who flock here in their legions during the summer months to look for the evasive Loch Ness Monster. Although Inverness city itself holds few major sights, it's a buzzing, attractive place to base yourself as you explore the other attractions in the surrounding area, including the possibility of spotting pods of dolphins in the Moray Firth. The city, however, is not without its own appeal, particularly the leafy banks of the River Ness, which runs through its heart, linking Loch Ness with the Moray Firth, and its fair share of fine accommodation and restaurants.

Arriving in Inverness → *Phone code 01463. Population 70,000.*

Getting there
There are daily flights from London Gatwick, Edinburgh, Stornoway and Kirkwall with British Airways (**Loganair**), and daily flights from London Gatwick, London Luton and Bristol with **easyJet**. There are regular flights from Stornoway, Birmingham, Exeter, Manchester, Southampton and Belfast with **Flybe**, whilst **Ryanair** flies from Nottingham (East Midlands) and **Aer Arann** from Dublin. The **airport** ① *T01667-464000, www.hial. co.uk*, is 7 miles east of the town at Dalcross. There's a daily **airport bus** ① *T01463-710555*, every 30 minutes to the town centre, which takes 20 minutes and costs £2.90. A taxi from the airport costs around £14. The **bus station** ① *just off Academy St, T01463-233371*, and the **train station** ① *east end of Academy St, T01463-239026*, have left-luggage lockers charging a maximum of £5 per item per day. ►► *See Transport, page 39.*

Getting around
Inverness town centre is compact and easy to explore on foot, and most of the hotels and guesthouses are within a 15-minute walk of the TIC. Loch Ness is not within walkable distance, so you'll either need your own transport, or you'll have to book a tour. ►► *See What to do, pages 37 and 60.*

Tourist information
The very busy **TIC** ① *T0845-225 5121, Easter-Oct Mon-Sat 0900-1800, Sun 0930-1600, call for winter opening hours*, is in an unattractive building at the foot of Castle Wynd, near Ness

Bridge, a five-minute walk from the train station. It stocks a wide range of literature on the area, can book accommodation and transport, and gives out free maps of the town and environs. There's also a bureau de change and internet access. Information (and possibly tickets) for the tours listed on the next few pages are available from the TIC. It's also worth visiting www.inverness-scotland.com.

Background

One of the old town's first visitors was that much-travelled cleric, St Columba, who came in AD 565 to confront the Pictish King Brude, whose fortress was reputedly at Craig Phadraig, a few miles west of Inverness. Around the mid-12th century King David I built the original castle and made Inverness a royal burgh on the strength of its growing importance as a trading port. Furs, hides, wool and timber were all exported as far afield as the Mediterranean. The town's economic prosperity and status as the most important northern outpost, however, made it a prime target for marauding Highland clansmen, and during the Wars of Independence in the 13th century Inverness was also a regular target for both English and Scots armies.

The town's renaissance came with the completion of the Caledonian Canal and rail links with the south in the 19th century. These improved communications heralded something of a tourist boom amongst the wealthy and fashionable who came north to the Highlands to shoot anything that moved in the name of sport. In the mid-19th century Queen Victoria decided to embrace all things Scottish, which only boosted the town's popularity. Over recent decades Inverness has grown rapidly, not only as a prime base for visiting tourists, but also as the main administrative and commercial centre for the Highlands. Since being conferred city status in 2000, Inverness has continued to enjoy a boom period. In 2006, the 750 seat **Ironworks** (see Entertainment, page 37) opened its doors, the Highland capital's first ever purpose-built live concert venue, and in 2008, the beloved **Eden Court Theatre** reopened after a £23 million refurbishment.

Places in Inverness → *For listings, see pages 34-40.*

The city is dominated by its red sandstone **castle** which now houses the **Sheriff Court**. Built in 1834, this Victorian edifice is very much the new kid on the block in terms of Scottish castles. The original castle dates from the 12th century and was built on a ridge to the east of the present structure. Nothing remains of the old castle, which is unsurprising given its bloody and eventful history. It was here that King Duncan of Scotland was slain by Macbeth, an event dramatically (and erroneously) portrayed in Shakespeare's eponymous work. The castle was occupied three times during the Wars of Independence in the 13th century, and when Robert the Bruce recaptured it in 1307 he destroyed it. In the mid-17th century Cromwell ordered his men to build a stone version on the same site. In 1715 James Francis Edward was proclaimed king there, but not long after it was destroyed by the Jacobites to prevent it from falling into enemy hands following the defeat of Bonnie Prince Charlie at Culloden, see box, page 43. On the castle terrace is a statue of Flora MacDonald, a poignant memorial to her role in helping the prince to escape. Directly across the road, is the **Castle Tavern**, beloved by real ale drinkers.

Below the castle, on Castle Wynd by the TIC is **Inverness Museum and Art Gallery** ① *Mon-Sat 1000-1700, free.* In recent years this interesting museum, complete with café, has undergone a £1 million refurbishment and now includes a wealth of exhibits that

Inverness

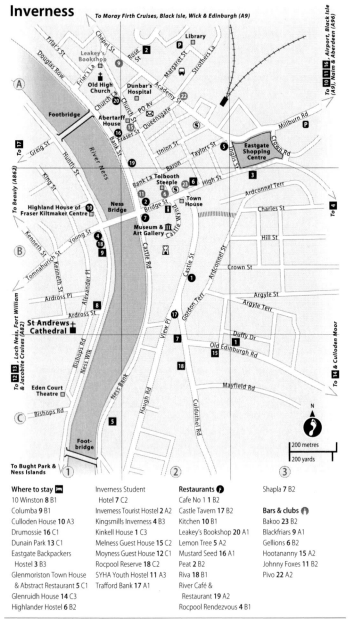

To Moray Firth Cruises, Black Isle, Wick & Edinburgh (A9)

To Airport, Black Isle (A9)/ Nairn & Aberdeen (A96)

Library

Leakey's Bookshop

Old High Church

Dunbar's Hospital

Footbridge

Abertarff House

To 17

Eastgate Shopping Centre

To Beauly (A862)

Highland House of Fraser Kiltmaker Centre

Ness Bridge

Tolbooth Steeple

Town House

Museum & Art Gallery

To 4

Ardconnel Terr

Charles St

Hill St

Crown St

Argyle St

Argyle Terr

To Loch Ness, Fort William / Jacobite Cruises (A82)

St Andrews Cathedral

Duffy Dr

Old Edinburgh Rd

To 14 & Culloden Moor

Eden Court Theatre

Mayfield Rd

Bishops Rd

Footbridge

To Bught Park & Ness Islands

N

200 metres
200 yards

Where to stay 🛏
10 Winston **8** B1
Columba **9** B1
Culloden House **10** A3
Drumossie **16** C1
Dunain Park **13** C1
Eastgate Backpackers
 Hostel **3** B3
Glenmoriston Town House
 & Abstract Restaurant **5** C1
Glenruidh House **14** C3
Highlander Hostel **6** B2

Inverness Student
 Hotel **7** C2
Inverness Tourist Hostel **2** A2
Kingsmills Inverness **4** B3
Kinkell House **1** C3
Melness Guest House **15** C2
Moyness Guest House **12** C1
Rocpool Reserve **18** C2
SYHA Youth Hostel **11** A3
Trafford Bank **17** A1

Restaurants 🍴
Cafe No 1 **1** B2
Castle Tavern **17** B2
Kitchen **10** B1
Leakey's Bookshop **20** A1
Lemon Tree **5** A2
Mustard Seed **16** A1
Peat **2** B2
Riva **18** B1
River Café &
 Restaurant **19** A2
Rocpool Rendezvous **4** B1

Shapla **7** B2

Bars & clubs 🍸
Bakoo **23** B2
Blackfriars **9** A1
Gellions **6** B2
Hootananny **15** A2
Johnny Foxes **11** B2
Pivo **22** A2

outline the social history of the Highlands, its wildlife, and ancient artefacts from the times of the Vikings and the Picts. Among the interactive displays is an opportunity to try your hand at speaking Gaelic. Just around the corner, on High Street, is the Gothic-style **Town House**, where Prime Minister Lloyd George held an emergency cabinet meeting in 1921, the first ever to be held outside London.

Opposite, on the corner of Bridge Street and Church Street, is the **Tolbooth Steeple**, which dates from 1791 and which had to be repaired after an earth tremor in 1816. Apparently, a (now blocked off) tunnel once led from the castle to a prison located below the Tolbooth. Among the cafés and bars to be found on historic Church Street – a fascinating part of the city local 'culture vultures' aim to steadily rejuvenate – is the town's oldest building, **Abertarff House**. Built around 1592, it is now a contemporary art and jewellery gallery. Almost opposite is the much-restored **Dunbar's Hospital**, built in 1688 as an almshouse for the town's poor. At the end of Church Street, where it meets Friar's Lane, is the **Old High Church** founded in the 12th century and rebuilt in 1772, though the 14th-century vaulted tower remains intact. In the adjoining atmospheric graveyard, prisoners taken at Culloden were executed, and you can still see the bullet marks left by the firing squads on some of the gravestones. At the far end of Church Street you'll also find **Leakey's Bookshop**, housed within a former church. Jam-packed with second-hand books, and with a delightful café upstairs, the owners estimate their towering shelves contain over 100,000 books.

The **Highland House of Fraser Kiltmaker Centre** ① *4-9 Huntly St, T01463-222781, www.highlandhouseoffraser.com, daily 0900-1700, factory tour Mon-Fri, £2, concessions and children £1*, still has a working kilt factory upstairs. In addition to watching kilts being made, two informative videos provide insights to the history of highland dress (including what Scotsmen wear under their kilts). In addition to mannequins dressed in period outfits, there are props used in the making of *Braveheart*. Nearby, directly opposite the castle, is the neo-Gothic **St Andrews Cathedral** which dates from 1869, and is worth a peek if you're passing by. Continuing south along Ness Bank, past the impressive glass frontage of the refurbished **Eden Court Theatre** (see Entertainment, page 37) you reach **Bught Park**, which overlooks the Ness Islands, joined by footbridge to both banks. The islands are attractively laid out as a park and are a favourite with local anglers. This also happens to be a lovely place for a peaceful evening stroll.

Inverness listings

For hotel and restaurant price codes and other relevant information, see pages 13-20.

⊖ Where to stay

Inverness *p30, map p32*

With an abundance of guesthouses, B&Bs and several good-quality hotels in and around Inverness, you shouldn't have much trouble finding somewhere to stay, though it does get very busy in Jul and Aug. Ideally, reserve ahead or consider booking through the TIC.

The best places to look are along both banks of the river south of the Ness Bridge, Old Edinburgh Rd and Ardconnel St (east of the castle) and around Bruce Gardens, Ardross St, Kenneth St and Fairfield Rd (the west bank). There are also several budget hostels in and around the centre, and a couple of campsites.

££££ Culloden House Hotel, Milton of Culloden, 3 miles east of town near the A9, T01463-790461, www.cullodenhouse.co.uk. Within this delightful Georgian mansion where Bonnie Prince Charlie prepared for battle at Culloden, you'll discover 1st-class accommodation and award-winning fine dining (**£££**).

££££ Rocpool Reserve Hotel, Culduthel Rd, T01463-240089. Inverness doesn't lack stylish, luxurious hotels and this boutique hotel, 10 mins' walk from the centre, is no exception. For those with deep pockets, its restaurant also offers exceptional food, including lunch (£15.50 for 2 courses).

££££-£££ Dunain Park Hotel, about 3 miles southwest of the town centre, just off the A82 Fort William Rd, T01463-230512, www.dunainparkhotel.co.uk. 11 rooms. An elegant Georgian mansion house within extensive gardens, with Victorian 4-poster beds, luxurious marble bathrooms and an excellent restaurant (see Restaurants, below). Can also arrange fishing, golf and riding.

££££-£££ Glenmoriston Town House Hotel, 20 Ness Bank, T01463-223777. With 30 individually styled rooms, this is a classy establishment. Its **Abstract** restaurant and more informal **Contrast Brasserie**, have both picked up notable awards and there are more than 25 malts available in the piano bar.

££££-£££ New Drumossie Hotel, 3 miles southeast of the town centre, Old Perth Rd, T0844-879 9017, www.drumossiehotel. co.uk. 44 rooms. Views over the Moray Firth and handy for Culloden Moor, this is a deluxe hotel in a rural setting with all the creature comforts including a lovely restaurant (**£££-££**).

£££ Kinkell House, 11 Old Edinburgh Rd, T01349-861270, www.kinkellhouse.co.uk. Clean, comfortable Victorian family home with spacious rooms close to all amenities.

£££-££ Columba Hotel, 7 Ness Walk, T01463-231391, http://columba-inverness. hotel-rv.com. Overlooking the river, this hotel from 1881 has been refurbished, and offers 76 comfortable rooms in a very central location.

£££-££ Glenruidh House Hotel, Old Edinburgh Rd South, 2 miles from the town centre and adjacent to Loch Ness Golf Course (phone for directions), T01463-226499, www. cozzeenessie-bed.co.uk. 5 rooms. Packed with history and character, this peaceful, friendly 'boutique' hotel serves organic, fresh produce in a secluded setting … and has over 40 species of birds in its garden.

£££-££ Kingsmills Hotel Inverness, Culca-bock Rd, 1 mile south of the city centre near A9, T01463-257100. Another higher end hotel, with 82 rooms. Parts of the building date back to the 17th century. Comfortable rooms and superb leisure facilities, including spa and a guest discount at the adjacent Inverness Golf Club.

£££-££ Trafford Bank, 96 Fairfield Rd, T01463-241414, www.traffordbankguest house.co.uk. 5 en suite rooms. Owners

Lorraine Feel and Koshal Pun continue to delight and win awards for their sumptuous guesthouse, which assures guests comfort, style and a very warm welcome.

££ Highland Voyages, Eala Bhan tall ship, T07786-106960, www.highlandvoyages. co.uk. When moored at Seaport Marina, this place offers on board B&B accommodation in 5 (bunk-bed) cabins. Also offers sailings, see What to do, page 37.

££ Melness Guest House, 8 Old Edinburgh Rd, T01463-220963, www.melnessie.co.uk. 4 rooms that include en suite and family. Clean and comfortable accommodation in an 18th-century building that long-ago was the 'Craigneish School for Young Ladies'.

££ Moyness Guest House, 6 Bruce Gardens, T01463-233836, www.moyness.co.uk. Fine Victorian villa in a quiet area near the theatre, with 7 very comfortable en suite rooms and nice touches like Botanics products in the bathrooms. During the 1920s this was the home of acclaimed Scottish author, Neil M Gunn.

££ Winston, 10 Ardross Terr, T01463-234477, www.winstonguesthouse.com. Friendly and comfortable guesthouse overlooking the river and minutes' walk from the **Eden Court Theatre**.

£ Eastgate Backpackers Hostel, 38 Eastgate, T01463-718756, www.eastgatebackpackers.com. 38 beds including 2 twins and 4 (6-bed) dorms. Secure, clean and central.

£ Highlander Hostel, 23a High St, T01463-221225, www.highlanderhostel.com. The new kid on the hostel block, with impressive facilities.

£ Inverness Student Hotel, 8 Culduthel Rd (at the top of Castle St), T01463-236556. Ok, hotel is pushing it but this is a great, lively hostel, close to the centre and just yards away from great food at the **Castle Tavern**.

£ Inverness Tourist Hostel, 2 mins from bus station, 24 Rose St, T01463-241962, www.invernesshostel.com. Don't let the dingy entrance fool you. This is an excellent backpacker rest stop with facilities including

satellite TV, internet access, friendly staff, terrific cooking facilities and complimentary tea and coffee. The budget traveller's dream.

£ SYHA Youth Hostel, Victoria Drive, off Millburn Rd, T01463 231771. 166 beds. Huge hostel in former school hall of residence. Good amenities, quieter location than many hostels but further from the city centre.

Self-catering

Easter Dalziel Farm Cottages, 7 miles east of Inverness, T01667-462213, www.easter dalzielfarm.co.uk. 3 comfortable, traditional cottages (sleep 4-6) on a 210 acre family farm. A 3-bedroom farmhouse B&B (**££**) is also available from £180-520 per week.

Camping

Bught Caravan and Camping Site, Bught Park, on the west bank of the river near the Inverness Aquadome, T01463-236920. Open Easter-Oct. The largest and most centrally located campsite, with good facilities, £7 per tent and £7 per head thereafter; £16 per caravan pitch with electricity; £3 for laundry.

Bunchrew Caravan and Camping Park, 3 miles west of Inverness, T01463-237802. Open Mar-Nov. Excellent campsite with views towards Ben Wyvis and the Beauly Firth and with good hot showers. 2 people can pitch a small tent for £14.50.

Restaurants

Inverness *p30, map p32*
As you'd expect in a major tourist centre, there's the usual plethora of pubs, cafés and restaurants serving cheap and basic food for the non-discerning palate, but those looking for a high standard of cuisine won't be disappointed either.

Takeaways and chain restaurant options are plentiful, particularly on Academy St, Eastgate, around the train station and on Young St, just across the Ness Bridge.

£££ Abstract, Glenmoriston Town House Hotel, 20 Ness Bank. Tue-Sat 1800-2200. The award-winning French-inspired cuisine from the à la carte menu comes at a price but for those who seek fine-dining in style, it's definitely worth it. 8-course tasting menu £50. Book ahead.

£££ Dunain Park Hotel, see Where to stay, above. Fine combination of elegance and Scottish cuisine, including fresh Scottish seafood. Take a post-dinner stroll in the lovely gardens.

£££ Rocpool Reserve, see Where to stay, above. The decor oozes style and chic. Just like the boutique hotel, the lunch and dinner cuisine here hits the mark – albeit at a price.

£££-££ The Kitchen, 15 Huntly St, T01463-259119, www.kitchenrestaurant.co.uk. One of the city's newer food haunts and the sister restaurant of **The Mustard Seed** (see below) across the river. Thoughfully prepared menu and lovely ambience for an evening meal. Good value set lunch (£5.95) and early bird (1700-1900) dinner (£10.95) offers.

£££-££ The Mustard Seed, 16 Fraser St, T01463-220220. Daily 1200-1500, 1730-2200. Cheery, stylish interior, and a lunch and dinner menu packed with local, freshly prepared produce.

£££-££ Peat, 20 Bridge St, T01463-701900, www.peat-by-the-bridge.co.uk. Overlooking the river, this trendy restaurant specializes in all things seafood. Look out for the fresh crab, lobster and langoustines at the entrance, which are destined for your plate.

£££-££ Riva, 4-6 Ness Walk, T01463-237377, www.rivainverness.co.uk. A stylish and good value riverside eatery that specializes in Italian food.

££ Contrast Brasserie, Glenmoriston Town House Hotel, see Where to stay, above. Daily 1200-1430, 1700-2100. A treat on a (slightly) more modest budget. Delicious food.

££ Rocpool Rendezvous, 1 Ness Walk T01463-717274. Stylish interior with attentive staff and fabulous food. Family friendly. Book ahead.

££ Shapla, 2 Castle Rd, T01463-241919. Daily 1200-2330. Good Indian restaurant with Tandoori and Balti menu and good views of the river in the upstairs lounge.

££-£ Café No 1, 75 Castle St, T01463-226200, www.cafe1.net. Mon-Sat 1200-1400, 1800-2130. Central location with reasonable selection of meat and vegetarian dishes. Early bird dinner offer (Mon-Fri 1730-1845).

££-£ The River Café and Restaurant, 10 Bank St, T01463-714884. Mon 1000-2030, Tue-Sat 1000-2130, Sun 1730-2030. Popular for lunches and delicious high tea.

£ The Castle Tavern, 1 View Pl, T01463-718178. Owned by renowned publican George MacLean, you can feast on hearty, good value and freshly prepared pub grub. There's a great selection of real ales downstairs and a beer garden. This is a CAMRA rated establishment, with a food menu (available until 2200) that changes daily and great views of the castle and river from upstairs.

£ Leakeys Bookshop, Church St, T01463-239947. After browsing through over 100,000 second-hand books and old maps, where better to sup on some home-made soup, a sandwich or simply a coffee before stocking up on your book collection.

£ The Lemon Tree, 18 Inglis St. Located in the pedestrianized town centre, this family-run café offers good home-baking and basic but filling meals. Popular with older visitors.

Bakeries

Ashers, Church St. A good bakery that prides itself on its famous whisky cakes.

🊋 Bars and clubs

Inverness *p30, map p32*
Bakoo, High St. Where the young clubbers let their hair down.

Blackfriars, Academy St. A decent pub that runs ceilidhs and live music for the backpacker fraternity on most nights.

Castle Tavern, View Pl. Excellent choice of real ales, good atmosphere and bar food.

Gellions, Bridge St. Claims to be the oldest pub in the highland capital. Good to try 'neeps and tatties' (£4.95) and for ceilidh's on a Wed and Sat.

Hootananny, 67 Church St. A great bet for all things Scottish, has live music including ceilidhs most nights. Don't be surprised if you find yourself dancing on the tables with the backpacker crowd. Probably the best pub atmosphere in Inverness.

Johnny Foxes, 26 Bank St. Irish folk music most nights in summer and great bar food.

Love 2 Love, Castle St. Another venue for the younger clubber.

Pivo, 38-40 Academy St. Enjoyed by those in search of the real Czech brews and a trendier atmosphere.

⊕ Entertainment

Inverness *p30, map p32*
Cinema
The cinema attached to **Eden Court Theatre**, see below, shows a programme of art house and newly released movies. Prices vary depending on the performance.

Warner Village, A96 Nairn Rd, 2 miles from town centre. 7 screens, tickets cost from £6.

Live music
The Ironworks, 122b Academy St, T08717-894173, www.ironworksvenue.com. The 1st purpose-built live music venue.

Theatre
Eden Court Theatre, Bishops Rd, overlooking the River Ness, T01463-234234. This renowned theatre and cinema re-opened in 2008 after a multimillion pound refurbishment. Diverse theatre and art-house productions. Also has a small café-bar.

⊛ Festivals

Inverness *p30, map p32*
There are numerous events held in and around Inverness throughout the year. These range from a humble pub ceilidh and a food festival to a full-blown Highland Games and the Baxters Loch Ness Marathon (Oct).

Feb/Mar Inverness Music Festival, T01463-716616.

Mar/Apr Folk festivals, T01738-623274. Local folk festivals held over Easter weekend.

Jun Rock Ness, www.rockness.co.uk. Live big bands play at Dores on the northern shores of Loch Ness.

Jul Inverness Highland Games, held in the 3rd week of the month.

⊙ Shopping

Inverness *p30, map p32*
Inverness is a good place to buy a kilt, or practically anything else in tartan. To find your own clan tartan, head for the **Highland House of Fraser Kiltmaker Centre**, see page 33. The **Eastgate Shopping Centre** has all the usual high-street shops such as **Gap** and **Marks & Spencer**.

Bookshops
Leakey's Bookshop, Church St. Mon-Sat 1000-1700. A brilliant second-hand bookshop, with a huge wood-burning stove in the middle of the shop and a café upstairs.

Highland dress and traditional gifts
Chisholm's Highland Dress, 47-51 Castle St, T01463-234599; Highland House of Fraser, Bridge St, T01463-222781; James Pringle Weavers of Inverness, 21 Bridge St, T01463-236517.

Market
Victorian Market, accessed off Church St and Academy St. Established in the 18th century, this market has a wide range of interesting and quirky shops although there is also the inevitable tartan tat.

⊕ What to do

Inverness *p30, map p32*
Boat tours
Caley Cruisers, Canal Rd, Inverness, T01463-236328, www.caleycruisers.com. If you fancy skippering your own power boat down Loch Ness and through the Caledonian Canal, you can do it in style

with friends and family start from £410 to £2050 for the bigger boats.

Highland Voyages, Eala Bhan tall ship, T01667-404441, www.highlandvoyages. co.uk. Aboard this converted wooden herring drifter, enjoy day sails from £48-£68. 5-day week living onboard from £380-£480.

John o'Groat's Ferries, contact the Inverness TIC, T01955-611353, www.jogferry. co.uk. For the ultimate day-trip, Orkney Islands Day Tours leave from Inverness every day throughout the summer, Jun-Sep (depart 0900, return 1945), £49, under 16s ½-price. Ancient sites include Skara Brae (older than the Egyptian pyramids) and the Ring of Brodgar. Booking essential.

Bus tours

Citysightseeing Inverness, leave from Bridge St outside the TIC, T01667-459849, www.city-sightseeing.com. Open-topped bus tours around the city, mid-Jun-Sep daily 1015-1700. Tickets valid for 24 hrs from the time of travel, and can be bought online or onboard. £6, concessions £4.50, children £3.

Exquisite Scotland, Cala na Sithe, Kirkhill, T01463-831643, www.exquisitescotland. com. Able to carry up to 8 passengers, this operator offers bespoke tours to suit your needs, whether it's visiting Culloden, Skye or finding a river to fish or a fairway to putt.

The Hebridean Explorer, Elmbank, Lewiston, Drumnadrochit, T07943-863292, www.thehebrideanexplorer.com. This family-run operator offers personal (for up to 5 people) and private (from £160 per day) tours to destinations including Loch Ness, upto £45 per person; Isle of Lewis, £125 per person; and Skye.

Highland Taxis, Farraline Park, T01463-222222, www.highlandtaxis.co.uk. Offers a highly personalized tour service (18 different tours), from exploring the far northwest for a day, £220 per person or £47.50 per person if 4 travel; Culloden Battlefield, £17.50 per person based on 4; and as far as the Cuillins of Skye, £55 per person based on 4 travelling.

Jacobite, Tomnahurich Bridge, Glenurquhart Rd, T01463-233999, www.jacobite.co.uk. Operates all kinds of informative tours that leave at 1030 from Inverness Bus Station. Also runs a courtesy bus from Inverness TIC to connect with their Loch Ness cruises. Offer a 6½-hr packed day-long tour (£37, concessions £34, children £25), which will see you sail on the dark waters of Loch Ness for 30 mins, pop into the Loch Ness Monster Exhibition Centre and visit atmospheric Urquhart Castle, before entering the 18th century engineering marvel that is the Caledonian Canal. Contact the operator for specific pick-up/drop-off points.

Puffin Express, tours leave from Castle Wynd, the narrow street between the Town House and the TIC, T01463-717181, www.puffinexpress.co.uk.

Cycling

Opened in 2002, the 73-mile-long Great Glen Way can be cycled. The stretch alongside the Caledonian Canal is flat and good for families. For a free leaflet, T01320-366322. To read about the Way, visit www.greatglenway.com.

Golf

There's an 18-hole public course at Torvean, 2 miles from town on the A82 to Fort William, T01463-711434.

History and ghost tours

Davey the Ghost, leaves from outside the TIC, T0845-2255121. Nightly 1900, £8, concessions £7. Tales of ghosts and ghouls.

Happy Tours, tours begin outside the TIC, T07828-154683, www.happy-tours.biz. Apr-Sep Mon-Sat, tours at 1100, 1300, 1500, 1700 and 1900. £10, children £5. Try the Riverside Rickshaw tour £30.

Iceskating

Ice Centre, Bught Park, T01463-235711, www.inverness-ice-centre.org.uk. Daily 1400-1630, 1900-21.30. £4.50, children £3.50.

Swimming
Aquadome Leisure Centre, Bught Park, T01463-667500. Mon-Fri 1000-2000, Sat-Sun 1000-1700. Competition-sized pool with flumes, wave machine and kiddies' pool. Also gym and other indoor sports facilities.

Ten-pin bowling
Roller Bowl, 167 Culduthel Rd, T01463-235100. Mon-Fri 1200-late, Sat-Sun 1100-late.

Tennis and squash
Inverness Tennis and Squash Club, Bishop's Rd, T01463-230751.

⊖ Transport

Inverness *p30, map p32*
Bus
Bus timetables and even operators on some routes change frequently. If in any doubt and for the latest information, call **Traveline Scotland**, T0871-200 2233, www.traveline scotland.com, or www.rapsons.co.uk.

There are regular daily buses to **Glasgow** and **Edinburgh** (via **Aviemore**), **Pitlochry** and **Perth** with Scottish Citylink, T08705-505050. Change at Perth for **Dundee**. There are regular daily Citylink buses to **Ullapool**, connecting with the ferry to **Stornoway**; also to **Fort William** and **Oban**. There are daily Citylink buses to **Kyle of Lochalsh**, **Portree** and **Uig** (connecting with ferries to **Tarbert** and **Lochmaddy**), and regular, daily Citylink buses to **Fort Augustus** via **Drumnadrochit** and **Urquhart Castle** (also with Rapsons, T01463-710555), and to **Scrabster**, for the ferry to **St Margaret's Hope**, via **Wick** and **Thurso**.

To **Ullapool** via **Dingwall** and **Braemore Junction**, there are 2 buses, Mon-Sat, Highland Country Buses, T01463-710555, in addition to the regular service operated by Citylink. **Scotbus**, T01463-224410, operate 1 bus daily, Jun-Oct, between **Inverness** and **Inverewe Gardens**, via

Achnasheen, **Kinlochewe**, **Loch Maree**, **Gairloch** and **Poolewe**. To **Tain** there is a daily service with **Citylink**, but to reach **Lairg** there's an irregular service with MacLeods and **Royal Mail**, T08457-740740. To **Tain** and **Helsmdale**, via **Dornoch** there are regular daily buses with Citylink. To **Lochinver** from **Ullapool** there's 1 bus, Mon-Sat, operated by Tim Dearman, T01349-883585, that departs Ullapool Ferry Terminal at 1055 and arrives in **Lochinver** at 1154. This bus continues to **Durness** via **Kylesku** and **Rhiconich** (for Sandwood Bay). Dearman Coaches carry a bike trailer on this route.

Between **Applecross** and **Inverness**, Skyeways, T01599-555477, operate a bus Mon, Wed and Sat via Lochcarron and Kishorn that also stops on request (Wed and Sat only) in **Shieldaig**. To **Grantown-on-Spey**, daily service with Highland Country Buses, T01463-710555. Stagecoach Inverness, T01463-239292, run services to places around **Inverness**, including **Beauly**, **Muir of Ord** and **Dingwall**. To reach **Tomich** (and **Glen Affric**) via Beauly use the Ross Minibuses service, T01463-761250. **Fort George** (No 11) and **Cawdor Castle** (No 12) are reached from Inverness with Highland Country Buses, T01463-710555. Stage-coach runs daily services to **Aberdeen** via **Nairn**, whilst the battle scene of Culloden and Cawdor Castle can both be reached using a Tourist Trail Rover ticket (from £6) with Highland Country Buses. It's worth noting that Rapsons, T01463-710555, www.rapsons.com, operate a 'Rack and Ride' scheme for some cyclists on certain routes including **Inverness** to **Aviemore**.

Car hire
Arnold Clark, 47 Harbour Rd and at the airport, T01463-236200 or T0845-607 4500; **Enterprise**, Harbour Rd, T01463-235525; **Focus**, an office at the airport, T01667-461212; **Turner Hire Drive**, office on Lotland St, T01463-716058, T0870-902 0200. Prices vary but expect to pay from £35 per day.

Cycle hire

Highland Cycles, Telford St, T01463-234789.
Mon-Sat 0900-1730.

Ferry

For details of connections to **Stornoway**
(Lewis) and **Lochmaddy** (North Uist),
contact **CalMac**, T0870-565000, T08000-
665000, www.calmac.co.uk. For **Scrabster**
to **Stromness**, Northlink Ferries, T01856-
851144, T08456-000449. For **John o'Groat's**
to **Burwick** (Orkney), John o'Groat's Ferries,
T01955-611353, www.jogferry.co.uk;
or for **Gill's Bay** to **St Margarets Hope**
(Orkney) aboard a superfast catamaran
(1 hr sailing), **Pentland Ferries**, T01856-
831226, www.pentlandferries.co.uk.

Taxi

Tartan Taxis, T01463-222777. Around £16
from the city centre to the airport.

Train

For more information, T0845-748 4950.
There are direct trains to **Aberdeen**,
Edinburgh (via **Aviemore**) and **Glasgow**.
There are several daily services to **London
King's Cross** (via **Perth**) and **Edinburgh**,
and a Caledonian Sleeper service to **London
Euston** or from London Euston to **Fort
William** via **Inverness**, ScotRail, T08457-
550033, www.firstscotrail.co.uk. There is
also a regular service to **Wick** and **Thurso**,
via **Tain**, **Lairg** and **Helmsdale**. The journey
from Inverness to **Kyle of Lochalsh** (for
Skye) is one of the most scenic in Britain.
There are 2-3 trains Mon-Sat.

❶ Directory

Inverness *p30, map p32*
Banks Most of the major banks can
be found in the town centre around
Inglis St. **Bank of Scotland**, opposite the
Town House on the High St; **Clydesdale**,
opposite the train station; **Lloyds TSB**,
Church St. **Royal Bank**, High St. **Currency
exchange** Money can be changed at the
TIC at 2.5% commission; **Thomas Cook**,
9-13 Inglis St, T01463-711921, Mon-Fri
0900-1700. **Internet** Inverness Library;
Mail Box Etc, 24 Station Sq; TIC. Several of
the backpacker hostels also provide internet
access. **Library** Inverness library, opposite
the bus station, with excellent genealogical
research unit. Consultations with the
resident genealogist cost around £14 per hr,
T01463-236463. The library also houses the
Highland archives, where you can research
the history and culture of the region, Jun-
Sep Mon-Fri 1000-1300, 1400-1700, Oct-May
1400-1700. **Medical services Hospitals**:
Raigmore Hospital, southeastern outskirts
of town near the A9, T01463-704000, for
accidents and emergencies. **Pharmacies**:
Boots, 14-16 Queensgate, T01463-233295,
Mon-Wed and Fri 0845-1800, Thu 0845-
1900, Sat 0830-1800, Sun 1100-1700;
also at Eastgate Shopping Centre, Fri-Wed
0900-1730, Thu 0900-1900.

Around Inverness

East of Inverness along the Moray Firth stretches a long coastline of clifftop walks, fine beaches, attractive old towns and many historic sites and castles. The Moray Firth is perhaps best known for its large resident population of dolphins. Scores of these beautiful and intelligent mammals live in the estuary, the most northerly breeding ground in Europe, and there's a very good chance of seeing them, particularly between June and August. The Moray Firth dolphins have become a major tourist attraction and several companies run dolphin-spotting boat trips. You can also see them from the shore. Two of the best places are on the southern shore of the Black Isle (see page 134) and Fort George, on the opposite shore (see below). The Kessock Bridge, which crosses the Moray Firth to the Black Isle, is another good dolphin-spotting location and also has a visitor centre, where you can listen in to their underwater conversations.

West of Inverness, the Moray Firth becomes the Beauly Firth, a relatively quiet little corner despite its proximity to Inverness, as most traffic heading north crosses the Kessock Bridge on the main A9. The A862 west to Beauly offers a more scenic alternative, and the chance to visit a 13th-century priory and a distillery. South of Beauly, the A831 leads to two of Scotland's most beautiful glens, Glen Strathfarrar and Glen Affric.

The Moray Firth → *For listings, see pages 47-49.*

Culloden

ⓘ *T0844-493 2159, www.culloden.org.uk. Site open daily all year, visitor centre open daily Feb-Mar 1000-1600, Apr-Oct 0900-1800, Nov-Dec 1000-1600, £10, concessions and children £7.50. Café/restaurant, educational rooms and a shop.*

The eerie and windswept Culloden Moor, 5 miles to the east of Inverness on the B9006, was the site of the last major battle fought on the British mainland. In 2007, the £8.5 million National Trust for Scotland visitor centre was opened, complete with its rooftop walk (10 minutes) with views over the restored battlefield, where on 16 April 1746 the Jacobean dream to place a Stuart, Prince Charles Edward Stuart (Bonnie Prince Charlie) back on the Scottish throne was brutally crushed by Hanoverian (largely English) forces amidst the heather and tussocky grass of Culloden Moor. This fateful battle was not simply Scotsmen fighting Englishmen but tragically, saw Scottish clan pitched against clan, whilst the Jacobean side included Irish and even English soldiers. Though the battle lasted barely an hour, the Hanoverian soldiers led by the Duke of Cumberland went on to commit appalling bloodshed across the Highlands, earning Cumberland the name, 'the Butcher.' Even to this day, his name is despised by many for the murderous post battle rampage he oversaw in a bid to forever stamp out sympathy for the Jacobites.

Fashioned from natural timbers and stone, the interior of the spectacular visitor centre combines artefacts and displays (including Jacobite swords and the Princes unfinished waistcoat) with cutting edge interactive displays (including a 'Battle Immersion Theatre' and 'voices' from witnesses of the battle) to provide visitors with an evocative and stirring account of the build up to the battle, the fateful day and the brutal consequences of a Jacobite/Hanoverean showdown that changed the face of Scottish history. From the visitor centre, walk along the paths (35 minutes), past clan graves marked by simple headstones. Next to the visitor centre, the restored cottage of Old Leanach – which was used by the Jacobites as a headquarters, and where 30 Highlanders were burnt alive – is arranged as it would have been at the time of the battle. A memorial cairn, erected in 1881, is the scene each April of a commemorative service organized by the Gaelic Society of Inverness.

Clava Cairns

This impressive and important Bronze Age site lies only a mile southeast of Culloden and is well worth a short detour. The 5000-year-old site consists of three large burial cairns encircled by standing stones, set in a grove of trees. The less imaginative visitor may see it as merely a pile of stones but no one can fail to be affected by the spooky atmosphere of the place, especially if no one else is around. To get there, continue on the B9006 past Culloden Moor, then turn right at the **Culloden Moor Inn** and follow the signs for **Clava Lodge**. Look for the sign on the right of the road.

Fort George

ⓘ *T01667-460232, Apr-Sep daily 0930-1730, Oct-Mar daily 0930-1630, £6.90, concessions £5.50, children £4.10, wheelchair access, café.*

Standing proudly on a sandy spit that juts out into the Moray Firth is Fort George, Europe's finest surviving example of 18th-century military architecture. In today's money it's estimated the mightiest artillery fortification in Britain would cost over £1 billion to build. Begun in 1748, it was the last in a chain of three such fortifications built in the Highlands – the other two being Fort Augustus and Fort William – as a base for George II's army to

Battle of Culloden

The second Jacobite rebellion of 1745 was ill-fated from the start. Bonnie Prince Charlie's expedition south lacked sufficient support and was turned back at Derby. After their long and dispiriting retreat north, the half-starved, under-strength army – exhausted after an abortive night attack on Hanoverian forces at Nairn – faced overwhelmingly superior forces under the command of the ambitious Duke of Cumberland at Culloden.

The open, flat ground of Culloden Moor was hopelessly unsuitable for the Highlanders' style of fighting, which relied on steep hills and plenty of cover to provide the element of surprise for their brave but undisciplined attacks. In only 40 minutes the Prince's army was blown away by the English artillery, and the Jacobite charge, when it finally came, was ragged and ineffective. Cumberland's troops then went on to commit the worst series of atrocities ever carried out by a British Army. Some 1200 men were slain, many as they lay wounded on the battlefield. Prince Charlie, meanwhile, fled west where loyal Highlanders protected him until he made his final escape to France.

But the real savagery was to come. Cumberland resolved to make an example of the Highlands. Not only were the clans disarmed and the wearing of Highland dress forbidden, but the Government troops began an orgy of brutal reprisals across the region. Within a century the clan system had ended and the Highland way of life changed forever.

prevent any potential threats to Hanoverian rule. It was completed in 1769, by which time the Highlands were more or less peaceful, but it was kept in use as a military barracks. Today it remains virtually unchanged, and as a functioning military base don't be surprised to find armed sentries at the main gate. You can walk along the ramparts to get an idea of the sheer scale of the place and also enjoy the sweeping views across the Moray Firth. You may even be lucky enough to see a school of dolphins. Within the fort are the barracks, a chapel, workshops and the Regimental Museum of the Queen's Own Highlanders, which features the fascinating Seafield Collection of arms and military equipment, most of which dates from the Napoleonic Wars.

Cawdor Castle

ⓘ *T01667-404401, May to early-Oct daily 1000-1730, £8.30 concessions £7.50, children £5.20. Highland Country Bus No 12 runs Mon-Sat to Cawdor Church from Inverness. It's a 10-min walk from there to the castle.*

Though best known for its legendary association with Shakespeare's *Macbeth*, Cawdor Castle post-dates the grisly historical events on which the great Bard based his famous tragedy. The oldest part of the castle, the central tower, dates from 1372, and the rest of it is mostly 16th or 17th century. But despite the literary disappointment, the castle is still one of the most appealing in Scotland. It has been in the hands of the Cawdor family for over six centuries and each summer they clear off, leaving their romantic home and its glorious gardens and Big Wood of native trees species open for the enjoyment of ordinary folks like us. There's also a nine-hole golf course and self-catering accommodation (£550 per week) on the estate at Banchor Cottage.

According to family legend, an early Thane of Cawdor, wanting a new castle, had a dream in which he was told to load a donkey with gold, let it wander around for a day and watch where it lay down, for this would be the best spot for his new castle. He duly followed these instructions and the donkey lay down under a thorn tree, the remains of which can still be seen in the middle of a vaulted chamber in the 14th-century tower.

Just to the west of Cawdor is **Kilravock Castle** ① *T01667-493258, www.kilravockcastle. com*. This 14th-century stately home (pronounced *Kilrawk*) is still the seat of the Rose family. In recent years Kilravock has opened its doors as a castle B&B and self-catering experience (see Where to stay, page 47). Guests can enjoy a guided tour of the castle Monday to Saturday 1000. From April to September there's delicious home-baking in the castle tea room.

Nairn and around → *Phone code 01667. Population 11,190.*

With two championship golf courses, the seaside town of Nairn also claims to have the driest and sunniest climate in the whole of Scotland. This alone should be reason enough visit, but there are other attractions besides the sunshine for there are miles of sandy beach stretching east to the Culbin Forest and two of the best castles in the country are within easy reach – Cawdor Castle, see above, and Brodie Castle, see below. Nairn is also only 5 miles from the airport and makes a pleasant alternative to staying in Inverness.

Nairn Museum ① *Viewfield House, Viewfield Dr, www.nairnmuseum.co.uk, Apr-Oct Mon-Fri, 1000-1630, Sat 1000-1300, £3, concession £1.50*, gives an insight into the area's history and includes the Fishertown Room, highlighting the lives of the hardy men and women who in the 18th and 19th century made their living from the herring trade.

About 2 miles east of Nairn, in the little village of **Auldearn**, is a 17th-century *doocot* (dovecote). Nearby the Boath Doocot information boards record the 1645 Battle of Aldearn in which the victorious troops of Charles I, led by the Marquess of Montrose, defeated and killed almost 2000 Covenanters.

From Nairn, Harbour **Phoenix boat trips** ① *T01667-456078, www.phoenix-boat-trips.co.uk*, offer enjoyable wildlife cruises out onto the Moray Firth to spot the seals off Ardersier and possibly dolphins.

Ten miles south of Nairn on the A939 to Grantown is **Dulsie Bridge**, a very popular local beauty spot which is a great place for a summer picnic or to swim in the River Findhorn. On the southern shores of the Moray Firth, just east of Nairn, is **Culbin Sands**, a stretch of sand home to a variety of birdlife and managed by the RSPB. The best time to visit is from autumn to spring when bar-tailed godwits, oystercatchers, knots, dunlins, ringed plovers, redshanks, curlews, shellducks, red-breasted mergansers, greylag geese and snow buntings, to name but a few, come here in their droves.

Brodie Castle

① *T0844-493 2156, castle open Apr daily 1030-1630, May-Jun Sun-Wed 1030-1630, Jul-Aug daily 1030-1700, Sep-Oct Sun-Thu 1030-1630. Grounds open all year. £9, concessions £6.50.*

Brodie Castle, 8 miles east of Nairn, just off the main A96 to Forres, is one of Scotland's finest castles. The oldest part of the castle, the Z-plan tower house, is 16th century, with additions dating from the 17th and 19th centuries, giving it the look of a Victorian country house. The interior of the house is the epitome of good taste, with fabulous ceilings, and you can look round several rooms, including the huge Victorian kitchen. The collections of French furniture and Chinese porcelain are wonderful but most notable are the outstanding paintings, which include Edwin Landseer and Scottish Colourists. The grounds, too, are a delight, especially in spring when the daffodils are in bloom and there are specially constructed hides to observe the wildlife.

Dolphin cruises

The waters in this area are renowned for their populations of that well-loved mammal, the dolphin. Buckie is the home of the **Moray Firth Wildlife Centre**, which houses a dolphin exhibition and where you can find out everything you ever wanted to know about them. Spey Bay (one hour east of Inverness) is the home of the **Whale and Dolphin Conservation Society (WDCS)**, T01343-820339. Its wildlife centre, complete with shop and café, is packed with information about the dolphins and their latest sightings. There's also a WDCS centre at North Kessock, from where you can try to observe dolphins in the Beauly Firth from the viewing window.

There are various dolphin-spotting cruises around the Moray Firth, but there is a code of conduct for boat operators. Before you choose a cruise, make sure the company is is signed up to the **Dolphin Space Programme (DSP)**, www.dolphinspace.org. **Moray Firth Dolphin Cruises**, Inverness, T01463-717900, www.inverness-dolphin-cruises.co.uk, Mar-Oct daily 1030-1800, £12.50, concessions £10, children £9. Boat departs from Shore Street Quay, Inverness harbour. Take the courtesy bus from the tourist office. Throughout the 90-minute tour, this professional operator provides a chance to spot the bottlenose dolphins while also pointing out common and grey seals and abundant birdlife. Take warm clothes. **Dolphin Trips Avoch**, Harbour office, Pierhead, Avoch, T01381-622383, £10, children (three to-12 years) £7, under 3s free. Run informative 60-minute wildlife cruises up to six times a day from April to October. **Ecoventures**, The Dolphin Centre, Cromarty, Black Isle, T01381-600323, www.ecoventures.co.uk, £22, concessions £16. Leave daily subject to weather conditions. Just 40 minutes north of Inverness by car over the Kessock Bridge (A9) and A832, this experienced operator uses a high-speed RIB boat for a thrilling ride out to spot the bottlenose dolphins and possibly minke whale.

The Beauly Firth → *For listings, see pages 47-49.*

Beauly and around → *Phone code 01463.*
① *The train station at Beauly has the shortest platform in the UK, so take care getting off.*
The sleepy little market town of Beauly is 10 miles west of Inverness, where the Beauly river flows into the Firth. It's a lovely wee place – hence its name. According to local legend, when Mary Queen of Scots stayed here, at the priory, in 1564, she was so taken with the place that she cried (in French, of course) "Ah, quel beau lieu!" (What a beautiful place!).

At the north end of the marketplace is the ruin of **Beauly Priory** ① *daily 1000-1800, free*, founded in 1230 for the Valliscaulian order but, like so much else of Scotland's ecclesiastical heritage, it was destroyed during the Reformation. Close by, the **Beauly Centre** ① *T01463-783444, daily 1000-1800*, provides information on the area, a genealogy service, web access, café, gifts, clan history and even contains a reconstructed 1920s village shop to highlight how locals lived in the last century.

Four miles east of Beauly, at Balchraggan just off the main Inverness road, is **Moniack Castle Winery** ① *Apr-Sep Mon-Sat 1100-1700, Oct-Mar 1100-1600,*, where you can try a range of wines, including elderflower and birch. Four miles to the north and just off the A832 is the **Glen Ord Distillery** ① *T01463-872004, www.discovering-distilleries.com, Jan-Mar, Oct-Dec Mon-Fri 1100-1600, Apr-Sep Mon-Fri 1000-1700, Jul-Sep Mon-Fri 1000-1700,*

Sat-Sun 1000-1600, £5 (including a dram), which was established in 1838. The malt tour is enjoyable – particularly the dram. If travelling by bus it's a 10-minute walk after taking the Nos 17, 18 or 19 Stagecoach bus from Inverness to Muir of Ord.

The River Beauly is one of Scotland's best salmon-fishing rivers, and 5 miles south of Beauly, at **Aigas**, is a **fish lift** ① *Mon-Fri 1000-1500*, where you can watch salmon bypass the dam with the aid of technology. Nearby, on the A831 Cannich road, golfers will love the picturesque and challenging nine-hole **Aigas Golf Course** ① *T01463-782942*.

Glen Strathfarrar

Southwest of Beauly are glens Affric and Strathfarrar. Glen Strathfarrar, the lesser known of the two, is unspoiled and considered by some to be the more beautiful. To get there, take the A831 9 miles south from Beauly to Struy and follow the signs. Access to the glen is restricted by the estates in the area to 25 cars at a time. As a general rule there's gate access from Easter to late summer but it's best to call (T01738-493942) for advice. Once you're in, there is a tremendous feeling of peace, and there's good climbing, fishing and walking. The little ungraded road runs for 14 miles all the way to the impressive **Monar Dam** at the head of the glen. Glen Strathfarrar can also be reached from Drumnadrochit, via Cannich (see below). Most of the walks and cycle routes here are covered by OS Landranger Nos 25 and 26.

Glen Affric → *OS Landranger Nos 25 and 26.*

The A831 continues south from Struy through Strathglass to the village of **Cannich**, gateway to glorious Glen Affric, a dramatic and beautiful gorge, with the River Affric rushing through it, and surrounded by Caledonian pine and birch forest – in fact this is one of the few places where you can still see the native Scots pine. There are few, if any, more stunning sights in the Scottish Highlands and it's perfect for walking, or even just to drive through and stop for a picnic on a sunny day. Thanks to Rapson's and Ross's Minibus, it's possible to reach the beautiful and remote inner reaches of Glen Affric. The best departure point is Inverness Bus Station (stand seven) where **Ross's minibus** ① *T01463-761250, T07801-988491*, departs at 0845 on a Monday, Wednesday and Friday (July-September) and travels via Beauly and Cannich to the upper car park in Glen Affric. Alternatively, catch the **Rapson's** ① *T01463-710555*, bus from Inverness that picks up passengers at Drumnadrochit Post Office and heads 10 miles west into Glen Affric via Balnain and Tomich Post Office. On a Monday, Tuesday, Wednesday and Friday in summer, Ross's minibus goes back down the glen to meet passengers off the Rapsons bus at Cannich (around 1210) and drives back up Glen Affric to the road end.

Beyond Loch Affric the serious walking starts. From **Affric Lodge**, 9 miles west of Cannich, begins a 20-mile trail west to **Morvich**, near Shiel Bridge, on the west coast near Kyle of Lochalsh, see page 96. This strenuous walk is for experienced hikers only, and takes around 10 hours. You can stop off halfway at one of the most remote youth hostels in Scotland, **Glen Affric Youth Hostel** at Allt Beithe, see Where to stay, below.

There are also many shorter, easier walks around Glen Affric. There are some short, circular marked trails at the end of the road which runs west from Cannich almost to Loch Affric, and also from the car park at the impressive **Dog Falls**, 4.5 miles from Cannich and a great place to stop for a picnic and swim. Cycling in the forests around Cannich is good too – you can hire bikes at the friendly **Cannich Caravan and Camping Park** (see Where to stay, below). The owner's a keen cyclist.

Glen Affric can also be reached from **Drumnadrochit** (see page 50), by heading west on the A831 through Glen Urquhart to Cannich. Just before Cannich, on the road from Drumnadrochit, a single-track road leads left (south), past the Caravan and Camping Park, to the tiny village of **Tomich**. From here, it's a 3-mile hike up a woodland trail to a car park. A few hundred yards down through the trees takes you to the 70-ft plunging **Plodda Falls**. An old iron bridge affords a spectacular view of the waterfall.

Around Inverness listings

For hotel and restaurant price codes and other relevant information, see pages 13-20.

⬤ Where to stay

Nairn and around *p44*
££££ The Boath House Hotel and Spa, Aldearn T01667-454896, www.boath-house. com. Apparently once described as the most beautiful regency house in Scotland, this stunning hotel with 6 tastefully appointed bedrooms combines award-winning dining with luxury spa treatments
£££-£ Kilravock Castle, 7 miles west of Nairn, Croy, T01667-493258, www.kilravock castle.com. Just like Mary Queen of Scots, you can be a guest of what has been described as a historical gem housing artefacts from Culloden. Beautiful garden and spooky dungeons in this atmospheric 14th-century castle. Also offers backpackers a budget stay.
££ Greenlawns, 13 Seafield St, T01667-452738, www.greenlawns.uk.com. A friendly, 7-bedroom guesthouse where you'll tuck into the likes of kedgeree, smoked salmon and scrambled eggs for breakfast, in a dining room crammed with antiques.
££-£ Bracadale House, Albert St, T01667-452547, www.bracadalehouse.com. Very fine B&B.

Camping
Nairn Camping and Caravanning Club, Delnies Wood, Nairn, T01667-455281. Open Apr-Oct. Clean with good amenities in a secluded spot, but it's 3 miles to the pub.

Beauly and around *p45*
£££-££ The Priory Hotel, the Square, on the main street, T01463-782309, www.priory-hotel.com. Delightful hotel (**£££** with dinner).
££ Lovat Arms Hotel, opposite end of the main street from **The Priory Hotel**, T01463-782313, www.lovatarms.com. A wonderful 22-bedroom country house with a relaxed air and a tartan touch. Try the terrific Scottish game and seafood in the restaurant (**£££-££**) or relax with a dram or cup of tea beside the log fire. Terrific Sun lunch (1230-1400).

Glen Affric *p46*
££ The Tomich Hotel, Tomich, T01456-415399, www.tomichhotel.co.uk. You'll find a friendly welcome and good food at this former Victorian hunting lodge that will appeal to the visitor in search of walking, stalking and fishing alike. There's even haggis on the breakfast menu.
££-£ Bearnock Country Centre, 6 miles west of Drumnadrochit, Glen Urquhart, T01456-476296, www.bcclochnesshostel. co.uk. Opened in 2007, it's beautifully furnished with solid oak furniture and provides free tea, coffee and bed linen. Ideal for mountain biking, fishing and hiking in the area.
£ Cougie Lodge, near Tomich, T01456-415459, www.cougie.com. Open Apr-Sep. It's a long walk from Tomich but call ahead and the owners of this delightful independent hostel will pick you up.
£ Glen Affric Backpackers, Cannich, T01456-415263. Closed Christmas and New Year. 70 beds and a great open fire.

Owner has extensive contacts for local activities and walks.

£ Glen Affric Youth Hostel, Allt Beithe, T0845-293 7373. Apr to mid-Sep.

Self-catering
Culligran Cottages, Glen Strathfarrar, T01463-761255. Enjoy your own cottage or chalet along 15 miles of private road, where you can spot deer, fish or ride bikes.

Camping
Cannich Camping and Caravan Park, Cannich, T01456-415364. Mid-Mar to Oct. Just 5 mins' walk from the Spar shop. Handy campsite with caravans for rent. Very friendly and bike hire available.

🍴 Restaurants

Cawdor Castle *p43*
££-£ Cawdor Tavern, close to the castle, T01667-404777. A very popular, traditional country pub serving excellent food in a friendly atmosphere. Perfect for lunch or dinner after visiting the castle.

Nairn and around *p44*
£££-££ The Boath House Hotel and Spa, see Where to stay, above. Dripping with awards for their cuisine, this delightful rural retreat is well worth a visit.
£ Asher's tea room, 2 Bridge St. It is recommended for a hot snack. Run by the same folk as the one in Inverness.
£ Classroom, Cawdor St. Great for coffee, tasty home-baking and sandwiches.

Beauly and around *p45*
£££-£ Lovat Arms Hotel, see Where to stay, above. Serves up terrific food in the restaurant or relax in the bar with tasty snacks.
£ Beauly Tandoori, the Square, T01463-782221. Good for a cheap curry.

⬤ What to do

Nairn and around *p44*
Cycling
If you have a mountain bike, bring it to Lochaber and Glen Affric. Glen Urquhart Forest has fantastic trails outside Cannich.

Golf
Aigas Golf Course, the best golf course in the area, see page 46.

Horse riding
Heatherfield Riding Centre, Lochloy Rd, T01667-456682. Offer pony trekking.
Highland Trekking and Trail Riding, Cougie, Tomich by Cannich, T01456-415323, www.cougie.com, www.glenaffric.org. Open all year. Ride in the stunning wilds of Glen Affric.

Mountain biking
Moray Monster Trails (southeast of Nairn); **Balnain Bike Park** in Urquhart Forest east of Cannich; and **Learnie Forest** (Black Isle) provide miles of forest/trail cycling for all standards on state-of-the-art tracks. See www.forestry.gov.uk for details.

⬤ Transport

Culloden *p42*
Bus Highland Country Bus (Rapsons) No 12 runs to **Inverness**, daily.

Fort George *p42*
Bus Highland Country Bus No 11 to **Inverness**, several daily Mon-Sat. Also buses to **Nairn**.

Cawdor Castle *p43*
Bus Highland Country Bus No 12, Mon-Sat to **Inverness**.

Nairn and around *p44*
Bus There are regular daily buses to **Inverness**, 30 mins, Highland Country Buses and Stagecoach/Bluebird, see page 39. There are also buses to **Fort George**. To

Cawdor Castle there's an infrequent service, Mon-Fri, No 252, **Forres Taxis**, T0800-834233.

Cycle hire Rafford Cycles, Forres, T01309-672811. Bikes for hire from £16 per day.

Train Nairn is on the **Aberdeen** to **Inverness** rail line, and there are several trains daily to Inverness, 20 mins.

Brodie Castle *p44*
Bus Bluebird/Stagecoach buses run to **Inverness** via **Nairn**, 45 mins.

Beauly and around *p45*
Bus To **Inverness**, daily, No 19, **Stagecoach**, T01463-239292. To **Muir of Ord** and **Dingwall**, take the **Inverness** bus.

Train You can take the train to **Inverness** from here, it stops on its way from **Thurso**.

Glen Affric *p46*
Bus To **Inverness** from **Cannich** and **Tomich** via **Drumnadrochit**, Mon-Sat, Highland County Buses, T01463-710555 (No 17); Ross's Minibus, T01463-761250, T07801-988491.

Ross's Minibus service leaves from Glen Affric car park Mon, Wed and Fri at 1700 and returns via **Cannich** and **Drumnadrochit** to **Inverness**. It is strongly recommended to call ahead to confirm the timetable. You only other option is to walk out of the glen to the village of Cannich and catch the No 17 **Rapson's** bus that runs 4 times Mon-Sat. On a Tue only, **Ross's Minibus** also runs from Cannich Post Office at 0945 to **Dingwall** via **Beauly** and **Muir of Ord**, arriving at 1039.

Loch Ness and around

One of Scotland's biggest attractions is the narrow gash of Loch Ness, Britain's deepest body of fresh water, stretching 23 miles from Fort Augustus in the south almost to Inverness in the north. The loch is scenic in its own right, with rugged hills rising steeply from its wooded shores, but visitors don't come here for the views. They come every year, in their hundreds of thousands, to stare across the dark, cold waters in search of its legendary inhabitant, the Loch Ness Monster. A huge tourist trade has grown up around 'Nessie', as the monster is affectionately known, and every summer the main A82, which runs along its western shore, is jam-packed with bus-loads of eager monster-hunters, binoculars trained on the loch surface, desperate for one glimpse of the elusive beast. If you do see it, bear in mind your photograph could be worth a fortune!

Arriving in Loch Ness

Getting around

The best way to see the loch is on a cruise from Inverness (page 37). There are also boat trips from Drumnadrochit and Fort Augustus (see page 60). Most of the tourist traffic uses the congested A82, built in 1933 and which offers few decent views of the loch. By far the best views of are from the quiet and picturesque B862/852, which runs along the eastern shore from Fort Augustus up to Inverness. It's possible to make a complete circuit of the loch, which is best done in an anti-clockwise direction heading south from Inverness on the A82, but you'll need your own transport (or take a tour), as there are no buses between Fort Augustus and Foyers. There are regular daily bus services between Inverness and Fort William, with additional buses between Invergarry and Fort Augustus. Fort Augustus is a convenient stopover between Fort William and Inverness. Citylink buses between Inverness and Kyle of Lochalsh stop at Urquhart Castle, Loch Ness Youth Hostel, Invergarry and Invermoriston. ▶▶ *See What to do, page 60, and Transport, page 61.*

Around the loch → *For listings, see pages 56-61.*

Drumnadrochit → *Phone code 01456.*

The Nessie tourist trade is centred on the village of Drumnadrochit, 15 miles south of Inverness, where the canny locals have cashed in on the enduring popularity of the monster myth. The monster hype is almost overpowering, with two rival Monster exhibitions and the inevitable souvenir shops selling all manner of awful tartan tat, including those scary-looking tartan dolls with flickering eyelids, the 'See-You-Jimmy' tartan bonnet, complete

The Great Glen Way

The Great Glen Way is a waymarked walking trail that runs for 73 miles between Inverness and Fort William. Panoramic views of Loch Ness can be seen at many of the sections between Fort Augustus and Inverness. Although a relatively easy walk, there are some fairly tough sections around Loch Ness and you'll need to be properly equipped and

have a good map. OS Landranger Nos 26, 34 and 41 cover the entire route. It should take four or five days to complete, depending on your level of fitness. It is probably better to walk it in 'reverse', from Fort William to Inverness, as the easiest section is then at the start. The Great Glen Way also has its own website, www.greatglenway.com.

with ginger 'hair', and not forgetting the Loch Ness Monster novelty hat. Fortunately, the very friendly **TIC** ① *in the car park, T01456-459076, Apr-Sep Mon-Sat 0900-1730, Sun 1000-1600, call ahead for winter hours*, can offer alternative suggestions, such as exploring peaceful Glen Affric (see page 46). There are also toilets a beside the TIC (daily 0700-1800).

One of the two Monster Exhibitions is the '**Original' Loch Ness Monster Visitor Centre and Lodge Hotel** ① *T01456-450342, www.lochness-centre.com, Jul-Aug daily 0900-2100, Sep-Jun daily 0900-1700, £5.50, concessions £4.35, students £4.50, children £4*, features a wide-screen cinema documenting the 'latest' facts and 'sightings' of Nessie. There's also a gift shop, but the most authentic experience of all is the restaurant's tasty home-baking. **Loch Ness Cruises** (*MV Nessie Hunter*) operates from here, see page 37. The rival exhibition is **Loch Ness 2000 Exhibition** ① *T01456-450573, Feb-May daily 0930-1700, Jun and Sep daily 0900-1800, Jul-Aug daily 0900-1830, Oct daily 0930-1700, Nov-Mar daily 1000-1530, £6.50, concessions £5, children £4.50*. This Nessie exhibition also details eye-witness accounts, but more pertinently provides a more elaborate audio-visual experience.

If it all gets too much, then fear not, for Drumnadrochit gives easy access to one of the most beautiful corners of Scotland. The A831 heads west from the village through Glen Urquhart to Cannich, about 12 miles away, at the head of Glen Affric, a great place for walking or enjoying a picnic (see page 46).

Castle Urquhart

① *T01456-450551, Apr-Sep daily 0930-1800, Oct-Mar daily 0930-1630, £7.20, concessions £5.70, children £4.30. Citylink bus (No 919) stops at Urquhart Castle.*

A few miles south of Drumnadrochit are the ruins of Castle Urquhart. The castle bears the scars of centuries of fighting but its setting, perched on a rocky cliff on the loch's edge, is magnificent and, not surprisingly, one of the most photographed scenes in Scotland. Dating from the 14th century, the castle was a strategic base, guarding the Great Glen during the long Wars of Independence. It was taken by Edward I, held by Robert the Bruce against Edward II, and was then almost constantly under siege before being destroyed in 1692 to prevent it from falling into Jacobite hands. Most of the existing buildings date from the 16th century, including the five-storey tower, the best-preserved part of the complex, from where you get great views of the loch and surrounding hills. The entire complex is accessed via the stunning visitor centre that in addition to the obligatory café includes an informative short-film about the history of the castle.

Great Monster Hunt

In a country full of myths and legends, the Loch Ness Monster is the greatest of them all. As elusive as a straight answer from a politician, Nessie has single-handedly sold more tins of tartan-wrapped shortbread to foreign visitors than Edinburgh Castle.

Tales of Nessie go way back to the sixth century, when St Columba is said to have calmed the beast after she had attacked one of his monks. But the monster craze only really took off with the completion of the A82 road along the loch's western shore in 1933. Since then there have been numerous sightings, some backed up with photographic evidence, though the most impressive of these – the famous black-and-white movie footage of Nessie's humps moving through the water, and the classic photograph of her head and neck – have been exposed as fakes.

In recent decades determined monster hunters have enlisted the help of new technology, such as sonar surveys but have failed to come up with conclusive evidence. Enter Cyber Nessie, the latest attempt to end the years of rumours, hoaxes and speculation. Nessie's very own website, www.lochness.co.uk, is a 24-hour real-time video watch of Loch Ness, and has already produced a couple of claimed sightings.

Invermoriston → *Phone code 01320.*

Between Drumnadrochit and Fort Augustus is the tiny village of Invermoriston, probably the most tranquil spot on the entire Inverness to Fort Augustus stretch of the A82. It's a beautiful little piece of Highland scenery, with a photogenic old stone bridge over foaming river rapids and with marked woodland trails leading off into the hills past some lovely waterfalls. There's an interesting **Clog and Craft Centre** ⓘ *T01320-351318*, where high-quality clogs and leather goods are made to measure. Just along the road is the **Glenmoriston Arms**, where, in addition to a resident ghost in the fabulous accommodation, the owner tempts the palette with fine food and a vast selection of malts.

At Invermoriston the A887 heads west through **Glen Moriston** to meet the A87, which runs from Invergarry (see page 53) all the way through the rugged and dramatic Glen Shiel and under the shadow of the Five Sisters of Kintail en route to Kyle of Lochalsh and Skye.

Fort Augustus → *Phone code 01320.*

At the more scenic southern end of Loch Ness stands the village of Fort Augustus, the former clan village of Kilchuimen until set up as a garrison after the Jacobite rebellion of 1715 to serve as the headquarters of General Wade's campaign to pacify the Highlands. Today, Fort Augustus is a very busy little place, full of monster-hunting tourists and boats using the flight of five locks to enter or leave Loch Ness on their journey along the Caledonian Canal. The TIC ⓘ *T01320-366779, Apr-Oct*, is in the car park next to the petrol station and cashpoint.

Like many visitors, you may find yourself drawn to the canal side, watching yachts and cruise boats negotiate the first of many locks to access/leave Loch Ness. Alternatively, pop into **The Clansman Centre** ⓘ *T01320-366444, Easter-Oct daily 1000-1800, £4.50, concessions £3.50*, where young guides in traditional dress provide a lively and entertaining presentation of 17th-century Highland family life in an old turf house. If you've time, pop into the **Caledonian Canal Heritage Centre** ⓘ *Jun-Sep daily, free*, with its history of the impressive canal system. Nearby, children may also enjoy the **Highland and Rare Breeds Croft** ⓘ *T01320-366433, £2, concessions £1.50*, where Highland cattle, red deer, Shetland sheep, ducks and rabbits can be spotted.

Fort Augustus to Dores

A very worthwhile detour from Fort Augustus is to take the B862/852 up the east shore of Loch Ness, a mostly single-track road that skirts the loch for much of its length to the village of Dores. It's a much quieter and more scenic route than the busy A82 and follows General Wade's original (and very straight) military road which linked Fort Augustus with Fort George. Though it makes a more interesting alternative to the more popular A82 route from Inverness to Fort Augustus, it's best done from south to north, if you have the time. Today, this road also attracts runners from around the world for the annual (October) Baxters Loch Ness Marathon. This route is only possible if you have your own transport. There are buses south from Inverness, but they only run as far as Foyers. If you're feeling very fit, it can be done by bike, as a tough trip from Fort Augustus or from Inverness, possibly using the one way bike hire service offered by **Off Beat Bikes** in Fort William (see What to do, page 73).

From Fort Augustus, the road winds its way up into rugged hills past Glendole where the largest hydroelectric scheme to be built in Scotland in 50 years recently became operational. Nearby is the good real ale house of the historic Whitebridge Hotel and the nearby 1732 White Bridge. The road then drops back to the lochside at **Foyers**. It's worth stopping here to see the impressive waterfall where the River Foyers plunges into Loch Ness or to enjoy an overnight stay at **Foyers House** (see Where to stay, page 57). To get there, follow the steep (and slippery) track down from opposite the shops. Three miles further north, at **Inverfarigaig**, is **Boleskine House**, once home of Alastair Crowley, who is said to have practised devil worship here. In the 1970s the house was bought by Jimmy Page of Led Zeppelin, but sold some years later after the tragic death of his daughter. Those of a nervous disposition may wish to pass on quickly and continue to the little village of **Dores**, at the northeastern end of the loch, where you can enjoy some fine forest walks or reasonable pub grub at the **Dores Inn**.

You can then continue to Inverness, or return via the beautiful hill road that leads up to **Loch Mhorand** back to Fort Augustus via the **Stratherrick Valley**. From **Errogie**, at the northern end of Loch Mhor, there's a dramatic section of road that winds down to the loch through a series of tight, twisting bends, reminiscent of an Alpine pass, and great for cyclists. There are also interesting marked woodland trails around Errogie.

Fort Augustus to Fort William → *For listings, see pages 56-61.*

South of Fort Augustus, the A82 leaves behind Loch Ness and runs along the west shore of Loch Oich and then the east shore of Loch Lochy, until it reaches Spean Bridge. Here the A82 continues south to Fort William, while the A86 branches east through Glen Spean to join the A9 Perth to Inverness road finally at Kingussie. All along this route are many opportunities to get off the beaten track and explore huge chunks of real wilderness, deserted since the Clearances and soaked in the blood of history.

Invergarry and around → *Phone code 01809.*

The old village of Invergarry stands where the A82 turns west to meet the A87. There's not much to see or do in the village, but the surrounding area merits some exploring, particularly the route west through Glen Garry, and there are several places to stay.

Inside the entrance to the **Glengarry Castle Hotel**, on the shores of Loch Oich (see Where to stay, page 58) stand the ruins of **Invergarry Castle**, once the stronghold of Clan Ranald of Glengarry and later destroyed by the Duke of Cumberland as he wreaked

Old as the hills

The Great Glen, which splits the Scottish mainland from Fort William in the south to Inverness in the north, is one of the world's major geological fault lines. The Glen was formed millions of years ago when the northern part of the Caledonian mountains 'slid' more than 60 miles south, leaving behind a massive glen with four freshwater lochs – Loch Linnhe, Loch Lochy, Loch Oich and Loch Ness.

The most famous of these is Loch Ness, which attracts hordes of visitors eager to catch a glimpse of its elusive monster. The renowned engineer, Thomas Telford, succeeded in connecting all these lochs when he built the impressive Caledonian Canal. The canal took 22 years to complete, and when it was opened in 1822 was the first in Britain to take ships from one coast to the other. It remains the only canal in the country capable of carrying ships of up to 500 tons. The best way to appreciate the glen is by boat, through the 38 miles of natural lochs and rivers and the 22 miles of canal, and every summer pleasure craft of all shapes and sizes ply its length. The main A82 runs from Inverness south to Fort William. The southern section, from Fort Augustus, follows the original line of the road constructed in 1727 by General Wade to link the military garrisons at Fort William and Fort Augustus (hence their names).

Another way to travel through the Great Glen is along the excellent cycle route, which follows the canal towpaths, forest trails and quiet minor roads to avoid the busy main road. The route is outlined in the Forestry Commission leaflet, available from most TICs.

revenge on the Highlands in the aftermath of Culloden (see box, page 43). The hotel was later built as the main house of the Ellice family, who made their fortune from the Hudson Bay Company in Canada and who were the main driving force behind the creation of the Victorian planned village.

A mile or so south of the village, at **North Laggan**, is a monument by the side of the road standing over **The Well of the Seven Heads**. This tells the grisly story of the Keppoch Murders, one of the most infamous clan murders which took place at **Roy Bridge** (see page 56) in the 17th century. It all began when the chief of the clan MacDonnell died, leaving two young sons, who were sent away to complete their education before returning to Roy Bridge to celebrate the elder brother's accession to chieftainship. Another branch of the clan present at the celebrations started a fight in which both brothers were killed. Believing they had been murdered, one of their cousins persuaded a fellow clan member to raise 50 men and march on the murderers' house at nearby Inverlair. The accused murderers – a father and his six sons – were duly slaughtered and their heads cut off, to be displayed before the local laird at Glengarry. On the way to his lodge, the heads were washed here in this well.

A few miles further south, at **Laggan**, where the A82 crosses to the east bank of Loch Lochy, is the site of the **Battle of the Shirts**. The A87 leads west from Invergarry through Glen Shiel to Shiel Bridge, on the way to Kyle of Lochalsh on the west coast, see page 96. About 7 miles along the A87, past the turning for Kinloch Hourn (see below), is the **Glen Garry viewpoint**, from where you get one of the most stunning, and famous, of all Highland views. From this angle Loch Garry looks uncannily like a map of Scotland, so get out the camera for that classic holiday snap.

Glen Garry to Kinloch Hourn

A mile or so before the Glen Garry viewpoint, where the A87 begins to leave the shores of Loch Garry, is the turning left for the road through Glen Garry, described as the longest and most beautiful cul-de-sac in Britain. The little single-track road turns and twists for 22 glorious miles along the shores of Loch Garry and Loch Quoich all the way to Kinloch Hourn at the head of Loch Hourn. Known as 'the loch of the devil' this sea loch forms part of the wonderful wilderness area of Knoydart aptly dubbed the 'Rough Bounds.'

Glen Garry is now virtually deserted but was once home to some 5000 people who were driven out during the infamous Highland Clearances in the 19th century. The road passes the tiny hamlet of **Tomdoun**, once the junction of the main road to Skye, until the massive post-Second World War hydroelectric schemes changed the landscape. Experienced hillwalkers can still follow the old route to Skye, through Glen Kingie, along Loch Hourn and then across the wild Knoydart Peninsula until they reach the tiny but welcoming settlement of **Inverie**. From here a little **ferry** ① *T01687-462320, Apr-Sep Mon-Fri, Oct-Mar Mon, Wed and Thu*, runs to Mallaig, see page 87.

Beyond Tomdoun the road passes a huge dam, built in the 1950s, which raised the waters of **Loch Quoich** by over 100 ft, flooding many of the old settlements. Also flooded was **Glen Quoich Lodge**, which can count Edward VII and Sir Edward Landseer among its notable guests. It was reputedly Glen Garry that gave Landseer the inspiration for his famous painting *The Monarch of the Glen*. The road then reaches its highest point, at 1200 ft, before descending to **Kinloch Hourn**, once a thriving crofting and fishing village.

Spean Bridge → *Phone code 01397.*

The main A82 runs down the east shore of Loch Lochy to the village of Spean Bridge, at the head of Glen Spean, beneath the towering Lochaber Mountains. The village gets its name from Thomas Telford's bridge across the River Spean. Two miles west are the remains of the old 'Highbridge', built in 1736 by General Wade, and the site of the first clash between Government troops and the Jacobites, three days before Prince Charles raised his standard at Glenfinnan.

Spean Bridge is only 8 miles north of Fort William so gets busy in the summer, but it still makes a more peaceful and attractive alternative base for exploring this astoundingly beautiful part of the Highlands. There's a **TIC** ① *T01397-712576, Easter-Oct*, just off the main road behind the **Spean Bridge Hotel**. This hotel, complete with its **Shinty Bar** watering hole, also houses the excellent **Commando Exhibition** ① *free*. The area is also the starting point for the excellent **Grey Corries ridge walk** (OS Landranger Map No 41).

Loch Arkaig and around → *Phone code 01397.*

A mile north of Spean Bridge on the A82 is the striking **Commando Memorial**, which commemorates the men who trained in the area from their secret base at Achnacarry during the Second World War and the 1700 commandos who lost their lives. It's worth lingering for a few moments to appreciate the fantastic views including (on a clear day) the summit of Ben Nevis. From here the B8004 branches west to **Gairlochy**, crossing the Caledonian Canal, then the B8005 heads north to Loch Arkaig, a long, deep and mysterious loch stretching west through the mountains. Bonnie Prince Charlie passed this way, before and after Culloden, through an area which has, for centuries, been the seat of the Camerons of Lochiel. The Camerons were fervent supporters of the Jacobite cause and when Prince Charles landed at Loch nan Uamh, on the road from Fort William to Mallaig, he called on Cameron of Lochiel to join him at Glenfinnan.

In the tiny township of **Achnacarry**, nestled between the shores of Loch Lochy and Loch Arkaig, you can find out about the Camerons and their involvement in the Jacobite rebellion of 1745 at the **Clan Cameron Museum** ① *T01397-712480, Easter to mid-Oct daily 1330-1700, Jul-Aug 1100-1700, £3.50 concessions £2, children free.* This interesting museum is housed in an old cottage, rebuilt after being burned by government troops in 1746.

Beyond the turn-off to Achnacarry, the single-track road runs through the Clunes Forest and The Dark Mile, a long line of beech trees which completely cuts out daylight. At the east end of Loch Arkaig, a stone bridge crosses the Caig Burn. Beside the bridge is a car park, from where a path leads up to the spectacular **Cia-Aig Falls** which tumble into a deep, dark pool known as **The Witch's Cauldron**. It was here that an old hag was accused of casting her evil eye over Lochiel's cattle, causing them to fall ill and die. But when she fell into the pool and drowned, the cattle miraculously began to recover from their illness. The road runs along the north shore of Loch Arkaig all the way to the head of the loch, from where experienced and well-equipped hill walkers can hike through the glens to Loch Nevis, 'the loch of heaven', and Knoydart.

Glen Roy and Loch Laggan → *Phone code 01397.*

From Spean Bridge the A86 runs east through dramatic Glen Spean to meet the A9 Perth to Inverness road which leads to Aviemore, see page 37. The road (and railway) passes through **Roy Bridge**, which is the turn-off for Glen Roy, noted for its amazing 'parallel roads'. These are not in fact roads, but three gravel ledges etched on to the mountains at different heights. The 'roads' marked the shorelines of a glacial lake formed during the last Ice Age. Roy Bridge was also the site of the infamous Keppoch Murders, see page 54.

The road continues east towards Loch Laggan. After a couple of miles it passes **Cille Choirille**, an ancient church built by a 15th-century Cameron chief as penance for a life of violence. The church fell into disrepair but was restored and reopened in 1932 and now attracts people of all creeds as it's said to inspire peace and spiritual healing. Further east, at the eastern end of Loch Laggan, is the massive **Laggan Dam**, built in 1933 to provide water for the aluminium smelter at Fort William. The water is piped through tunnels up to 15 ft in diameter carved through the core of Ben Nevis. The road runs along the north shore of the loch, past the **Creag Meagaidh National Nature Reserve**, where you can see herds of red deer right by the reserve car park. A path leads from here up to **Lochan a' Choire** (about four hours). Note that there are no bus or postbus services between Spean Bridge and Laggan.

Loch Ness and around listings

For hotel and restaurant price codes and other relevant information, see pages 13-20.

🛏 Where to stay

Drumnadrochit *p50*

£££ Loch Ness Inn, Lewiston, T01456-450991, www.staylochness.co.uk. Fabulous and beautifully appointed accommodation and restaurant, 1½ miles south of the TIC in Drumnadrochit, and with connections to the acclaimed **Applecross Inn**. In addition to 12 comfortable bedrooms, this former rustic brewery, just off the main road, has a **Brewery Bar** serving the likes of Isle of Skye real ale and a menu (**£££-££**), of hand-dived scallops, Applecross Bay prawns and all manner of locally sourced produce.

££ The Benleva Hotel, T01456-450080, www.benleva.co.uk. A former manse, this small, atmospheric hotel prides itself on a fine range of real ales and its use of freshly

prepared local produce. Each Sep, it helps host the **Loch Ness Beer Festival** so book ahead. The 400-year-old chestnut tree outside the front door was the former hanging tree.
££ Gillyflowers, T01456-450641, gillyflowers@cali.co.uk. Good-value guesthouse in converted croft.
££-£ Loch Ness Backpackers Lodge, Coiltie Farmhouse, Lewiston, T01456-450807, www.lochness-backpackers.com. A terrific, low-budget option run by friendly, helpful owners who can arrange boat trips and walks in the area.
£ Bearnock Country Centre (Loch Ness Hostel), 6 miles west of Drumnadrochit towards Cannich, T01456-476296, www.bcc lochnesshostel.co.uk. This backpackers oozes quality and style. Beautifully furnished, fully en suite and with great facilities, this place is within reach of both Loch Ness and Glen Affric. Highly recommended.

Invermoriston p52
£££ Glenmoriston Arms Hotel, T01320-351 206, www.glenmoristonarms.co.uk. Formerly a 17th-century drovers inn, this comfortable, 8-bedroom hotel on the route of the Great Glen Way is proud of its freshly prepared cuisine that draws on local produce (**£££-££**) and there are 150 malt whiskies behind the bar. Johnson and Boswell were guests during their 18th-century tour of the Highlands and it's said there's a resident ghost.
£ SYHA Loch Ness Youth Hostel, a few miles north, on the main A82, T01320-351274. Mid-Apr to end Oct. Fantastic views across Loch Ness.

Self-catering
Lann Dearg B&B and Studios, Invermoriston, T01320-351353, www.lanndearg.com. Right by the the Great Glen Way, this delightful B&B (**££**) with adjoining, fully equipped self-catering studios (£60 per studio per night) offers a luxurious stay after a hard days hike by the lochside. There's even the option of a 'breakfast basket' if you can't be bothered rolling out of bed.

Camping
Loch Ness Caravan & Camping Park, 1.5 miles south of Invermoriston, and 6 miles north of Fort Augustus, T01320-351207. Open Mar-Jan. On the shores of the loch with great views and excellent facilities.

Fort Augustus p52
£££-££ Caledonian Hotel, T01320-366256. Directly opposite the **Lovat**, this is another lovely place to dine (**£££-££**) and enjoy a comfortable sleep (10 en suite rooms).
£££-££ Lovat Arms Hotel, T01463-782313. Beautiful, family-run mansion house, which has been refurbished at considerable expense to ensure you enjoy a luxurious stay and delicious food (**£££-££**). They also run the acclaimed
Loch Torridon Hotel.
££ Auchterawe House, Fort Augustus T01320-366228. Open all year. 6 en suite rooms. Comfortable and friendly.
££ Sonas, on the Inverness Rd, T01320-366291. Run by Mrs Service who certainly lives up to her name.
£ Morag's Lodge, Bunoich Brae, T01320-366289, www.moragslodge.com. Open all year. Friendly, good value – another excellent option along Loch Ness.

Fort Augustus to Dores p53
££ Evergreen Guest House, Inverfarigaig T01456-486717, www.evergreenlochness. co.uk. The very friendly owners of this east-shore guesthouse also offer dinner, B&B and innovative car and walking tours around the Loch Ness area (see What to do, below).
££ Foyers House, Foyers, T01456-486405. Small guesthouse that prides itself on its view of Loch Ness from the decking and tasty evening treats such as game pie. They do not accommodate children or babies. (**££**).
££ Whitebridge Hotel, 3 miles south of Foyers, T01456-486226. Old-world hotel with comfortable accommodation. Also serves good real ales and bar food.

Camping

Fort Augustus Caravan and Camping, at the southern end of the village, T01320-366618. A good option for campers.

Invergarry and around p53

£££ Glengarry Castle Hotel, T01809-501254, www.glengarry.net. Mar-Nov. 26 tastefully appointed bedrooms set in 60 acres of woodland running down to Loch Oich. The hotel prides itself on its traditional Highland hospitality with the daily changing dinner menu (**£££-££**) serving up the best of local Scottish produce.

££ Forest Lodge, South Laggan, south of Invergarry and 24 miles north of Fort William, T01809-501219, www.flgh.co.uk. A welcoming and comfortable B&B that can also rustle-up a 4-course Scottish dinner (£17 per person), whilst you enjoy the scenery.

£ Invergarry Lodge, Mandally Rd, Invergarry, T01809-501412, www.invergarrylodge.co.uk. Open all year. Independent hostel sleeping up to 26 in 4-6 bed rooms. Fully equipped kitchen and safe cycle shed.

Self-catering

Faichmard Farm Chalets, Invergarry, T01809-501314, www.glengarryselfcatering.co.uk. Rustic, secluded, cosy and peaceful. Sleeps 3 at a modest price. £220 plus per week.

Camping

Faichem Park, Ardgarry Farm, lodge and cottages, 15 mins' walk from the village, T01809-501226, www.ardgarryfarm.co.uk. There's a fabulous double room in the farmhouse offering B&B (**££**), and options for 4-6 people to enjoy self-catering (£290-560 per week) in well equipped lodges with spectacular views.

Glen Garry to Kinloch Hourn p55

The **Cluanie Inn** (see page 97 for details), sits in an isolated spot before the road presses further westward into Glen Shiel under the mighty Sisters of Kintail. 30 mins further west is the turn-off towards Loch Hourn and the remote, roadless wilds of the beautiful Knoydart Peninsula. With the lodge at Skiary now closed, call the Knoydart Foundation rangers office at Inverie (T01687-462242) for details of accommodation options near Loch Hourn and around the peninsula.

Spean Bridge p55

There's no shortage of accommodation in Spean Bridge.

££££ Corriegour Lodge Hotel, 9 miles north of Spean Bridge on the A82, T01397-712685, www.corriegour-lodge-hotel.com. Open Feb-Dec. 9 rooms. Lovely Victorian hunting lodge on the shores of Loch Lochy, with fine views and an excellent restaurant, £49 for a 5-course candlelit dinner.

££££ Old Pines Hotel and Restaurant, just past the **Commando Memorial** on the B8004, T01397-712324, www.oldpines.co.uk. This delightful boutique hotel is where discerning guests will experience a truly personal touch. Each of the 8 rooms is individually appointed to a very high standard. The warm scones and tea on arrival are just a hint of the treat in store at dinner where venison, local lamb, prime beef and shellfish feature. It's not inexpensive but for a touch of class in an unpretentious manner this could be a fine choice for an overnight stay or just for dinner (**£££**).

££ Corriechoille Lodge, 2 miles north of Spean Bridge, T01397-712002, www.corriechoille.com. Apr-Oct. This secluded former fishing lodge offers a very comfortable stop for the night and a roaring open fire.

££ Invergloy House, T01397-712681. A friendly, comfortable former coach house converted into a B&B, which is set in 50 acres of gardens and offers 2 en suite rooms.

£ Smiddy House, T01397-712335. A comfortable guesthouse with a small restaurant (**££**). Self-catering also available in the adjacent **Old Smiddy**.

Camping
Gairlochy Holiday Park, west towards Gairlochy, T01397-712711. Open Apr-Oct. Camping and self-catering chalets from £250-620 per week.
Stronaba Caravan & Camping, north of the village, T01397-712259. Apr-Oct.

Glen Roy and Loch Laggan *p56*
£ Aite Cruinnichidh, Achluachrach, 1.5 miles from the village, T01397-712315. This comfy bunkhouse even has a sauna.
£ Grey Corrie Lodge, Roy Bridge, T01397-712236. Very handy for the nearby pub, transport and local shop.
£ Station Lodge, 5 miles east at Tulloch train station, T01397-732333. Ideal if arriving by train or planning to hike in the hills. The friendly owners will even cook very early breakfasts to accommodate walkers and climbers. The trains stop practically at the door.

❷ Restaurants

Drumnadrochit *p50*
The hotels all tend to serve decent bar food and some B&Bs offer evening meals.
£££-££ The Loch Ness Inn, 1 mile north of Urquhart Castle, T01456-450991. Lovely setting and offering fresh seafood, locally sourced produce and a good range of real ales.
££-£ Karasia, Balmacaan Rd, T01456-450003. Scotland's love-affair with curry has even reached the shores of Loch Ness. Great food.

Fort Augustus *p52*
££ Lock Inn, by the canal. A good place for a drink and serves good pub food.
££ Poachers, Richmond House Hotel, Main St. For a drink and good pub grub.
££-£ Bothy Bite, down by the canal bridge, T01320-366710. A cosy choice serving simple but tasty bistro-style meals.

Spean Bridge *p55*
There's a chip shop and the **Spean Bridge Mill Coffee Shop**, T01397-712260, around the back of the Spean Bridge Hotel.
£££-££ Old Station Restaurant, Station Rd, T01397-712535, www.oldstationrestaurant.co.uk. Sep-Jun Thu-Tue, Jul-Aug daily. As long ago as 1894, trains on the West Highland Railway Line puffed up to its door, and now the railway station has been converted it serves delicious evening meals from 1800 in a fascinating interior.
££-£ Spean Bridge Hotel, T01397-712250, www.speanbridgehotel.co.uk. Aside from its **Commando Museum** and reasonable food, it's also worth popping into the refurbished **Shinty** bar. Here you can share a real ale or some pub grub with the locals whilst admiring the local shinty team's silverware.

Glen Roy and Loch Laggan *p56*
£££-££ Best Western Glenspean Lodge Hotel, 1.5 miles east of Roy Bridge, T01397-712223. For those in search of sustenance, this tastefully modernized hunting lodge rustles up a tasty bar lunch (1200-1400) and dinner.
££-£ Stronlossit Inn, Roy Bridge, T01397-712 253, www.stronlossit.co.uk. Serves reasonable meals and a good range of real ale and malts. Also has rooms (**££**).
£ Bunroy Caravan Park, in a secluded spot, Roybridge, T07909-850724. Directly opposite the **Stronlossit Inn**, handy for the train station.

❁ Festivals

Fort Augustus *p52*
Jun-Sep Highland Gatherings. Late Jun and Jul, mid-Aug and early Sep is the period when Fort Augustus hosts the Highland Gatherings, featuring traditional dancing and piping competitions, tossing the caber and sheep dog trials.

⚙ What to do

There are various monster-spotting tours of Loch Ness which leave from the tourist office in Drumnadrochit or Fort Augustus.

Drumnadrochit *p50*
Boat trips
Castle Cruises Loch Ness, Temple Pier, T01456-450695, T01456-450205, www.loch nesscruises.com. Offers 60-min cruises (£10) on Loch Ness, leaving from Drumnadrochit aboard the *MV Morag*.

Jacobite, Tomnahurich Bridge, Glenurqu-hart Rd, Inverness, T01463-233999, www.jacobite. co.uk. Tours depart from the Clansman Hotel, about 5 miles north of Drumnadrochit. Loch Ness cruises that incorporate Castle Urquhart, the Caledonian Canal and a visit to the Loch Ness Monster 2000 Exhibition. Its Discovery tour includes a 3½-hr cruise on the loch (£26); its Temptation option offers a 30-min cruise and 60-min tour of the castle (£21). Contact the operator for specific pick-up/drop-off points.

Horse riding
Highland Riding Centre, Borlum Farm, Drumnadrochit, T01456-450220, www. borlum.com. Children must be over the age of 4 to ride.

Fort Augustus to Fort William *p53*
Boat trips
Cruise Loch Ness, Knockburnie, Inchnacardoch, Fort Augustus, T01320-366277, www.cruiselochness.com. Sailing out of Fort Augustus by the Caledonian Canal for the past 40 years, this renowned operator has catered for Hollywood and Scottish stars alike and uses onboard 3D underwater imaging to relay 'real time' information about what is lurking in the peaty depths of Loch Ness. Mar-Nov hourly, 1000-1600, Jul-Aug 1000-2000, 1 hr, £11, children £6.50.

Fingal of Caledonia, The Slipway, Corpach, Fort William, T01397-772167, www.fingal-cruising.co.uk. Runs all-inclusive 4- and 6-day cruises in a converted Dutch 'spitz' barge that gently ploughs its way through the 60-mile waterway of the Great Glen. In addition to sailing the length of the loch, and wildlife tours of Loch Linnhe, its Great Glen Way tour allows guests to walk up to 14-mile sections of the route each day before meeting the barge each evening at prearranged points. On board, guests can make use of mountain bikes, canoes, sailing dinghies and wind-surfers lashed to the deck. Guides and instructors are included. Cruises operate Apr-Oct and cost from £350-725 per person.

George Edwards, contact **Castle Cruises Loch Ness**, T01456-450395, www.lochness-cruises.com, or **'Original' Loch Ness Monster Visitor Centre**, see page 51. George takes would-be monster-spotters out on the loch in his boat, *Nessie Hunter*, which is based near Drumnadrochit. He not only once caught a glimpse of Nessie but also discovered the deepest part of the loch (812 ft), now known as Edward's Deep. Cruises run hourly Apr-Oct 1000-1800. Trips last 1 hr, £10, children £6.

Climbing
Nevis Guides, Bohuntin, Roy Bridge, T01397-712356.

Mountain biking
Laggan Wolftrax Mountain Bike Centre, 20 miles west of Roy Bridge, T01528-544786, www.laggan.com. Has miles of purpose-built trail in Strathmashie Forest, bike hire from £18 plus and an excellent café.

Fishing
Loch Arkaig in particular is renowned for its trout fishing.
Fishing Scotland, Roy Bridge, T01397-712812, T07737-627907, www.fishing scotland.co.uk. Jimmy Coutts runs professional fly-fishing courses for the expert and novice alike, giving them the opportunity to learn to fly fish or fish for wild salmon and trout on select lochs and rivers.

Horse riding
Old Pier House, Fort Augustus, T01320-366418. Offers guests 2-hr horse riding for around £50 and the chance to hire canoes. Non-guests can ride if they phone and request in advance.

Tour operators
Evergreen B&B and Car Tours, see Where to stay, above. Fiona and Graeme Ambrose run fabulous car tours to some of the Highlands' most beautiful locations. Even if you're not staying at their guesthouse, you can arrange to be picked up in Fort Augustus. Depending on the season and conditions, trips explore around Loch Ness, as far south as Fort William and Glencoe and even northwest to romantic Plockton and Loch Carron. From £45 for a ½-day tour of southern Loch Ness to £160 for a full blown odyssey to the far northwest of Scotland complete with your own chauffeur and guide (for guests only)
Highland Activities, Keepers Cottage, Inverlair, Tulloch near Roy Bridge, T0845-094 5513, T07850-323267, www.highland activities.co.uk. Offer the chance (from £45) to go canyoning, quad biking, mountain biking, fun yakking and rafting.

Watersports
Monster Activities at Great Glen Water Park, east shore of Loch Oich, near South Laggan, T07710-540398. An outdoor activities centre, with hostel accommodation nearby, offering adventure sports including whitewater rafting, canoeing, mountain biking, rock climbing, sailing, windsurfing, hillwalking and water skiing. Self-catering lodges for rent too.

⊖ Transport

Drumnadrochit *p50*
Bus Citylink buses between **Inverness** and **Fort William** stop here several times daily in either direction. There are also buses (No 17

and No 306) from Inverness to **Cannich** and **Tomich**, via **Drumnadrochit**.

Fort Augustus *p52*
Bus Several buses daily (No 919) to **Fort William** or **Inverness**, 1-hr. The same service stops at **Invergarry** daily.

Cycle hire Monster Activities, 25 miles north of Fort William at the southern edge of Loch Oich, T01809-501340. You can hire bikes (and boats).

Invergarry and around *p53*
Bus Invergarry is on the **Fort William** to **Inverness** bus route, which stops in **Fort Augustus**. It is also on the main **Fort William** to **Kyle of Lochalsh** (and Skye) **Citylink** route (Nos 915, 916) and a couple of buses pass through daily in both directions. For times T08705-505050.
   Unfortunately, there's no longer a postbus service that runs from **Invergarry** to **Kinloch Hourn**. Your best option is to catch the Scottish Citylink (No 915, No 91 and No 917), which runs 4 times daily and request to be dropped off at the turn-off for the long walk into the glen.

Spean Bridge *p55*
Bus There are regular buses to **Fort William** and **Inverness**. Spean Bridge is also on the **Fort William** to **Glasgow** railway line.

Loch Arkaig and around *p55*
Bus At least 1 bus per day (Mon-Sat) travels the route to **Fort William** via **Banavie** and **Gairlochy**, T01397-702373, for details.

Glen Roy and Loch Laggan *p56*
Bus There is a No 40 bus to **Fort William** from **Roy Bridge**, 3 times daily Mon-Fri, 1 on Sat. **Roy Bridge** is also on the **Fort William** to **Glasgow** railway line.

Fort William and around

Fort William, the self-proclaimed 'Outdoor Capital of the UK', is also the gateway to the Western Highlands and one of the country's main tourist centres. It stands at the head of Loch Linnhe, with the snow-topped mass of Ben Nevis towering behind. You could be forgiven for assuming that it's quite an attractive place, but you'd be wrong. Despite its magnificent setting, Fort William has all the charm of a motorway service station. After passing a string of B&Bs on the southern outskirts the visitor finds a dual carriageway running along the lochside past uninspiring 1960s- to 1970s-era concrete boxes masquerading as hotels. Unsurprisingly, the majority of Fort William's attractions are out of town. The surrounding mountains and glens are amongst the most stunning in the Highlands and attract hikers and climbers in their droves: Ben Nevis – Britain's highest peak at 4406 ft – and also the very beautiful Glen Nevis, which you may recognize from movies such as *Braveheart* and *Rob Roy*. There are also snowsports on the slopes of nearby Aonach Mor, one of Scotland's top ski areas. Here, in and above, Leanachan Forest, you'll find world-class cross-country and downhill mountain biking. Since 2002, Fort William has hosted the annual Mountain Bike World Cup.

Arriving in Fort William

Getting there

Fort William is easily reached by bus, from Inverness, Glasgow and Oban, and by train, direct from Glasgow via the wonderful West Highland Railway, see box, page 72. The train and bus stations are at the north end of the High Street, next to the supermarket. If you're driving, parking can be a problem. There's a big car park beside the loch at the south end of town, and another behind the tourist office. You can also walk to Fort William, if you have a week to spare, from just north of Glasgow, along the 95-mile-long West Highland Way, see box, page 72.

Getting around

The town is strung out for several miles along the banks of Loch Linnhe though the centre is compact and easy to get around on foot. Many of the B&Bs and several backpacker hostels and camping options are within Glen Nevis or around Corpach, 1.5 miles to the north. Both areas are serviced by frequent buses from the town centre. There are buses every 20-30 minutes to and from Caol and Corpach, and every hour on Sunday and in the evening. Monday to Saturday there is a two-hourly service (No 42) to Glen Nevis Youth Hostel (fewer on Sunday). Buses No 41 and No 42 run daily to Nevis Range during the summer. During the ski season there are at least three daily buses (from 0745) to Nevis Range with the last return journey at 1630. ▸▸ *See Transport page 71.*

Tourist information

The very busy TIC ⓘ *Cameron Sq, just off the High St, T0845 2255121, Apr-May Mon-Fri 0900-1700, Sun 1000-1700, May-Jun Mon-Sat 0900-1800, Sun 0930-1700, Jun-Sep Mon-Sat 0900-1830, Sun 0930-1830, Sep-Nov Mon-Sat 0900-1700, Sun 1000-1600*, stocks a good range of books, maps and leaflets covering local walks. Staff will also help arrange transport to more remote Highland parts.

Places in Fort William → *For listings, see pages 67-73. Phone code 01397.*

Though it's not a pretty sight, Fort William is the largest town hereabouts and has all the services and facilities you'd expect. There are banks with ATMs on the pedestrianized High Street, as well as a supermarket, a good bike shop and outdoor-equipment outlets.

There's little of real interest in the town, although the **West Highland Museum** ⓘ *Cameron Sq by the TIC, T01397-702169, Jun and Sep Mon-Sat 1000-1700, Oct-May Mon-Sat 1000-1600, Jul-Aug Mon-Sat 1000-1700, Sun 1400-1700, £3.50, concessions £2.50, children £1, under 12s free*, is a worthwhile exception. It contains excellent exhibits of Jacobite memorabilia, including a 'secret' portrait of Bonnie Prince Charlie which is revealed only when reflected in a cylindrical mirror. There are also fine displays of Highland clans and tartans, wildlife and local history. The fort from which the town gets its name was built in 1690 by order of William III to keep the rebellious Scottish clans in order. The garrison fought off attacks by Jacobites during the rebellions of 1715 and 1745 but was then demolished to make way for the railway line. Remnants of the forts outer walls are all that remain and can be seen by the lochshore.

Ben Nevis Distillery ⓘ *T01397-700200, www.bennevisdistillery.com, Mon-Fri 0900-1700, Easter-Sep Mon-Sat 1000-1600, Jul-Aug Mon-Fri 0900-1800, Sat 1000-1600, Sun 1200-1600, tours £4, children £2*, is at Lochy Bridge, at the junction of the A82 to Inverness and the

Fort William

To Ben Nevis
Distillery, Banavie,
Corpach, Mallaig
(A830) &
Inverness (A82)

River Lochy

River Nevis

Nevis Bridge

To Glen Nevis

North Rd

Fort William Shinty Field

Glen Nevis Pl

Croft Rd

Lochaber Leisure Centre

Morrisons Supermarket

Camanachd Crescent

Nevis Ter

Mary St

Belford Rd

Dougkas Pl

Alma Rd

Mamore Cres

Wallace Pl

Nevisport

Parade Rd

Bank St

Linnhe Rd

High St

Fassifern Rd

Viewforth

Hill Rd

Victoria Rd

Bruce Pl

Kennedy Rd

West Highland Museum

Cameron Square

Off Beat Bikes

Fassifern St

Cameron Rd

Argyll Rd

Seaview Terrace

Union Rd

Glasdrum Rd

Glasdrum Drive

To Camusnagul

Loch Linnhe

High St

Heatherdon Rd

Argyll Terr

Achintore Rd

Grange Rd

Lundavra Rd

Connoch Rd

Drumfada Terr

N

200 metres
200 yards

To Glen Coe &
Glasgow (A82)

To 4

Where to stay 🛏
6 Caberfeidh **1**
Alexandra **2**
Bank Street Lodge **10**
Calluna **3**
Crolinnhe **4**
Distillery House **5**
Fort William Backpackers **6**
Glenlochy Guesthouse **11**

Grange **13**
Lime Tree **7**
Mrs Johnalda Macleod **12**

Restaurants 🍴
Cafe Chardon **1**
Crannog Seafood **2**
Grog & Gruel **3**

A830 to Mallaig, about a mile north of the town centre. It's a bit too polished for some though the imaginative audio-visual display that features the mythical giant Hector McDram provides light amusement. There's also a pleasant café and restaurant. Just before the distillery, on the left, are the 13th-century ruins of **Inverlochy Castle**.

Three miles from the town centre along the A830 to Mallaig, in the suburb of Banavie, is **Neptune's Staircase**, a series of eight linked locks on the Caledonian Canal. The locks lower the canal by 90 ft in less than 2 miles between Loch Lochy and Loch Eil and comprise the last section of the canal which links the North Sea with the Irish Sea. It's a pretty dramatic sight, with equally dramatic views of Ben Nevis and its neighbours behind Fort William. In fine weather, **The Moorings Hotel** (see page 67) by the canal is great for watching boats come and go as you enjoy a midday bite. You can also walk or cycle along the canal towpath from here. For details on the **Great Glen Way** ① *www. great glenway.fsnet.co.uk*, which links Fort William with Inverness, see box, page 51.

Further along the A830 to Mallaig, in the village of Corpach, is **Treasures of the Earth** ① *T01397-772283, Oct-Jun 1000-1700, Jul-Sep daily 0930-1900, £4.99, concessions £3.99, children £3.99*, an exhibition of crystals, gemstones and fossils displayed in a huge simulated cave.

Glen Nevis → *For listings, see pages 67-73.*

Only 10 minutes' drive from Fort William is one of Scotland's great glens, the classic Glen Nevis. If you can forget the sight of streams of campervans on the road and distant figures threading their way up the steep track towards the summit (dress appropriately) you could almost be mesmerized by the sparkling Water of Nevis as it tumbles through a wooded gorge, closed in by the steep, bracken-covered slopes of the magnificent hulk of Ben Nevis.

The whole scene is both rugged and sylvan, and some may say the nearest you'll get to a Himalayan valley in the Scottish Highlands. It's not surprising, then, that this is a favourite with movie directors and has featured in films such as *Rob Roy*, *Braveheart*, *Highlander III* and *Harry Potter and the Philosopher's Stone*.

There are many walks in and around the glen, not least of which is the return trek up to the summit of Britain's highest mountain. Aside from the walks described below, there are several easy, marked forest walks which start from the car park at the **Glen Nevis Visitor Centre** ① *open daily*, about half a mile up the Glen. Here, you'll also find toilets and an interesting interpretive display. Pick up a leaflet here or at the TIC (£1) for scenic walks around the area or check out www.forestry.gov.uk. There are buses into Glen Nevis, as far as the youth hostel, from Fort William bus station.

Ben Nevis → *OS Landranger No 41*.

Every year many thousands of people make the relatively straightforward ascent of Ben Nevis, and every year a frighteningly high percentage end up injured, or lost, or dead. Don't let the infamous ascent by a Ford Model T car in 1911 fool you. It's reported an average of four people perish on the mountain every year. Whatever the figure, it's vital that anyone venturing up the Ben is appropriately dressed and equipped for the hike. It should be remembered that the weather in Scotland's mountains can change at an alarming speed. Though it may be 20°C in the Glen Nevis car park when you set off, even far from the summit you may quickly find yourself in a disorientating blizzard or hill fog. It goes without saying that you need to be well prepared. You will need a good, strong pair of boots, warm clothing, waterproofs, food and drink. You should also take a map and a compass. Allow six to eight hours for the return trip. In the winter months the top part of the mountain is covered in snow. You should not attempt the walk unless you are an experienced hill climber.

The main tourist path, built as a pony track to service the long-gone observatory on the summit, starts from the car park at Achintee Farm, on the north side of the river, reached by the road through Claggan. It climbs gradually at first across the flank of Meal an t-Suidhe, before joining the alternative path from the youth hostel. This latter route is shorter but much steeper.

The trail continues to climb steadily as it begins to follow the Red Burn, until it reaches a junction, with Lochan Meal an t-Suidhe down to the left. Here, an alternative route down from the summit heads left under the north face of the mountain (see below). This is the halfway point of the main route. The path crosses the Red Burn and then climbs by a series of long and seemingly never-ending zigzags up to a plateau. If you're tired, consider that the record for the annual 10-mile run from Fort William to the summit and back is one hour 25 minutes! The path splits in two, but both paths take you up to the summit, marked by a cairn and emergency shelter, on the ruins of the old observatory. Note that on the upper sloping plateau the path can 'disappear' in mist and snow, and some cairns and beacons have been removed by vandals masquerading as purists. If conditions deteriorate, a compass is a life-saver. There is a form of shelter on the summit but ensure you're carrying extra clothes.

To return simply retrace your steps all the way. If the weather is settled enough and you have time, you can follow the alternative route below the north face. This leads right round the mountain to the Charles Inglis Clark mountain hut, then heads down into the Allt a' Mhuilinnglen which leads all the way down to the distillery on the A82, a mile north of the town centre. Note that this route adds an extra 3 or 4 miles to the descent and should only be attempted by fit and experienced hillwalkers.

Steall Falls → *OS Landranger No 41.*

A fairly easy low-level walk is to the spectacular 300-ft-high Steall Falls at the head of the glen. It's a popular walk, especially in the summer but this doesn't detract from its stunning natural beauty.

The path starts at the end of the twisty road, at the second car park. Before setting off you might like to note the sign by the steep waterfall that cascades down to the edge of the car park. It reads 'Warning! This is not the path to Ben Nevis'. If you need to be warned against attempting to climb up Ben Nevis through a waterfall, you probably shouldn't be left alone in possession of this book, never mind let loose on the Scottish mountains. Once you've shaken your head in disbelief at the apparent mind-numbing stupidity of some of your fellow travellers, follow the track alongside the Water of Nevis. The path climbs steadily through the woods and becomes rocky, with the river thundering below through the steep gorge. It runs close to the river before emerging from the gorge and opening up into a wide, flower-filled meadow, with a high waterfall at the far end. It's a beautiful, tranquil place and ideal for a picnic. Follow the path across the valley floor until it crosses the river via a precarious bridge that consists of three ropes of thick wire in a V-shape. The path then leads to the bottom of the falls. You can also head left at the bridge and continue up the valley to some ruins. From here the path leads to Corrour station, 14 miles away. However, it's for fit, well prepared and experienced hillwalkers only. You can then catch a

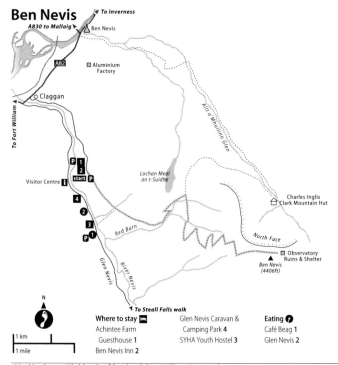

Ben Nevis

◄ *To Inverness*

A830 to Mallaig ►

■ Ben Nevis

A82

□ Aluminium Factory

○ Claggan

To Fort William ◄

Allt a' Mhuilinn Glen

P 1 2
start P

Visitor Centre ℹ

4

2

3

P 1

Lochan Meall an t-Suidhe

□ Charles Inglis Clark Mountain Hut

Red Burn

North Face

Glen Nevis

River Nevis

□ Observatory Ruins & Shelter
▲ Ben Nevis (4406ft)

N ▲

1 km
1 mile

◄ *To Steall Falls walk*

Where to stay 🛏
Achintee Farm Guesthouse **1**
Ben Nevis Inn **2**

Glen Nevis Caravan & Camping Park **4**
SYHA Youth Hostel **3**

Eating 🍴
Café Beag **1**
Glen Nevis **2**

train back to Fort William. It's a very popular route, and there's even accommodation at the end of it, near the train station.

Nevis Range

ⓘ *T01397-705825, www.nevis-range.co.uk. Gondola Sep-Oct, mid-Dec to Jun 1000-1700, Jul-Aug 0930-1800. Gondola prices: £10.50 return, concessions £9, children £6, under 5s free; day ticket £13, children £7.50. There is wheelchair access and guide dogs ride free.*

Nevis Range, 3 miles north of Fort William at Torlundy, just off the A82 to Inverness, is situated on the mountain of **Aonach Mhor** (4006 ft) and is Scotland's highest skiing and snowboarding resort. The ski area is reached by Scotland's only gondola lift system and in a good season it permits skiing between Christmas and May. The 1½-mile (15-minute) ride is a popular attraction, not only with wintersport enthusiasts, but also with summer hillwalkers keen to gain easy access to the mountains. A couple of easy walks lead from the gondola station to Sgurr Finnisgaig (40 minutes) and Meal Beag (one hour), both of which offer stunning views from the top. Beside the top gondola station there's a small shop and a large self-serving **Snowgoose restaurant (££-£)** providing fantastic vistas across Lochaber. Mountain bikers come for some truly world-class riding (see page 71).

Fort William and around listings

For hotel and restaurant price codes and other relevant information, see pages 13-20.

○ Where to stay

Fort William *p63, map p64*

Fort William has an abundance of accommodation, ranging from large luxury hotels to modest guesthouses and B&Bs. You'll find B&Bs and hostels on the road north towards Corpach and Banavie whilst the southern entrance to Fort William on Achintore Rd is truly packed with B&Bs and hotels. Running parallel is Grange Rd, which is also lined with B&B accommodation. Nearer to the town centre, Fassifern Rd and Alma Rd are also a hive of hostel and B&B activity. Wherever you search for a pillow, remember that as a tourist hub Fort William gets extremely busy in the high season and during key events (see Festivals, page 70). Ideally, book ahead or through the tourist office for a small fee. The TIC carries copies of the *Fort William and Lochaber Accommodation Guide*.

South of Fort William, on the A82, the villages of Onich and North Ballachulish, make an attractive alternative.

££££ Inverlochy Castle Hotel, 3 miles north of town on the A82 to Inverness, T01397-702177, www.inverlochy.co.uk. This is your castle in the Highlands. A luxurious stay is assured; unsurpassed elegance, impeccable service and superb food (see Restaurants page 69), all set in 500 acres of grounds.
£££ The Grange, Grange Rd, T01397-705516, www.grangefortwilliam.com. Delightful 4 bedroom escape in a Victorian town house with views over Loch Linnhe.
£££ The Lime Tree, Achintore Rd, T01397-701806. Offers 9 beautifully appointed bedrooms – hardly surprising as its co-owned by a resident artist and includes an art gallery. In addition, fabulous lunches and dinner are served. It's fantastic and deserves its growing reputation for a quality stay. Recommended.
£££ The Moorings Hotel, 3 miles out of town in Banavie, on road to Corpach and Mallaig, T01397-772797, www.moorings-fortwilliam.co.uk. Overlooks Neptune's Staircase; well situated and comfortable with a reasonable Jacobean restaurant (**£££-££**).
£££-££ Crolinnhe, Grange Rd, T01397-702709. Mar-Nov. 10 mins' walk from town, this grand Victorian villa is a luxurious B&B.

The welcome is friendly and the food delicious but don't dare take those muddy boots into the hall! If you opt for the luxury double your room includes a jacuzzi.
££ 6 Caberfeidh, Fassifern Rd, T01397-703756. A friendly B&B that will prepare packed lunches after you've slept in your 4-poster bed.
££ Alexandra Hotel, The Parade, T01397-702241. This large sandstone hotel provides a reasonable standard of accommodation and food (**££**). Very handy for the town centre.
££ Distillery House, Nevis bridge, T01397-700103, www.visit-fortwilliam.co.uk/distillery-house. Situated between the Glen Nevis and Achintee turn-offs, this smart, comfortable guesthouse will appeal to those who seek a touch of class close to the town centre. Also offers self-catering in nearby cottages for £200-490 per week.
££ Glenlochy Guesthouse, Nevis Bridge, North Rd, T01397-702909. Almost directly opposite Distillery House. This substantial villa with 10 (including family) rooms is another smart choice for those in search of a friendly welcome, good food and relaxation.
££ Mrs Johnalda Macleod, 25 Alma Rd, T01397-703735. Open all year. Unpretentious and comfortable.
££ Rhiw Goch, Banavie, T01397-772373. Unbeatable views of Ben Nevis (when not shrouded in mist) and overlooking the Caledonian Canal. Owners are welcoming and serve a terrific breakfast in this small B&B about 500 yds north of the **Moorings Hotel**. Also hire kayaks.
£ Bank Street Lodge, Bank St, T01397-700070, www.bankstreetlodge.co.uk. 42 beds. Open all year. Independent, centrally located backpackers' hostel with family/double rooms and en suite.
£ Fort William Backpackers, Alma Rd, 500 yds from the train station, T01397-700711, www.scotlandstophostels.com. Packed with information and young backpackers.
£ Snowgoose Mountain Centre & Smiddy Bunkhouse, Station Rd, next to the Corpach

train station, 4 miles west of Fort William on A8309 to Mallaig, T01397-772467, www.highland-mountain-guides.co.uk. Alpine-style bunkhouse accommodation for up to 12, plus hostel for 14, fully self-catered.

Self-catering
Calluna, Heathercroft, about a 15-min walk from the TIC, T01397-700451, www.fortwilliamholiday.co.uk. Open all year. 2 modern, semi-detached apartments have been configured to suit groups or families, whilst the ground-floor will suit a wheelchair-bound visitor and carer. Run by experienced mountain guide, Alan Kimber. 6-bed apartment from £300 per week, 8-bed apartment from £400 per week.
The Old School Chalet, Duisky, 16 miles from Fort William, T01397-722227. Perfect peace and quiet assured in this basic (centrally heated) log cabin by the sea loch of Loch Eil. Forget shops, think nature. Sleeps 6. From £195-275 per week.

Glen Nevis *p64, map p66*
Glen Nevis is excellent for camping, whilst Achintee at the start of the Ben walk has several excellent guesthouses and accommodation options.
£ Achintee Farm Guesthouse, by the start of the path to Ben Nevis, T01397-702240, www.achinteefarm.com. Lovely setting and terrific welcome. Recommended.
£ Ben Nevis Inn, above Achintee Farm; across the river and up the steep steps from the visitor centre, T01397-701227, www.ben-nevis-inn.co.uk. An independent hostel where you'll find walkers and climbers enjoying banter, a real ale and hearty food (**££-£**) beside a roaring fire in this 17th-century inn. The hostel's little cramped, but upstairs you'll find the best atmosphere in Fort William. Worth the walk.
£ Farr Cottage Lodge and Activity Centre, Corpach, T01397-772315, www.farrcottage.com. This lively set-up can accommodate individuals or groups in bunkhouse or self-catering style. Terrific facilities, including

internet and laundry, and hearty breakfast and dinners. Can organize everything from hillwalking and mountain biking trips to sea-fishing, kayaking, go-karting and canyoning.

£ SYHA Youth Hostel, 3 miles out of town, near the start of the path up Ben Nevis, Glen Nevis, T0870-0041120, www.syha.org. uk. Though remote, this popular hostel is an excellent choice if you plan to hike on the Ben. Book ahead.

Camping
Glen Nevis Caravan & Camping Park, 2 miles up the Glen Nevis Rd, T01397-702191, www.glennevisholidays.co.uk. Mid-Mar to late Oct. Good facilities. With option to rent cottages.

❷ Restaurants

Fort William *p63, map p64*
Finally, Fort William and its environs can boast several real culinary gems ready to reward your taste buds. Be wary though, for there are also those still earning a crust off run-of-the-mill bar lunches and uninspiring dinners. Note that many places stop serving after 2200 – in which case it's a chippy dinner at the likes of **Sammy's** in Caol, Fort William, Mon-Sat 1700-2300. A 10 mile taxi ride from Fort William is the **Lochleven Seafood Café** (**££**), which serves excellent seafood. See page 81 for details.

£££ Crannog Seafood Restaurant, Town Pier, T01397-705589. Great seafood by the pier with views across Loch Linnhe. Based in an old smokehouse it has a great ambience, delicious food and there's a good wine list to help wash down delicious lobster or salmon. Book ahead.

£££ The Eagle Inn, Laggan Locks, northern end of Loch Lochy. The original owner has moved on but this lovingly restored Dutch barge, complete with a clean, cosy galley and fabulous wooden bar is the perfect place to enjoy a light bite or evening meal.

£££ Inverlochy Castle Hotel, see Where to stay, above. Here you'll experience exquisite fine dining – at a price. Will it be the black pudding with white truffles and scrambled eggs? Perhaps the saddle of rabbit or poached loin of venison? The food and wine list is 1st class – and so is the view out the window. Dress to impress. Built in 1863, it's regarded as one of Scotland's and indeed Europe's best country house/castle hotels.

£££-££ The Lime Tree, see Where to stay, above. In addition to its beautifully appointed bedrooms, this relative newcomer to Fort Bill's gastro scene promises to serve up a flavoursome, freshly prepared dinner (including slow cooked aromatic lamb) and a hearty lunch. Recommended.

£££-££ The Moorings Hotel, 3 miles out of town, Banavie, on road to Corpach and Mallaig, T01397-772797, www.moorings-fortwilliam.co.uk. Good-value bar meals, whilst the more formal Jacobean restaurant serves up reasonable evening treats.

£££-££ Old Pines, by the Commando Monument, Spean Bridge, T01397-712324, www.oldpines.co.uk. Enjoys a lovely wooded setting, where guests are pampered and can feast on organic, freshly prepared dinners made using local seafood and game. Book ahead.

££ The Grog & Gruel, 66 High St, T01397-705078. Open until 2400. There's a good atmosphere in this traditionally styled bar that serves a range of cask ales, a good selection of malt whiskies and bar meals. The younger crowd may prefer the **Ben Nevis Bar** across the road.

£ Café Chardon, just off High St. The best freshly prepared sandwiches in town.

Glen Nevis *p64, map p66*
££-£ The Ben Nevis Inn, Achintee, T01397-701227, www.ben-nevis-inn.co.uk. Yes, it's a long walk into the glen but many of the lunch and dinner treats, including venison, are filling and freshly prepared. There's often live music and a generally great atmosphere. Best in the area.

££-£ Glen Nevis Restaurant, 200m from the SYHA hostel, T01397-705459. Apr-Oct daily 1200-2200. Serves a standard 2-course lunch and 3-course dinner.

£ Café Beag, down from the SYHA, T01397-703601. Sep-Jun Tue-Sun 1000-1700, Jul-Aug daily. A cosy place with a fire, home-baking, baked potatoes and organic ice-cream.

✪ Festivals

Fort William *p63, map p64*
As the self-proclaimed Outdoor Capital of the UK, Fort William annually hosts a number of high profile events.

May/Jun UCI Mountain Bike World Cup, www.ridefortwilliam.co.uk. Since 2002, this has been held annually at Nevis Range, 6 miles north of town. Watched by over 20,000 spectators, the downhill riders descend the 2-mile long course at an electrifying speed.

Jul Lochaber Highland Games. Caber tossing and Highland dancing.

Sep Ben Nevis Race, www.bennevisrace. co.uk. 500 runners undertake the gruelling 10-mile run from Fort William to the summit of Ben Nevis and back. Staged for over 100 years, the record stands at 1 hr 25 mins.

✪ Shopping

Fort William *p63, map p64*
Nevisport, High St, T013967-704921. Has a huge selection of books, maps and guides, a bureau de change and good café-bar.
West Coast Outdoor Sports, High St, T01397-705777. A good outdoor activity equipment shop.

✪ What to do

Fort William *p63, map p64*
Adventure sports
There are several good whitewater rivers around Fort William ranging in difficulty from Grade I-VI, or you can paddle the Caledonian Canal. For advice on operators and lessons,

see www.canoescotland.com. There's also an indoor climbing wall at the Lochaber Leisure Centre, Belford Rd, T01397-704359.
Rhiw Goch, Top Locks, Banavie, T01397-772373, www.rhiwgoch.co.uk. Close to Neptune's Staircase. Hires out sea kayaks for £25 per day.
Snowgoose Mountain Centre, Station Rd, next to the Corpach train station, 4 miles west of Fort William on A8309 to Mallaig, T01397-772467, www.highland-mountain-guides.co.uk. Offers lessons in mountaineering, canoeing, kayaking, skiing and mountain biking. Also hires equipment.
Vertical Descents, Inchree, 8 miles south of Fort William, T01855-821593, www.vertical descents.com. There are many excellent outdoor adventure operators in Scotland – this is one of them. Offers canyoning, whitewater rafting, mountain biking and fun yakking, amongst others.

Boat trips
Crannog Cruises, Town Pier, T01397-700714, www.crannog.net. Run trips of 1½ hrs from Mar-Oct, £10, children £5. Board the *Souter's Lass* in Fort William (daily 1000, 1200, 1400, 1600) for a chance to spot local marine wildlife including seals, otters and seabirds.
Sea Ventures, 3 Kincardine Pl, T07766-138538, www.seaventuresscotland.com. Thrilling fast-boat trips from 60 mins to 1 week in search of dolphins, whales, seals and birdlife or simply to explore the Isles of Staffa and Mull. Cruises start from £15 for the Loch Linnhe experience and they'll be happy to arrange a customized itinerary subject to sea conditions.

Hiking and climbing
Fort William is a mecca for hikers and climbers and boasts one of the highest concentrations of guides and instructors in the land. For information on the climb up Ben Nevis and walks around Glen Nevis, see page 65. Nevis Range offers some of the most accessible winter climbs in

the country for experienced climbers. For details of the gondola ride, see page 67. If you want to hire a guide, note that the information board/staff in Nevisport (see Shopping, above) can provide useful advice. **Abacus Mountaineering**, www.abacus mountaineering.com, T01397-772466; **Alan Kimber at West Coast Mountain Guides**, T01397-700451; **Alpha Mountaineering**, T07748-275825, www.alphamountaineering. co.uk; **Mountain Motion**, T01397-701731; **Snowgoose Mountain Centre**, see Adventure sports, above.

Mountain biking

It's easy to see why Scotland is now regarded as one of the world's top mountain biking destinations. The Leanachan Forest, below Aonach Mhor, 3 miles north of town, covers a huge area with over 25 miles of mountain bike trails, ranging from easy to demanding and including the (world-class) Witch's Trail. These are free cross-country routes run by the Forestry Commission (www.forestry.gov.uk, or www.ridefortwilliam.co.uk).

Nevis Range is also home to the 2-mile-long World Cup downhill mountain bike course. Not for the faint-hearted or inexperienced. Bikers (over 12s) and bikes reach the top of this steep descent using the resort's gondola system (see page 67). Adult single £12, multi-trip £28, single youth £8, multi-trip £19. Track open May-Sep daily 1015-1600 (subject to weather).

A more gentle alternative is the Great Glen Cycle Route, mainly off-road, running from Fort William to Inverness. See box, page 51. If you want to cycle this long-distance route, **Off Beat Bikes** in Fort William (see Cycle hire, below) offer an excellent one-way bike hire service.

Sea kayaking

Rockhopper Scotland, 2 Montrose Mansions, Corpach, Fort William, T07739-837344, www.rockhopperscotland.co.uk. Whether a beginner or expert, the friendly,

fully qualified guides at Rockhopper are available for a ½-day (£40), full day (£70) or even overnight sea kayaking adventure in Ardnamurchan. Paddle down Loch Sheil, across the narrows to Ardgour or along the remote northern coastline off Glenelg with the chance to spot eagles and basking sharks. Highly recommended.

Skiing

Nevis Range Ski Centre, see page 67. Nevis Range hires all the snowboard and ski equipment required. You can also try **Nevisport**, High St, T013967-704921.

Swimming

Lochaber Leisure Centre, Belford Rd, T01397-704359. Mon-Fri 0930-0900, 1230-2000 Sat-Sun 1230-1600.

Tour operators

Jacobite SteamTrain, contact **West Coast Railway Company**, T01524-737751, T01524-737753, www.steamtrain.info. Runs from Fort William to Mallaig, Jun to mid-Oct Mon-Fri, Jul-Aug daily, departing Fort William at 1020, arriving in Mallaig at 1225, departing Mallaig at 1410 and arriving back in Fort William at 1600. Day return £31, children £17.50, 1st-class return £49, children £25 (see box, page 72).

⊖ Transport

Fort William *p63, map p64*
Bus For the Fort William area contact **Highland Country Buses**, T01463-710555, www.rapsons.co.uk.

Long-distance services include several daily **Citylink** buses to **Inverness**, 1 hr 50 mins, £7.20; to **Oban**, 1 hr 30 mins, £10.40, via **Glencoe**, 30 mins; and to **Uig**, 3½ hrs, via **Portree** and **Kyle of Lochalsh**, 1 hr 50 mins, £19. **Citylink** buses several times daily to **Glasgow** via **Glencoe** and **Tyndrum**, 3 hrs, £17.80; and to **Edinburgh**, 4 hrs, £25.20, via **Stirling**, 3 hrs. There is a bus to **Mallaig** via **Lochailort** (for **Ardnamurchan**), Mon-Sat,

Riding the rails

Running from Glasgow to Mallaig via Fort William, the **West Highland Railway** is only 164 miles long but is widely acknowledged as one of the most scenic railway journeys in the world. The great thing about this journey is its variety, taking you from the distinctive red tenements of Glasgow and the former ship-building areas of the River Clyde, to the windy wilderness of Rannoch Moor and the chilly splendour of the hills. It's about an hour after leaving Glasgow that you get your first taste of Highland scenery when the train hugs the eastern bank of sinewy Loch Long. Then it's on past the 'bonnie banks' of Loch Lomond, Britain's largest body of inland water. It's impossible not to pass this serene loch without thinking of the famous ballad about two Jacobite soldiers captured after the '45 rebellion. The soldier taking 'the low road' is due to be executed, his companion taking the 'high road' is due to be released.

After Ardlui, at the top of Loch Lomond, the countryside gets more rugged. Wherever you look you see something of interest: a waterfall, a buzzard surfing on the breeze, perhaps a herd of Highland cattle wallowing in a river.

The **West Highland Way**, the long-distance footpath from Glasgow to Fort William, is close to the line now and at stations such as Crianlarich, Upper Tyndrum and Bridge of Orchy you can often spot footsore walkers with muddy boots – who get on the train looking slightly guilty and collapse on their seats with sighs of relief.

The landscape gets wilder and bleaker as the railway crosses the lonely, peaty wastes of Rannoch Moor and on to Corrour, which featured in the film version of Irvine Welsh's cult book *Trainspotting*. Then you descend to the lusher country around Tulloch, before pulling in to Fort William. This is a popular visitor centre as it's close to Ben Nevis, Britain's highest mountain, and beautiful Glen Nevis, which has featured in films such as Braveheart and Rob Roy. Now comes the most spectacular part of the journey. Leaving Fort William, the train crosses Thomas Telford's Caledonian Canal – where you can see an impressive series of eight locks known as 'Neptune's Staircase' – hugs the shore of Loch Eil, then crosses the magnificent Glenfinnan Viaduct, a masterpiece in concrete. You soon get superb views of the evocative Glenfinnan Monument that commemorates the start of the 1745 rebellion, before pulling in to Glenfinnan Station. The train now takes you through a landscape of craggy hills and glacial lochs etched with birch and pine trees. You pass Loch nan Uamh, from where Bonnie Prince Charlie fled from France after his defeat at Culloden, then draw in to Arisaig, the birthplace of the man who inspired RL Stevenson's Long John Silver. Next is beautiful Loch Morar, Britain's deepest inland loch and home – so legend has it – to a mysterious monster. Soon you get great views across the water to the craggy islands of Eigg and Rùm, before finally pulling in to the port of Mallaig.

1 hr 10 mins, £5, Shiel Buses, T01967-431272. To **Kinlochleven**, via **Glencoe**, daily, 50 mins, Highland Country Buses. Unfortunately, there's no longer a **postbus** service to **Glen Etive** so you'll need to walk or cycle in.

Car hire Hawco Volkswagen Rental, Caol Industrial Estate T01397-700900. **Practical Car & Van Hire**, Slipway Autos, Corpach, T01397-772404, www.practical. co.uk. Prices from around £35 per day.

Cycle hire Off Beat Bikes, 117 High St, T01397-704008, www.offbeatbikes.co.uk. Offer an excellent one-way bike hire service (including panniers and spares) from £40 per day, including the option to start your ride in Inverness. Also offer bikes sales, repairs and advice. Bikes from £17 per day to £110 for a full-on downhill bike to tackle the World Cup course at Nevis Range. Kids and tandem bikes, helmets and armour also available. **Rhiw Goch**, Top Locks, Banavie, T01397-772373, www.rhiwgoch.co.uk. Close to Neptune's Staircase, hires out bikes (£12).

Ferry There is a passenger-only ferry service to **Camusnagaul**, on the opposite bank of Loch Linnhe, from the Town Pier. It sails Mon-Sat 0745-1740 and takes 10 mins, £1.50, children 75p. The **Corran Ferry**, T01855-841243, to **Ardgour** (see page 83) is 8 miles south of Fort William, just off the A82. Throughout the year the ferry makes the 5-min crossing every 20-30 mins from 0710 and every hour thereafter until 2100

(Fri-Sat until 2130). Single £6.40, pedal bikes free. Slight timetable variation in winter. For further details contact Corran Ferry, ask the TIC or look at www.lochabertransport.org.uk.

Taxi Al's Tour and Taxi Service, T01397-700700.

Train There are 2-3 trains daily to **Glasgow**, 3 hrs 45 mins, via **Crianlarich**. To **Mallaig**, 1 hr 20 mins, to connect with ferries to **Armadale** on Skye. To **Oban**, daily, occasionally changing at Crianlarich. There is a sleeper service to **London Euston** (see page 8), but you'll miss the views.

❶ Directory

Fort William *p63, map p64*
Banks Plenty of ATMs on the High St. Note that if you planning to travel into remoter areas such as Ardnamurchan or Knoydart, banks are few and far between.
Internet Library, High St.

Glen Coe

There are many spectacular places in the Scottish Highlands,
but few, if any, can compare to the truly awesome scenery of
Glen Coe. No-one could fail to be moved by its haunting beauty,
with imposing mountains, their tops often wreathed in cloud,
rising steeply on either side from the valley floor. The brooding
atmosphere of the landscape is only enhanced by the glen's tragic
history. Once you've heard of the Glen Coe Massacre it sends a
shiver down the spine every time you pass this way. Scotland's
most famous glen is also one of its most accessible, with the A82
Glasgow to Fort William road running through it. Much of the
area is owned by the National Trust for Scotland and is virtually
uninhabited, leaving huge tracts of glen and mountain which
provide outstanding climbing and walking. There's also skiing at the
Glencoe Mountain Resort and canoeing on the rivers Coe and Etive.

Onich, North Ballachulish and Kinlochleven

The A82 south from Fort William passes through tiny Onich and the car ferry for
Ardnamurchan at Corran before the B863 turns east at North Ballachulish and heads past
the excellent **Lochleven Seafood Café** (see Restaurants, page 81) to Kinlochleven, at
the head of Loch Leven. It can also be reached on the same road from Glencoe village,
7 miles west. Until the late 1990s a huge, unsightly aluminium factory dominated and was
the lifeblood of the community. Fortunately, the entrepreneurial ingenuity of a Lochaber
climber has since transformed the defunct factory into **Ice Factor**, the world's largest
indoor ice-climbing facility (see What to do, page 81) and there's even the **Atlas microbrewery** next door. Industrialists can find out all about the history of aluminium-working
in Kinlochleven at **The Aluminium Story** ⓘ *Linnhe Rd, T01855-831663, Apr-Sep Mon-Fri
1000-1300, 1400-1700, free.*

The West Highland Way passes through the village and many walkers spend the night
here before setting out on the last stretch before Fort William. There are also good walks
in the surrounding hills and glens of the Mamores, a few of which are described below.

Walks near North Ballachulish

Five miles north of the village of North Ballachulish and having turned off the road for
Inchree and **Vertical Descents** (see What to do, page 82) a moderate one-hour circular
walk up to Inchree Waterfall begins at the car park just 100 yds past the Vertical Descents
bothy. A clearly marked trail, the huge waterfall is very dramatic to the eye, particularly
when it's in spate. So too are the views back towards Loch Linnhe. The path continues up
past the waterfall to the forest road which leads back downhill to the car park.

A stab in the back

Glen Coe is probably best known as the scene of one of the most shameful and notorious incidents in Scottish history.

Following his succession to the throne, William III wanted all the clans to swear an oath of allegiance by 1 January 1692. After much hesitation, the Jacobite clans of the West Highlands agreed to do so. However, Maclain of Glencoe, chief of a small branch of the MacDonalds, was not only late in setting off on the journey, but mistakenly went to Fort William to sign, instead of Inveraray. By the time he reached Inveraray it was 6 January and the deadline had passed.

The government decided that the rebellious clan be punished, in order to set an example to other clans, some of whom had not taken the oath. A company of 120 soldiers, under the command of Campbell of Glenlyon, were sent to Glen Coe and, since their leader was related by marriage to Maclain, the troops were billeted in MacDonald homes, in keeping with the long-standing Highland tradition of hospitality.

There they stayed for almost two weeks, until the cold-blooded order came through to "… put all to the sword under seventy". And so, on a cold winter's night, in the early hours of 13 February 1692, the Campbells ruthlessly slaughtered their hosts. Maclain and 37 men, women and children were slain in their beds, while many others fled into the hills, only to die of hunger and exposure. It was a bloody incident which had deep repercussions and proved to be the beginning of the end of the Highland way of life.

There's a monument to the fallen MacDonalds in the village of Glencoe, where members of the clan still gather on 13 February each year. For a powerful and evocative account of the Massacre, read *Glencoe* by John Prebble (Penguin, first published 1966).

Walks around Kinlochleven → *OS Landranger No 41.*

There are some relatively easy short walks from Kinlochleven up the glen of the River Leven, including the one to the impressive **Grey Mare's Tail waterfall**. It's a short walk of under an hour, signposted from the village.

Dressed for the outdoors, a rewarding half-day walk is to follow the West Highland Way south from the village to the top of the **Devil's Staircase** (named by the 400 soldiers who had to endure severe hardship while building it in the 17th century), where it meets the A82 at the eastern end of Glen Coe. The well-signposted route begins at the wooden bridge north of Ice Factor and climbs gradually on a dirt jeep-track up to Penstock House, at 1000 ft. At the top, near the house, the track forks to the right and continues on a rough but well maintained footpath to the Devil's Staircase. The path is marked with the West Highland Way thistle sign, so it's easy to follow uphill to the top of the pass (1804 ft), from where you get great views of Loch Eilde Mór and the Mamores to the north. The path then descends down the staircase to Glen Coe, with breathtaking Buachaille Etive Mór in front of you all the way. You'll have to return to Kinlochleven by the same route, or you could carry on to the **Kingshouse Hotel** (see Where to stay, page 80). The return trip from Kinlochleven should take four or five hours, or you can start out from Glencoe (see below). Before leaving, ensure you are properly equipped. This section of the West Highland Way was once part of the old military road which ran from Fort William to Stirling.

Another good hike, though more strenuous, is to **Beinn na Callich** (2507 ft). You'll need to be fairly fit as it's a steep climb; allow around six to seven hours for the return trip.

The route is well marked and starts from the West Highland Way footpath opposite the school, which is on the road heading northwest out of the village towards Fort William. The path climbs steeply at first, crosses the tarmac road to **Mamore Lodge**, then continues until it joins General Wade's old military road, which takes the West Highland Way on its final 11 miles to Fort William. From here, you'll see the path zigzagging up the mountain. Continue along the old military road for about 400 yds until you cross a wooden bridge. Then follow a path down to another wooden bridge, where the ground is quite boggy. Cross the bridge and the path begins to zigzag uphill until it levels out on to a plateau, before continuing relentlessly upwards through a long series of zigzags to the summit, marked by a couple of cairns and a commemorative plaque. The views from the top make the tiring climb worthwhile. You can see down on to Loch Leven, over to Glen Coe and across the magnificent Mamores.

Fit and experienced hillwalkers can access the **Mamores** from the **Mamore Lodge** road. Once you're up there you have the opportunity to bag several Munros, via a series of

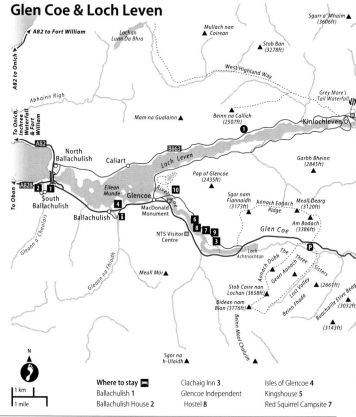

Glen Coe & Loch Leven

A82 to Fort William
A82 to Onich
A82 to Oban

Lochan Lunn Da Bhra

Mullach nan Coirean ▲

Sgurr a' Mhaim ▲ (3606ft)

Stob Ban ▲ (3278ft)

West Highland Way

Abhainn Righ

Grey Mare's Tail Waterfall

To Onich, Inchree Waterfall & Fort William

Mam na Gualainn ▲

Beinn na Callich ▲ (2507ft) ❶

Kinlochleven ○

A82

North Ballachulish

Caliart

B863

Loch Leven

Garbh Bheinn ▲ (2845ft)

To Oban

A828

South Ballachulish

Eilean Munde

Glencoe

River Coe

Pap of Glencoe (2435ft) ▲

Sgor nam Fiannaidh (3173ft) ▲

Aonach Eagach Ridge

Meall Dearg ▲ (3120ft)

Ballachulish ℹ

❹

MacDonald Monument

❿

❻ ❽ ❼ ❾ ❸

Am Bodach ▲ (3386ft)

Glen Coe

Gleann a' Chaolais

NTS Visitor Centre

Loch Achtriochtan

Aonach Dubh

Gearr Aonach

The Three Sisters

▲ (2661ft)

Gleann na Fhiodh

Meall Mór ▲

Stob Coire nan Lochan (3658ft) ▲

Beinn Fhada

Lost Valley

Buachaille Etive Beag ▲ (3032ft)

Bidean nam Bian (3776ft) ▲

Beinn Maol Chaluim

▲ (3143ft)

Sgor na h-Ulaidh ▲

N

1 km
1 mile

Where to stay 🛏
Ballachulish 1
Ballachulish House 2

Clachaig Inn 3
Glencoe Independent
Hostel 8

Isles of Glencoe 4
Kingshouse 5
Red Squirrel Campsite 7

excellent ridge walks connecting **Am Bodach** (3386 ft) with **Stob Coire a' Chairn** (3219 ft), **Na Gruagaichean** (3461 ft), **An Gearanach** (3222 ft), **Sgor An Iubhair** (3285 ft), **Sgurr a'Mhaim** (3606 ft) and **Stob Ban** (3278 ft). These peaks and ridges can also be reached from Glen Nevis, see page 64. As well as the proper equipment, take a map and a compass.

Ballachulish

On the southern shore of Loch Leven, a mile or so west of Glencoe village on the A82, is the old slate quarrying village of Ballachulish. Aside from interpretive panels at the TIC, there's 550 yds of wheelchair accessible path to view the quarry and its history where for 300 years Gaelic speaking locals toiled to excavate the slate. There are a few B&Bs and a couple of hotels close by. In the car park just off the main road is the **TIC** ① *T01855-811866, Mar-May Mon-Sat 0900-1700, Sun 1000-1700, May-Oct daily 0900-1800,* with a good coffee shop. Here, you can also find out all about the quarries.

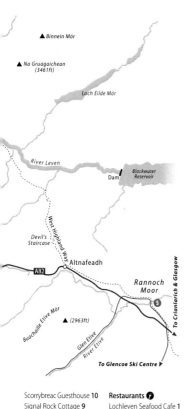

Glencoe village

At the western entrance to the glen, on the shores of Loch Leven, is Glencoe village, 16 miles south of Fort William just off the A82. There are several places to stay in and around the village, as well as a post office and in stark contrast to the Spar general store next door there's also the thatched **Glencoe Folk Museum** ① *late May-Sep daily 1000-1730, £2.50,* which has collections of 17th- to 18th-century costumes, military memorabilia and, according to the owner, a chair that once belonged to none other than the Young Pretender. The most significant development in recent years has been the revamped and impressive **National Trust for Scotland Visitor Centre** ① *1 mile south of Glencoe village, T0844-493 2222, Jan-Mar Thu-Sun 1000-1600, Apr-Oct daily 0930-1730, Nov-Dec Tue-Sat 1000-1600, £6, concessions £5.* There are interesting interpretive displays, information about the area's history (including the massacre), geology, fauna and flora. During the summer, the ranger service organizes guided walks and Landrover safaris. This eco-friendly building also boasts a lovely café.

Climbing and hiking in Glen Coe → *OS*

Landranger No 41. www.glencoemountain.com.
Glen Coe offers some of Britain's most challenging climbing and hiking, with some notoriously treacherous routes and unpredictable weather conditions that

Scorrybreac Guesthouse **10**
Signal Rock Cottage **9**
SYHA Youth Hostel **6**

Restaurants 🔵
Lochleven Seafood Cafe **1**

claim lives every year. The routes described below are some of the least strenuous, but you'll still need a map, good boots, warm clothing, food and water, and you should take the usual precautions, including checking on the weather forecast, see page 26.

One of the most popular walks is the relatively straightforward hike up to the **Lost Valley**, a secret glen where the ill-fated MacDonalds hid the cattle they'd stolen. Allow around four hours for the return trip. Start from the car park by the large boulder (see map), opposite the distinctive **Three Sisters**. Head down to the valley floor and follow the gravel path which leads down to a wooden bridge across the River Coe. Cross the bridge and follow the path up and over the stile. From here there's a choice of two routes. The less obvious route heads right and offers an easier climb into the valley. This eventually meets the lower, well-worn track, which involves a bit of scrambling but is more exciting as it follows the rushing waters of the **Allt Coire Gabhail**. The upper and lower paths meet a few miles further up and here you cross the river by some stepping stones. Proceed up the steep scree slope until you reach the rim of the **Lost Valley**, where many of the MacDonalds fled on the night of the infamous massacre. Once in the valley there are great views of Glencoe's highest peak, Bidean nam Bian ('pinnacle of the mountains') at 3776 ft, Gearr Aonach and Beinn Fhada and you can continue for a further 50 minutes to the head of the valley. From here it's possible to climb Bidean, but you'll need to be fit, experienced and well equipped.

Glen Coe also offers one of Scotland's classic ridge walks, the **Aonach Eagach**. With potentially fatal drops it's not for the inexperienced or faint-hearted as there are some very exposed pinnacles you must climb around. The exposed ridge runs almost the entire length of the glen, starting at **Am Bodach** and ending at **Sgor nam Fiannaidh**. Don't make the mistake of descending from the last summit straight down to the **Clachaig Inn**. Instead, take the safer marked route.

Another difficult route is to the summit of **Buachaille Etive Mór**, one of the most photographed mountains in Scotland and one you'll probably recognize immediately the first time you see it from the A82, especially on the road north up to Glencoe. The mountain is best viewed from the **Kingshouse Hotel** and the route starts from Altnafeadh, a couple of miles west of the hotel. This is also the start or finish point for the fairly easy half-day walk over the **Devil's Staircase**, which is part of the West Highland Way. For a description of the route, see page 75. **Glen Etive** runs southwest from the hotel. It's a very beautiful and little-visited place, and great for wild camping. Unfortunately, there's now no postbus so you'll need to walk in or cycle.

Finally, there are some short, pleasant walks around **Glencoe Lochan**, an artificial loch created in the mid-19th century by Lord Strathcona for his homesick Canadian wife. Take the left turning off the minor road to the youth hostel just beyond the bridge over the River Coe. There's a choice of three walks of between 40 minutes and an hour, all detailed at the car park (or see www.forestry.gov.uk).

Glencoe Mountain Resort
ⓘ *T01855-851226, www.glencoemountain.com. Chairlift Dec-Oct daily 0930-1700, £10, during the winter ski season an adult day pass is £25, children £20.*
The **Glencoe Ski Centre** is just over a mile from the **Kingshouse Hotel**, on the other side of the A82, on **Meall A'Bhuiridh** (3636 ft). Established in 1956, it is Scotland's oldest ski centre and remains one of the best. The aptly titled Flypaper is the steepest 'black' marked piste in Scotland. In the summer months, for £20 mountain bikers can enjoy all day (lift) access to its downhill course.

Glen Coe listings

For hotel and restaurant price codes and other relevant information, see pages 13-20.

⊜ Where to stay

Onich, North Ballachulish and Kinlochleven *p74, map p76*

There's a wide selection of places to stay in the villages of Onich and North Ballachulish, mostly with good views of the loch. They make an attractive alternative to Fort William and you may catch sight of gannets, seals, porpoises, and even sea otter in and around Ballachulish Bay and Loch Leven.

££££ The Lodge on the Loch Hotel, Onich, T01855-821237, www.lodgeontheloch.com. For guests who expect that little bit extra (at a price), with some rooms (including 4-poster beds) giving views over the sea loch. Handy for Glencoe and Fort William. Reasonable dinners from daily 1830-2100.

£££ Cuilcheanna House, Onich, T01855-821226. Easter-Oct. A comfortable guesthouse just off the main road with a reputation for a warm welcome and tasty food.

£££ Onich Hotel, Onich, T01855-821214. Standard hotel rooms, some with loch views and a great panorama over Loch Linnhe from the conservatory. Good range of meals (**££**), including hot sandwiches (1200-1700) in its busy bar.

£££-££ Allt-nan-Ros Hotel, Onich, T01855-821210, www.allt-nan-ros.co.uk. James and Fiona Macleod's Victorian country house overlooks Loch Linnhe with views across to Appin and the hills of Ardgour and Morvern. There are pretty gardens, great food (**£££-££**), and even a 10% discount on the 'Dragon's Tooth' Ballachulish 9-hole golf course.

££ Camus House, Onich, T01855-821200. Mar-Oct. Lovely guesthouse with sea views.

££ The Inn at Ardgour, Ardgour, T01855-841225. This historic watering hole that also serves good value lunches and dinners is just 300 yds across the water from the Corran Ferry.

££ MacDonald Hotel, Fort William Rd, Kinlochleven, T01855-831539. Year-round. A welcoming, 10 bedroom hotel with a Bothy bar and restaurant serving reasonable food (**££**), open to residents and campers alike. Round the back of the hotel the owners have added several modern but small bunk bed-based cabins (from £22 per person) and space for 11 camp pitches £6 per night. Campers can also enjoy a full Scottish breakfast (£7).

££ Woolly Rock B&B, North Ballachulish, T01855-821338. Open all year. 4 rooms with sea views over Loch Linnhe. Good-value guesthouse.

££-£ The Corran Inn, 6 miles south of Fort William, right by the Corran ferry slipway off the A82, T01855-821235. A warm welcome is assured in this small hotel that also serves up great value hearty lunches and dinners (**££-£**). Nip into its wee (former Temperance) bar, complete with tin roof for a dram or real ale. Behind the hotel is the 32-bed **Corran Bunkhouse** (**£**), T01855-821000.

£ Blackwater Hostel, Lab Rd, Kinlochleven, T01855-831253, www.blackwaterhostel. co.uk. Based in a row of old stone cottages, this is a friendly, well-run backpackers' hostel. 30 camping pitches outside the door (beware of the midges). The **Ice Factor** is only 200 yds away and the West Highland Way is at your feet.

£ Inchree Hostel, Inchree, on the A82 to Fort William, T01855-821287, T0800-3101536, www.inchreecentre.co.uk. Buses stop 100 yds from the hostel. Dorms, and twin and double rooms. Good facilities and on-site bistro and bar (**££-£**). **Vertical Descent** is just up the road.

£ Tigh-na-Cheo Guest House, Garbhein Rd, Kinlochleven, T01855-831434. Friendly, with a superb outlook over Loch Leven and the Mamores. Very close to **Ice Factor** and the West Highland Way.

Ballachulish *p77, map p76*

As well as one of the most historic hotels in Scotland, there's a wide selection of cheaper B&Bs and guesthouses in the village.

££££ Ballachulish House, some 200 yds beyond the **Ballachulish Hotel** on the A828 to Oban, T01855-81126. 8 rooms. This is a beautiful hotel, oozing style and an eclectic history, including an alleged role in inspiring RL Stevenson's *Kidnapped* classic and possibly once host to the treacherous officers who slaughtered the MacDonald's in Glencoe. Today, the fine bedroom decor is complemented by personal touches such as the home-made shortbread and Arran Aromatics toiletries. The recipient of a Michelin star, this retreat's style and taste extends seamlessly to the restaurant (**£££**).

££££-££ Ballachulish Hotel, South Ballachulish by the bridge, T01855-831500, www.ballachulishhotel.com. 54 rooms. With a touch of tartan, the rooms are tasteful with some affording stunning loch views. However, it's the **Bulas Bar & Bistro (£££-££)** that attracts many, try its daily *bulas* (Gaelic pot) creations, including venison and seafood pie using fresh, locally sourced produce.

£££ The Isles of Glencoe Hotel, T01855-811602, www.islesofglencoe.com. 39 rooms. A modern hotel and leisure complex adjacent to **Lochaber Watersports** on the shores of the loch. Lovely sea views from the 'top-deck' bedrooms whilst families will enjoy the excellent facilities, including heated pool, sauna and outdoor adventure play area. The restaurant is open for lunch from 1200 (**£**) and dinner (**££**) from 1830-2130. Non guests can swim and use the sauna after a minimum spend of £7.50 on the premises.

££ Fern Villa, T01855-811393. A good-value guesthouse.

Glencoe village *p77, map p76*

There are several B&Bs and guesthouses in the village and quite a few options around.

££ Clachaig Inn, about 3 miles south just off the A82 on the old 'B' road that winds back to the village, T01855-811252, www.clachaig.

com. Though more highland twee than its rustic beginnings of yesteryear, this remains a popular haunt for walkers. There's good-value accommodation and self-catering in chalets (from £485 per week) but it's the real ales from Kinlochleven's Atlas Brewery, live music and hearty pub grub (**££-£**), including wild boar sandwiches, that attracts people.

££ Kingshouse Hotel, east end of the glen, almost opposite the turn-off to the **Glencoe Ski Centre**, T01855-851226. From Glencoe village you'll need to walk 15-20 mins to the road entrance of the White Corries (Glencoe) ski area where Citylink buses pull over. This is Scotland's oldest established inn and, judging by the decor it feels like it. However, thanks to the congenial, cosy **Climber's Bar** and the West Highland Way which passes its door, it's little wonder that this historic hotel is popular with the many who camp across the old stone bridge. The sign on 'The Kingy' hotel door is telling: it advises non patrons there's a toilet in the village (10 miles away!).

££ Scorrybreac Guesthouse, 1 mile from Glencoe village, T01855-811354, www.scorrybreac.co.uk. Dec-Oct. Pleasant guesthouse.

£ Glencoe Independent Hostel, near the SYHA Youth Hostel, T01855-811906, www.glencoehostel.co.uk. This is a basic but friendly bunkhouse complete with open fire. It's a 10- to 15-min walk for food or a pint at the **Clachaig Inn**.

£ Signal Rock Cottage, 1.5 miles from Glencoe village down the old road, T01855-811295. This timber-clad B&B is set amidst the trees in 50 acres of land. Secluded but worth the walk.

£ SYHA Youth Hostel, on the same road as Clachaig Inn, about 2 miles from the village, T01855-811219. Excellent hostel very popular with cyclists and climbers. Book ahead.

Camping

Glencoe Camping and Caravanning Club Site, T01855-811397. Mar-Oct. At the westernmost edge of Glencoe village with views down the loch towards Ballachulish.

Red Squirrel Campsite, T01855-811256.
Open year-round. If walking south from
Glencoe village on the 'B' road you'll reach
this modest campsite before the hostels
further along the road.

🍴 Restaurants

Onich, North Ballachulish and
Kinlochleven *p74, map p76*
£££ Ballachulish House, some 200 yds
beyond **Ballachulish Hotel**, just off the A828
to Oban, T01855-811266, www.ballachulish
house.com. Mar-Oct. 8 rooms. Steeped in
history, delicious game and seafood are just
some of the tempting dishes. Book ahead.
££ Inchree Bistro and Bar, Inchree, T01855-
821393. Open daily. A friendly and informal
place that produces good food and attracts
a fun-loving outdoor crowd.
££ Lochleven Seafood Café, 4.5 miles
along the B863 from North Ballachulish,
Onich, T01855-821048, www.lochleven
seafood cafe.co.uk. May-Aug 1200-1430,
1800-2100 and snack menu 1430-1600.
Superb, mouth-watering and excellent. The
seafood at this simple but stylish restaurant
is unrivalled. Feast on caught oysters,
scallops, langoustines and a gargantuan
seafood platter. There are non fishy treats
too but as the latest catch in the tanks
highlights, affordable tasty seafood is the
star attraction. Book ahead. Recommended.
££-£ Bothan Bar and Bistro, Ice Factor,
Kinlochleven, T01855-831100. Daily 1100-
late. A hip post-climb gathering place witha
delicious restaurant menu, including venison
and Loch Leven shellfish, tasty bar snacks,
and refreshing real ales from Kinlochleven's
own Atlas microbrewery on tap; Blizzard,
Sisters and Latitude. There is a wonderful
wood-burning stove, the chance to watch
fellow climbers on the walls and enjoy the
view of Loch Leven and the Mamores.
£ Fishnet fish and chip shop, Kinlochleven,
opposite the **Tail Race Inn**. Open all year.
Proudly proclaims to be the West Highland
Way's only chip-shop. Great portions.

Glencoe village *p77, map p76*
For Restaurants options,
refer to Where to stay, above.

🍸 Bars and clubs

Onich, North Ballachulish and
Kinlochleven *p77, map p76*
Bothan Bar, Ice Factor, Kinlochleven
and the **Tail Race Inn** (the local worthies'
haunt) both serve beer from the local
Atlas microbrewery. It's also worth
popping into the cosy bar in the
MacDonald Hotel along the road.

🛍 Shopping

Glen Coe village *p77, map p76*
Crafts
Crafts and Things, in a delightful old whitewashed croft at the northern end of Glencoe
village. Has expanded to offer both an array
of woollens, crafts and excellent home-
baking and light bites (**£**) in its homely café.

🎯 What to do

Onich, North Ballachulish and
Kinlochleven *p74, map p76*
Brewery Tours
Atlas Brewery, Kinlochleven, T01667
404555, www.atlasbrewery.com. Easter-
Sep. Free tour of the microbrewery at 1730.
Formerly the carbon bunker for the massive
aluminium smelter, Atlas microbrewery
produced its first beers in Feb 2002 and
now sells its finest tipples far and wide.

Climbing
For advice, contact the Mountaineering Council
of Scotland (MCofS) on T01738-493942,
www.mountaineering-scotland.org.uk.
Ice Factor, Kinlochleven, T01855-831100,
www.ice-factor.co.uk. Tue-Thu 0900-
2200, Fri-Mon 0900-1900. Housed in
a former aluminium smelter, the world's
largest indoor ice-climbing facility is truly
spectacular. A giant refrigerated toy-box

for anyone in search of vertical fun, over 500 tons of snow are packed onto the 15-m-high vertical walls. Novice (under instruction) or expert, the ice wall simulates as closely as possible outdoor conditions. There are also 15-m-high rock-climbing walls, a bouldering area, a well-stocked equipment shop and even a sauna and steam room, before you reflect on your day in the **Bothan Bar and Bistro** upstairs (see Restaurants, above). Annual membership £10, £5 for14-17 year olds. Daily rates vary according to the activity, with beginners only permitted to climb under instruction or expert supervision. Call for rates and times. A competent climber can enjoy all-day rock climbing for £9; or 2 hrs ice-climbing for £20, children £17.50. It's £5 for the sauna and steam room, £3.50 if also climbing.

Climbing guides Ice Factor's professional climbing staff also run outdoor mountaineering and climbing courses.
Alan Kimber, West Coast Mountain Guides, Calluna, Heathercroft, T01397-700451, www.westcoast-mountainguides.co.uk. Recommended professional climbing guide.
Mike Pescod, Abacus, 6 Hillview Dr, Corpach, www.abacusmountainguides.com. Recommended professional climbing guide.

Mountain biking
Vertical Descents, see Watersports, below. Mountain bikes, £15 for ½-day, £20 for full-day.

Golf
Ballachulish House, T01855-811695. This challenging and scenic 9-hole golf course (from £15 per round) is open to the general public.

Glencoe Mountain Resort *p78*
Snowsports
Glencoe Ski Centre is the oldest resort in Scotland and has pistes suitable for beginners and experts. The Flypaper is reportedly the steepest black-marked run in Scotland and is definitely for experts only. It affords stunning views southwards over Glencoe. There is also a small café (winter only) above the first chairlift.

Watersports and other activities
Lochaber Watersports, next door to the Isles of Glencoe Hotel, North Ferry View, Old Ferry Rd, Onich T01855-811931, T07760-793894, www.lochaberwatersports.co.uk. Double open kayak, £30 for 3 hrs; 2-person dinghy, £35 for 3 hrs; and fast (RIB) power-boat two day course £230 per person.
Vertical Descents, Inchree Falls, Onich, T01855-821593, www.verticaldescents.com. Yes, it can rain in Scotland but who cares if you've a wetsuit on and are having fun experiencing the thrills and spills of fun-yakking (£50, a mix of rafting and kayaking) or the adrenalin-pumping activity of canyoning (from £50). After a day climbing (or jumping off) waterfalls or blasting through the water in a kayak you're certain to come back refreshed.

⊖ Transport

Onich, North Ballachulish and Kinlochleven *p74, map p76*
Bus Highland Country Buses, T01397-702373, run Mon-Sat 6 times a day, Sun 3 times, between **Kinlochleven** and **Fort William**, 50 mins. En route these (No 44) buses stop at **Onich** and **Corran Ferry**. They also stop at **Glencoe Junction** (the southern edge of the village). You can also catch the **Scottish Citylink** service to **Glasgow**, which leaves Fort William 4 times a day and stops at **Glencoe village**.

Glencoe village *p77, map p76*
Bus There are daily Citylink buses to **Glasgow** and **Fort William**, 2½ hrs.

West of Fort William

West of Fort William lie some of the Britain's most extravagantly scenic landscapes and some of its most remote places. From southernmost Morvern, through the ruggedly handsome Ardnamurchan Peninsula, across the evocatively named 'Road to the Isles', through the haunting and tragic 'Rough Bounds' and on to the hopelessly isolated and utterly wild lands of Knoydart, this is serious wilderness, with little pockets of accessible and user-friendly Highlands thrown in for good measure.

Ardgour, Ardnamurchan and Morvern → *For listings, see pages 89-93.*

This lonely, southwestern corner features a dramatic landscape of rugged mountains, ancient forest, wild moorland and near-deserted glens, fringed by a coastline of sparkling white beaches and clear turquoise seas with wonderful views across to the isles of Mull, the Small Isles and Skye. This is one of the least-populated areas in Britain, mainly due to the legacy of the Highland Clearances in the mid-19th century, when whole communities were evicted by landlords in favour of more profitable sheep. Today, the issue is more finding people willing to stay year-round instead of leaving villages like Kilchoan with all too many homes run only as seasonal self-catering or second home hideaways. With so few people around, the whole peninsula is a haven for wildlife with a huge variety of birds and animals, such as deer, pine martens, wildcats and eagles. If you have both the time and the energy, it's worth exploring by car, foot or even kayak (see What to do, page 92) and there's a myriad of (Forestry Commission Scotland) footpaths to explore. However, distances can be deceptive and if driving, ensure you've enough fuel.

Arriving in Ardgour, Ardnamurchan and Morvern

Getting around Once you leave the A830 Fort William to Mallaig road, buses are few and far between, so it's not easy to get around quickly without your own transport. You'll need your own transport to reach Ardnamurchan Point and Sanna Bay as there are no buses beyond Kilchoan. If driving, note most of the roads are single-track. If you're travelling by car, access is via the A861, leaving the A830 before Glenfinnan or at Lochailort. You can also make the five-minute ferry crossing to Ardgour from the Corran Ferry, about 8 miles south of Fort William on the A82, see page 84. From Corran, the ferry sailings are frequent and leave daily from around 0700-1800. The journey costs £6.40 for a car and driver, pedestrians and cyclists travel free. ▶▶ *See Transport page 92.*

Tourist information The website www.ardnamurchan.com, has lots of information on walks, as well as local events and attractions. Some 40 walks in the area are listed in a local guidebook, *Great Walks* (£4), available at tourist offices. OS Explorer Maps 383, 390 and 391 cover the entire region. See also What to do, page 92.

Ardgour → *Phone code 01967.*

The name Ardgour means 'height of the goats', and you can still see feral goats in this huge, sparsely populated wilderness bordered by Loch Shiel, Loch Eil, Loch Linnhe and Loch Sunart. Access is via the A861 south from Kinlocheil, or on the Corran Ferry to the tiny lochside villages of **Corran** and **Clovulin**.

The attractive little village of **Strontian** on the shores of Loch Sunart gave its name to the element strontium, which was first discovered in the nearby lead mines in 1790. These now-abandoned mines also produced most of the lead shot used in the Napoleonic wars. Strontian is the largest settlement in these parts and has a small grocery shop, post office, petrol pumps and a **TIC** ① *T01967-402131, Mar-Jun Mon-Sat 1000-1600, Jun-Aug Mon-Sat 1000-1700, Sun 1000-1600, Sep-Oct Mon-Sat 1000-1600.* One mile north of the village is the **Ariundle Nature Reserve**, which offers a pleasant two-hour nature trail through the glen and a 40-minute forest walk. It's all well signposted and there's a café/bistro.

Morvern → *Phone code 01967.*

Just east of Strontian the A884 leads south through the dramatic, wildlife rich landscape of Morvern to the tiny remote community of **Lochaline** on the Sound of Mull, departure point for the CalMac ferry to Fishnish. About 3 miles before Lochaline is the turning left for the track which leads down the side of Loch Aline to the 14th-century ruins of **Ardtornish Castle**. First you'll come to **Kinlochaline Castle** (keys available at the cottage) and **Ardtornish House**. This house stands on the site of the original house, which was visited on several occasions by Florence Nightingale, who was a family member of the original owners. The author John Buchan spent many summers here in the 1930s. There's a path which leads from the estate office uphill across open moorland for an hour until it reaches **Loch Tearnait**. In the centre of the loch is a 1500-year-old crannog, an artificial island built for defensive purposes. This walk is detailed in the tourist board's leaflet, along with the Ariundle Nature Trail (see above). During the stalking season (1 July to 20 October) check at the estate office before setting out on the walk to the Loch.

Ardnamurchan Peninsula and Moidart → *Phone code 01972 and 01967.*

The main places of interest in this area are to be found on the rugged Ardnamurchan Peninsula (from the Gaelic *Aird nam Murchan*, meaning 'Point of the High Seas'), the end of which is the most westerly point on the British mainland. The winding A861 runs west from Strontian along the north shore of Loch Sunart to **Salen**, where the single-track B8007 branches west and runs all the way out to the tip of the peninsula. The A861 meanwhile turns north and twists and turns along a spectacular single-track road to Acharacle.

The first settlement as you head west out to Ardnamurchan Point is **Glenborrodale**. Before you reach the tiny hamlet look out on the left for the castellated late-Victorian towers of **Glenborrodale Castle**, once the property of a certain Jesse Boot, who founded a chain of chemist shops which you may have heard of. Just west of Glenborrodale is the excellent **Glenmore Natural History Centre** ① *T01967-500254, Apr-Oct Mon-Sat 1030-1730, Sun 1200-1730,* should be on the list of everyone with the faintest interest in the peninsula's wildlife and nature – for which Ardnamurchan is renowned. The 'Living Building' with turf on the roof and bark on the floor ensures you will see birds and animals (including pine martens) up close, whilst the interactive displays are both fun and informative for all ages. It's a good place for kids, and a life-saver when the weather is just too bad to venture outside. There's a good little **Antler Tearoom** (£) serving home-baking and light lunches, and a decent gift shop. In addition, this is the base of the wonderful

Sunart Suppers ① *T07772-850133*, frozen gourmet food, made to order and available to collect or be delivered. It's self-caterers and campers heaven with the likes of highland venison and fish pie. A mile to the east is the **RSPB Reserve** where you can see golden eagles, otters and seals. You can take a two-hour wildlife trip to the seal colonies – or further afield to Tobermory on Mull or Staffa and the Treshnish Islands (see What to do, page 92). A few miles west of the centre, the B8007 turns away from the coast. Here you'll see the beautiful bay of **Camas nan Geall** (Bay of the stranger or pledge, the precise meaning is unclear). It's worth stopping at the car park to admire the fantastic views, or take the path down to the beach. Between Glenborrodale and Kilchoan, a road runs to the north coast of the peninsula and the beautiful beaches at **Fascadale**, **Kilmory** and **Ockle**.

The straggling crofting village of **Kilchoan** is the main settlement on Ardnamurchan. Shortly after passing the sign for the village, you can turn left to the scenic ruin of **Mingary Castle**, built around the 13th century. There's a **TIC** ① *T01972-510222, Easter-Oct daily*, which provides information on local scenic walks and will help with accommodation. Beyond Kilchoan the road leads to the lighthouse at mainland Britain's most westerly point, with stunning views (on a clear day) across to the small isles of Rùm, Eigg, Muck and Canna, with the Cuillins of Skye rising behind Rùm. The former (36 m high) lighthouse was designed by Alan Stevenson, father of Robert Louis, and built in 1849. The buildings have been converted into the **Ardnamurchan Lighthouse Visitor Centre** ① *T01972-510210, www.ardnamurchan.u-net.com, Apr-Oct daily 1000-1700, £5.50*, where you can learn about the history and workings of lighthouses. There's self-catering accommodation, a café and gift shop.

A mile northwest of Kilchoan a road branches to the right to the beautiful long, white beach at **Sanna Bay**. It's worth making the trip here just to walk on the beach, but this is also a good place to spot whales and dolphins. On the road to Sanna Bay is the tiny settlement of **Achnaha**, which is famed for its rare 'ring-dyke' system, a huge, natural rock formation which is the crater of an extinct volcano.

North of Salen on the A861 is the scattered crofting township of **Acharacle**, at the western end of Loch Shiel surrounded by rolling hills. The village has several shops, a post office, garage and plenty of places to stay. A couple of miles to the west a road leads to beautiful **Kentra Bay**. Cross the wooden bridge, follow the footpath round the side of Kentra Bay and then follow the signs for Gortenfearn, where you'll find the famous 'singing sands'. Not only is the beach music to the ears as you walk its length, but the view across to Skye and the small isles is a feast for the eyes.

Three miles north of Acharacle is **Loch Moidart**. Here, perched on a rocky promontory in the middle of the loch, is the 13th-century ruin of **Castle Tioram** (pronounced 'Cheerum'), one of Scotland's best-loved castle ruins. This was the seat of the MacDonalds of Clanranald, until it was destroyed by their chief in 1715 to prevent it from falling into Hanoverian hands while he was away fighting for the Jacobites. There are plans to restore the castle, but you can visit it (free) via the sandy causeway that connects it to the mainland at low tide. You can paddle the seal rich, crystal clear waters in the Sound of Arisaig with **Rockhopper Seakayaking** ① *www.rockhopperscotland.co.uk*. The A861 follows the shores of Loch Moidart, into the region of the same name, before joining the A830 Fort William to Mallaig road at Lochailort.

Raising standards

It all started on 19 August 1745 at Glenfinnan, 19 miles west of Fort William at the head of Loch Shiel. Less than a month earlier, Prince Charles Edward Stuart had landed on the Scottish mainland for the first time, on the shores of Loch nan Uamh, between Lochailort and Arisaig. He had come to claim the British throne for his father, James, son of the exiled King James VII of Scotland and II of England.

The clan chiefs had expected French support, but when the Prince arrived with only a handful of men they were reluctant to join the cause. Undeterred, the prince raised his standard and his faith was soon rewarded when he heard the sound of the pipes and Cameron of Lochiel, along with 800 men, came marching down the valley to join them. It must have been an incredible moment.

The Road to the Isles → *For listings, see pages 89-93.*

The Road to the Isles, the 46-mile stretch of the A830 from Fort William to Mallaig, runs through a series of magnificent glens before emerging on a coastline of vanilla-coloured beaches and sinuous bays backed by machair and washed by turquoise seas, with views across to Rùm, Eigg and the Cuillins of Skye. This is also the route followed by the West Highland Railway (see box, page 72), frequently hailed as one of the great railway journeys in the world. Either way – by road or rail – this is a beautiful journey, through a landscape that resonates with historical significance. For this is Bonnie Prince Charlie country, where the ill-fated Jacobite Rising began, and ended, with the Prince's flight to France.

Glenfinnan → *Phone code 01397.*

Some 17 miles west of Fort William, at the head of Loch Shiel, is Glenfinnan, a kind of single-malt distillation of Highland beauty. A grand monument marks the spot where Bonnie Prince Charlie raised the Jacobite standard in 1745. It was erected in 1815 by Alexander MacDonald of Glenaladale in memory of the clansmen who fought and died for the Prince. You can climb to the top (mind your head, though) for even better views down the loch. There's a powerful sense of history here and as you gaze across eerie Loch Shiel stretching into the distance, veiled by steep mountains, you can almost hear the wail of the bagpipes in the distance, through the mist. On the other side of the road is the **National Trust for Scotland Visitor Centre** ① *T01397-722250, Apr-Jun, Sep-Oct daily 1000-1700, Jul-Aug daily 0930-1730, £3.50, concessions £2.50*, which has displays and an audio programme of the Prince's campaign, from Glenfinnan to its grim conclusion at Culloden. The Glenfinnan Games are held here in mid-August.

A mile away, in Glenfinnan village, is the **Station Museum** ① *T01397-722295, Jun-Oct daily 0900-1700, other times by appointment, £1*, which is housed in the railway station on the magnificent Fort William to Mallaig railway line. It has displays of memorabilia from the line's 100-year history. You can also sleep and eat here (see below). The 1000-ft span of the **Glenfinnan Viaduct**, between the visitor centre and the village, is one of the most spectacular sections of the famous West Highland Railway, see box, page 72.

About 10 miles west of Glenfinnan the road passes through the tiny village of **Lochailort**, complete with the pleasant Lochailort Inn and where the A861 branches south to the remote Ardnamurchan Peninsula, see above. A couple of miles further on, is **Loch nan Uamh**, where Prince Charles first landed on the Scottish mainland (he first landed on Eriskay in the Outer Hebrides) and from where, a year later, he fled for France following the disastrous defeat at Culloden, see box, page 43. A path leads down from the car park to the Prince's Cairn, which marks the beginning and the end of the Jacobite cause. A few years ago, scientific imaging proved that contrary to reports, a horse and cart were not entombed in the concrete foundations of the Glenfinnan Viaduct following an accident during its building. However, it did prove the horse and cart lie encased under the Loch nan Uamh Viaduct.

Arisaig and Morar → *Phone code 01687.*
At the western end of the Morar Peninsula is the little village of Arisaig, scattered around the head of a sheltered bay with An Sgurr's knobbly peak peering above the narrow mouth. The village has sleeping and eating options, as well as a post office, general store (with ATM) and doctor's surgery and is a useful service centre for the many self-catering cottages and caravans that line this stretch of coastline. There are some nice beaches around, and the road west from the village out to the **Rhue Peninsula** is great for seal spotting. You can also take a cruise from Arisaig to the islands of Rùm, Eigg and Muck, see Transport, page 92.

Arisaig was the birthplace of Long John Silver, who worked on the construction of the nearby lighthouse at Barrahead, one of many designed by the father of Robert Louis Stevenson who met Silver and was so impressed that he immortalized him in his classic *Treasure Island*.

The main A830 bypasses Arisaig on its way to Mallaig, while a wiggly single-track road hugs the coast and heads north, past the golf course and on past beautiful Camusdarach beach (which featured in the film *Local Hero*) before joining the main road by the tiny village of Morar. A single-track road leads up behind the village of Morar to dark, mysterious **Loch Morar**, the deepest inland loch in the country and home of Morag, Scotland's other, lesser-known, but more attractive (according to the locals) monster. Two locals reported seeing her in August 1969 and a scientific investigation two years later uncovered a remarkable number of eye-witness accounts. You could always try to elicit further information from the locals over a wee dram in the bar of the **Morar Hotel**. The road runs along the north shore of the loch for 3 miles until it reaches the pretty little hamlets of **Bracora** and **Bracorina**. Here the road stops, but a footpath continues all the way to **Tarbet** on the shores of Loch Nevis, from where it's possible to catch a boat back to Mallaig, see Transport, page 92. It takes about three hours to walk to Tarbet – where there's now a bothy – and you'll need to get there by 1530 for the boat.

Mallaig → *Phone code 01687.*
The end of the road – and railway line – is Mallaig, a busy fishing port and main departure point for ferries to Skye. It's a no-nonsense, workmanlike place, with little in the way of worthwhile diversions, but there are decent facilities and at least the train and bus stations and CalMac ferry office are all within a few yards of each other. Also close by are banks with ATMs and the post office. The TIC ① *by the harbour, T01687-462170, Apr-Oct daily, Nov-Mar Mon, Tue and Fri,* has a café.

Beside the train station is the **Mallaig Heritage Centre** ① *T01687-462085, Apr-Jun and Oct Mon-Sat 1100-1600, Jul-Sep Mon-Sat 0930-1630, Sun 1230-1630, Nov-Mar Wed-Sat 1200-1700, £2, concession £1.50 under 16s free*, with interesting descriptions of the local Clearances, the railway line and the fishing industry.

Knoydart Peninsula → *For listings, see pages 89-93. Phone code 01867.*

The Knoydart Peninsula, the most remote and unspoilt region in Britain and one of Europe's last great wildernesses, literally lies between Heaven and Hell, for it is bordered to the north by Loch Hourn (Loch of Hell) and to the south by Loch Nevis (Loch of Heaven). Knoydart is not for wimps. It can only be reached on foot, or by boat from Mallaig, and consequently attracts walkers, who can wander for days around a network of trails without seeing another soul. If you've time and love the outdoors it's worth the trip.

Arriving in Knoydart Peninsula

Bruce Watt Sea Cruises ① *T01687-462320, www.knoydart-ferry.co.uk*, run trips to the remote village of Inverie (45 minutes), and Tarbet on Loch Nevis. They sail on Monday, Wednesday and Friday all year and from Monday to Friday in summer. On a Monday and Friday the boat calls in at Tarbet (all year, also on a Wednesday in summer). If you intend to catch the boat at Tarbet you must contact them in advance to confirm numbers There's also a ferry service from Arnisdale, on the north shore of Loch Hourn, to Barrisdale To arrange a crossing, contact Billy Mackenzie in Arnisdale, T01599-522247. It's a passenger only fast boat (also takes bikes) that sails subject to sea conditions and that can also be hired for wildlife spotting.

If approaching Knoydart from the Glenelg road, there's a **MacRae Kintail bus** ① *on request, T01599-511384*, that runs Monday to Friday from Shiel Bridge to Glenelg (see page 95), from where you can take a ferry across to Kylerhea on Skye. Note: if planning to explore the Knoydart Peninsula it's advisable to call **Knoydart Foundation** ① *T01687-462242*, for travel and accommodation advice, including information on stalking activity.

Walking on the Knoydart Peninsula

A two-day hiking route starts from Kinloch Hourn, reached by bus from Invergarry, see page 53. The trail winds its way around the coast to Barrisdale and on to Inverie. Another route into Knoydart starts from the west end of Loch Arkaig, and runs through Glen Dessarry. Both are tough hikes and only for fit, experienced and well-equipped hillwalkers. An easier way in is by boat (see Transport, page 92).

The peninsula's only settlement of any size is tiny **Inverie**, with just 60 inhabitants, one of only a few villages in Scotland which can't be reached by road, but still has a post office, a shop, a few places to stay and Britain's most remote pub. Much of the peninsula is mountain, with four peaks over 3000 ft. Its 85 square miles is a mix of private sporting estate, conservation trust and community partnership. Almost a decade ago one chunk of the peninsula, the 17,000-acre **Knoydart Estate**, was rescued from a succession of indifferent landlords by a community buy-out, funded by public money and individual donations. The Knoydart Foundation's trustees include the conservationist Chris Brasher and impresario Cameron Mackintosh, and if you sit outside the **Old Forge** long enough, one of them might pass by, or stop for a chat. Equally possible is the sighting of otters in the Sound of Sleat or golden eagles soaring overhead.

West of Fort William listings

For hotel and restaurant price codes and other relevant information, see pages 13-20.

● Where to stay

Ardgour *p83*

££££-£££ Kilcamb Lodge Hotel, Strontian, T01967-402257, www.kilcamblodge.com. Mid-Feb to Dec. This luxurious Victorian country house standing in its own grounds just north of Strontian on the shores of Loch Sunart has its own private beach. The perfect bolthole, with only the occasional otter or eagle to disturb the peace, also serves superb food.

£££-££ The Inn at Ardgour, Ardgour, next to Corran Ferry, 9 miles from Fort William, T01855-841225, www.ardgour.biz. 12 en suite rooms. Small hotel dating from 1746. Cosy, lively bar with a fine selection of malts and good value lunches and dinners. Good choice for walkers, with lovely views. Recommended.

££ Ben View Hotel, 1 mile west of Strontian, T01967-402333, www.benviewhotel.co.uk. In addition to its 9 comfortable bedrooms, enjoy views over Loch Sunart, a dram in the bizarre pine panelled bar and delicious locally sourced food. Also has 2 self-catering cottages by the hotel that sleep 2 (from £220 per week).

££ Strontian Hotel, Strontian, T01967-402029, www.thestrontianhotel.co.uk. You can't miss this 6-bedroom hotel, right by the shores of Loch Sunart and with breathtaking views over the sea loch from its restaurant (**££**). Dinner until 2100.

£ Heatherbank, Upper Scotstown, Strontian, T01967-402201, www.heatherbankbb.co.uk. Open Easter-Oct. 3 en suite rooms. Modern house with great views to the Ardgour hills. Spacious guest lounge with log fire. Discounts for longer stays.

Ardnamurchan Peninsula and Moidart *p84*

£££ Meall Mo Chridhe, Kilchoan, T01972-510238. Year-round. A beautiful 3-bedroom 17th-century converted manse set in over 40 acres with great sea views and fine cooking. Dinner available for non-residents (**£££**), but booking essential.

£££-££ Strontian Hotel, by Strontian, T01967-402029. Fabulous 18th-century inn that looks right down Loch Sunart. Opportunities to spot seals and otters, fish, dine or simply relax in one of 6 comfortable bedrooms.

£££-£ Glenuig Inn, Glenuig, by Loch Ailort, T01687-470219, www.glenuig.com. 18th-century inn that has undergone extensive renovation. Offers comfortable bunkhouse accommodation for £25 (plus £10 breakfast) per person. Also en suite accommodation for families or groups. Reasonable lunches and dinners (including lamb and fish) served in the inn's restaurant (until 2100). Good bar and terrific views of loch. Owner is a keen sea-kayaker and has links with local operators. Great area to spot seals and basking sharks.

££ Cala Darach, Glenmore by Glenborrodale, T01972-500204. Open Mar-Oct. 3 en suite rooms. Lovely country house with views across Loch Sunart.

££ Kilchoan House Hotel, Kilchoan, T01972-510200, www.kilchoanhotel.co.uk. 7 en suite rooms. Comfortable option with views of Mull from most of the rooms. Also good meals served 1200-1400 and 1800-2030, in the bar or dining room. 3-course dinner from £15.95.

££ Loch Shiel House Hotel, Acharacle, T01967-431224. 8 en suite rooms. Comfortable hotel serving decent bar meals (**££-£**). Contact them for details of cruises on Loch Shiel.

££ Salen Inn, Salen, T01972-431661, www.salenhotel.co.uk. Open all year. Decent hotel accommodation and good food (**££**), with the likes of seafood, lamb and venison on the menu. Cosy bar and information on walks.

££-£ Sonachan Hotel, a few miles beyond Kilchoan, on the road to Ardnamurchan

Point, T01972-510211, www.sonachan.
u-net.com. Open all year. The most westerly
hotel on the UK mainland, close to the
lighthouse and beaches and surrounded
by 1000 acres of grounds with walking
and fishing opportunities. Good food
available and children welcome. Also has a
4-bedroom self-catering house and 2 rooms.

Self-catering
Glenmore House and Cottage, Port An
Aiseig, Glenborrodale, T01972-500263,
www.holidayardnamurchan.co.uk. Luxury
self-catering cottage and lodge on shores
of Loch Sunart, facilities include whirlpool
baths and sauna. Available all year, £400-
£1500 per week.
Shoreline Cottages, Glenborrodale, T01972-
500248. Great views out to sea from 2 lovely,
secluded cottages set in 13 acres of grounds.
Fabulous opportunities to spot wildlife and
enjoy a true escape from the daily stresses
of urban life. From £545 per week.

Camping
Branault Croft Caravans, Achateny by
Acharacle, T01972-510284. Apr-Oct. Offers
3 static (luxury) caravans on a working
croft at the northern edge of the peninsula.
A peaceful escape and ideal for young
children, with acres of space to play in and
explore. Lovely views across the sea towards
Eigg and Skye. £110-170 per week.
Resipole Farm Caravan Park, 1 mile or
so east of Salen, Resipole, T01967-431235,
www.resipole.co.uk. Self-catering chalets,
caravan and tent pitches, and caravans for
rent. Also has a restaurant and bar on site.
Fantastic views over the sea. Gets busy but
highly recommended.

Glenfinnan *p86*
£££ Glenfinnan House Hotel, off the main
road, T01397-722235, www.glenfinnan
house.com. Mar-Oct. 17 en suite rooms.
Charming house dating back to mid-1700s
with fabulous bedrooms, lovely meals
(1800-2030) and a bar that serves the likes of

venison sausages (1200-2100). Great place
to hear local folk music, fish or relax over
an intimate dinner (**£££**). Recommended.
£££ The Prince's House, main road, ½ mile
past monument on the right, heading west,
T01397-722246, www.glenfinnan.co.uk.
Mar-Nov. 9 en suite rooms. Comfortable old
coaching inn which offers good food (**££**).
£ Glenfinnan Sleeping Car, at the train
station, T01397-722400. Bunkhouse
accommodation for 10 people. Also offers
mountain bike hire and you can eat here
in the Glenfinnan Dining Car (**££-£**).

Arisaig and Morar *p87*
£££ Arisaig Hotel, Arisaig, T01687-450210,
www.arisaighotel.co.uk. Open all year.
18th-century former coaching inn with
13 en suite rooms and good sea views.
Meals (**££**) served in the restaurant and
2 bars (**£**). Child-friendly, with separate
playroom,10% off green fee at Traigh
golf course (3 miles away).
£££ The Old Library Lodge, Arisaig,
T01687-450651. Apr-Oct. 6 en suite rooms.
Lovely food in restaurant (**£££**), with well-
furnished rooms. Recommended.

Mallaig *p87*
£££ West Highland Hotel, T01687-462210,
www.westhighlandhotel.co.uk. Apr-Oct.
Centrally located with 40 reasonable rooms.
The restaurant is proud of its seafood
dishes and this is the place to order a
'West Highland Coffee' liqueur prepared
to the hotels secret recipe (**££**).
££ Western Isles Guesthouse, follow the
road round the harbour to East Bay,
T01687-462320. Jan-Nov. Excellent-value
guesthouse which serves dinner to guests.
££-£ Glencairn House, East Bay, T01687-
462359, www.glencairn-house.co.uk.
Apr-Sep. 2 en suite rooms. Comfortable
rooms with TV and DVD.
£ Sheena's Backpackers' Lodge, Station Rd,
T01687-462764, www.mallaigbackpackers.
co.uk. The cheapest place to stay is this
friendly, easy-going independent hostel,

with dorm beds, double rooms and
kitchen facilities.

Knoydart Peninsula *p88*

There's a growing number of options,
see www.knoydart-foundation.com.
Other than those listed below, there are
3 or 4 additional great value (**£**) backpacker
options on the peninsula, including
the **Kilchoan Barn**, T01687-462724;
and **The Old Byre**, T01687-460099.

£££ Doune Stone Lodge, 3-4 miles up the
peninsula's only road, standing in splendid
isolation, T01687-462667, www.doune-
knoydart.co.uk. 3 en suite rooms, all with
bunk beds for 2 children. Minimum stay
3 nights. Price includes breakfast, packed
lunch and dinner. The food is superb and
cannot be praised highly enough. Guests are
picked up by boat from Mallaig (around £20),
where you can leave your car. The owners
also run the nearby **Doune Bay Lodge**, with
shared facilities, for parties of up to 14 (from
£575 per person). Can be self-catered, fully
catered, or somewhere in between. Also the
option to charter the *TSMV Mary Doune* boat
for £2940. Highly recommended.

£££ The Gathering, Knoydart, T01687-
460051. A fabulous B&B, only opened a few
years ago, offers stylish rooms and great
breakfasts. Friendly host. Recommended.

£££ Pier House, Inverie, T01687-462347,
www.thepierhouseknoydart.co.uk. 4 rooms,
2 en suite, 2 with extra beds for children.
Price includes dinner. Good, old-fashioned
hospitality and wonderful local seafood (**££**).

£ Knoydart Foundation Backpackers,
15 mins' walk from the pier and pub,
T01687-462242. Basic but good value
at only £14 per bunk.

£ Torrie Shieling, Inverie, T01687-
462669. It's a bit more expensive than
most other hostels, but is very comfortable,
and popular with hikers. They also have
their own transport for trips around the
peninsula and will collect guests from
Mallaig by arrangement.

🍴 Restaurants

Ardgour *p83*

£££-££ The Inn at Ardgour, Corran,
T01855-841225, www.ardgour.biz. Family-
run, atmospheric inn serving good value
bar food, full à la carte menu and takeaway
snacks. Dogs and children welcome.
Informal dining with fantastic sea views.
Recommended.

££ Ariundle Centre, Strontian, T01967-
402279, www.ariundle.co.uk. Daily 0900-1730.
Licensed tea room/restaurant serving soups,
salads and snacks. Also does candlelit suppers
during the summer, phone for details.

Morvern *p84*

££ Lochaline Hotel, Lochaline, T01967-
421657. Hotel serving decent bar meals.

££ Whitehouse, Lochaline, T01967-421777.
Open Mon-Sat for lunch and dinner (till
2100). Local organic produce.

Ardnamurchan Peninsula and
Moidart *p84*

All the hotels listed under Where to stay
serve good food.

££ Glenuig Inn, 5 miles from Loch Ailort
and tucked back from the shoreline of
the Sound of Arisaig, T01687-470219.
Has undergone extensive refurbishment.
Hearty lunches and dinners in a friendly,
simple setting with a couple of real ales
on tap. Dinner until 2100.

££-£ Clanranald Hotel, at Mingarry, T01967-
431202. Tasty food is also available here.

Arisaig and Morar *p87*

Very good meals can be found at the **Arisaig
Hotel**, although the **Old Library Lodge and
Restaurant** definitely has the edge – see
Where to stay, above.

£ Café Rhu, Arisaig, next door to the Spar
store, T01687-450707. Open daily 1000-
1800. Snacks, soups, filled rolls and burgers,
also offers takeaway. Internet available £1
per hr. Friendly and good with kids.

Mallaig *p87*

If you're heading across to Skye you could buy some delicious peat-smoked salmon from **Andy Race**, by the harbour, T01687-462626, www.andyrace.co.uk, and eat it on the ferry with some brown bread. Alternatively, grab some excellent fish and chips or freshly caught scallops at the Cornerstone chippy.

££ Cabin Seafood Restaurant, by the harbour. Serves decent meals and a great value 'teatime special'.

£ Tea Room, below Sheena's Backpackers (see Where to stay, above). Great value meals, including a print of prawns and all manner of daytime hearty snacks.

Knoydart Peninsula *p88*

£££-££ The Old Forge, Inverie, T01687-462267. The most remote pub on mainland Britain, where you can enjoy some tasty local seafood and a pint of real ale in front of an open fire. The craic among the locals and visitors also produces a terrific atmosphere. There's even the occasional impromptu ceilidh. Mercifully devoid of wannabe city slickers, this isn't the place to dress to impress – think more walking boots, waterproofs and midge cream'. Recommended.

✪ What to do

Ardgour, Ardnamurchan and Morvern *p83*
Boat trips
Ardnamurchan Charters, T01972-500208. Offers a 2-hr wildlife trip to the seal colonies – or further afield to Tobermory on Mull or Staffa and the Treshnish Islands.

Sea kayaking
Rockhopper Scotland, based in Fort William (see page 71). Offer sea-kayaking adventures in Ardnamurchan. Highly recommended.

Glenfinnan *p86*
Loch Shiel Cruises, Jim Michie, Marnoch, Roshven, Lochailort, T01687-470322,

www.highlandcruises.co.uk. Runs a variety of cruises down Loch Shiel, from Glenfinnan to Acharacle. Sailings most days from Apr-Oct. Parking available at the **Glenfinnan House Hotel**, see Where to stay, page 90. Prices from £8 for 1 hr and £22 for a full loch cruise, with the possibility of spotting golden eagles. Cyclists can also join a cruise and disembark at the Polloch Pontoon to cycle back along the banks of the loch to Glenfinnan.

Arisaig and Morar *p87*
Arisaig Marine, The Harbour, Arisaig, T01687-450224, www.arisaig.co.uk. Trips to Eigg, Muck or Rùm aboard *MV Sheerwater*. Varied wildlife and spectacular scenery.

Mallaig *p87*
MV The Grimsay Isle, Ewen Nicholson, 6 Gillies Park, T01687-462652, T07880-815158, www.road-to-the-isles.org.uk/grimsayisle.html. Available for fishing charters and ferry service.

⊖ Transport

Ardgour, Ardnamurchan and Morvern *p83*
Bus Shiel Buses, T01967-431272, run most of the bus services. There's a bus once a day on Tue, Thu and Sat to **Fort William** from **Lochaline**, 2 hrs. There's a bus (No 500) once a day, Mon-Sat to **Fort William** from **Acharacle**, 1½ hrs, via Lochailort. The No 500 and No 502 also runs Mon-Sat from **Mallaig**, 1½ hrs, to Fort William. There's a bus, if you are very patient and super organized (to **Fort William** from **Kilchoan**, Mon-Sat, 2 hrs 25 mins, via **Glenuig**, 1 hr; **Acharacle**, 1 hr 20; and **Glenborrodale**, 2 hrs. There's also one service (No 506), Mon-Fri to **Fort William** from **Kilchoan**, 2½ hrs, via **Ardgour** and **Salen**.

Ferry For details of the ferry from Lochaline to Fishnish on Mull and from Kilchoan to Tobermory.

Arisaig and Morar *p87*
Ferry Arisaig Marine, T01687-450224, www.arisaig.co.uk, sails from Arisaig pier to **Rùm**, **Eigg** and **Muck** daily Mon-Fri all year and also Sat-Sun from Jun-Aug. The islands are visited on different days, though there is a boat to Eigg every day except Thu in summer. You can visit all 3 islands in a day, allowing 2-5 hrs ashore. Fares range from £18 return to Eigg, £19 to Muck and £24 return to Rùm (children 2 and under free to all islands, 3-10 years £10, 11-16 years £13). These trips cater for the island's residents as much as tourists, so don't expect a running commentary, though hot and cold drinks are served on board.

Mallaig *p87*
Bus Shiel Buses, T01967-431272, runs 2 buses daily Mon-Sat from **Mallaig** to **Fort William,** Jul-Sep, 1½ hrs, £5, and on Mon, Thu and Fri the rest of the year. The West Highland Flyer, T07780-724248, runs daily, Mar-Oct between **Oban** (0945) and **Mallaig** (1215) via Fort William (1100) and connects with the ferry to Skye and the Small Isles. It's possible to get off and on at **Onich**, **Fort William** and **Glenfinnan** but book in advance and call for the latest prices (from around £17 one way).

Ferry CalMac, T01687-462403, ferries run throughout the year to **Armadale** on Skye, to **Lochboisdale** and **Castlebay** (see page 60), and to the **Small Isles**.

Train There are several services daily (1 on Sun) to **Fort William**, with connections to **Glasgow**. There's also a steam train which runs in the summer months (see box, page 72).

Knoydart Peninsula *p88*
There are no roads through Knoydart so the only means of accessing and leaving the area is on a (very) long walk north from **Inverie** via the hamlet of **Barrisdale** to the road end at **Kinloch Hourn**. Alternatively, call Billy Mackenzie in Arnsdale, T01599-522247, to arrange for a passenger only (and bikes) pick-up from **Barrisdale**, across **Loch Hourn** to **Arnisdale** from where you can walk out to the bus at **Glenelg**.

Ferry To return to **Mallaig** from **Inverie**, contact Bruce Watt Sea Cruises, T01687-462320, www.knoydart-ferry.co.uk, which runs passenger only sailings on Mon, Wed and Fri Oct-Apr and Mon-Fri May-Sep. On a Mon and Fri the boat calls in at **Tarbet** on Loch Nevis and returns to Mallaig 1745. The Wed sailing to Tarbet only takes place from mid-May to mid-Sep. Though billed as a wildlife cruise, this is essentially a working ferry and fares are £11 return, and £16 for the afternoon sailing.

Great Glen to Kyle of Lochalsh

The A87 is one of the main Highland tourist routes, connecting the Great Glen with the west coast and the Isle of Skye. It runs west from Invergarry between Fort Augustus and Fort William, through Glen Moriston and Glen Shiel to Shiel Bridge, at the head of Loch Duich, and on to Kyle. At Shiel Bridge a road branches off to Glenelg, from where you can enjoy a magical and short ferry crossing to Skye. It's a beautiful journey and by far the best way to reach the island.

Arriving in the Great Glen
Getting there Unfortunately, there's no longer a postbus service between Kyle and Glenelg so you'll need to call **MacRae Kintail** (No WR61) ① *T01542-836363*, which runs one trip (Monday and Friday only) from Kyle of Lochalsh to Glenelg via Ratagan Youth Hostel. On demand it will continue to Arnisdale and Corran. There's also a bus (No 62 and No 64) to Plockton from Dornie via Kyle of Lochalsh, which runs three times a day, starting at 0830 from Kyle.

Glen Shiel → *OS Landranger No33.*
The journey from Invergarry to **Shiel Bridge** is worth it for the views alone. Glen Shiel is a sight to make the heart soar as high as the 3000-ft peaks that tower overhead on either side. This is one of the most popular hiking areas in Scotland, with the magnificent and much-photographed **Five Sisters of Kintail** on the north side of the glen, and the equally beautiful South Glen Shiel Ridge on the other.

There are several excellent hiking routes in Glen Shiel, but these mountains are to be treated with great respect. They require fitness, experience and proper equipment and planning. None of the routes should be attempted without a map, compass and detailed route instructions. You should be aware of the notoriously unpredictable weather conditions and also check locally about deer stalking. The season runs from August to October, but for more details contact the local stalkers (T01599-511282). A good trekking guide is the *SMC's Hill Walks in Northwest Scotland*.

The **Five Sisters Traverse** is a classic ridge route. It starts at the first fire break on the left as you head southeast down the glen from Shiel Bridge and finishes at Morvich, on the other side of the ridge. Allow a full day (eight to 10 hours). You can also hike from Morvich to **Glen Affric Youth Hostel** at Cannich. It's a strenuous 20-mile walk, but you can stop off midway at the remote **Allt Beithe Youth Hostel**. For details, see Glen Affric, page 46.

The magnificent **South Glen Shiel Ridge** is one of the world's great hikes. It starts from above the **Cluanie Inn**, see Where to stay, page 97. From here, follow the old public road to Tomdoun; it then meets up with a good stalking path which climbs to the summit of the first Munro, Creag a' Mhaim (3108 ft). The ridge then runs west for almost 9 miles and gives you the chance to pick off no fewer than seven Munros. Allow a full day for the walk (nine to 10 hours), and you'll need to set off early.

Glenelg and around → *Phone code 01599.*

One of the most beautiful journeys in Scotland and certainly overlooked by the majority of tourists is the road from Shiel Bridge to the sublime little outpost that is Glenelg; a tiny village on the shores of the Sound of Sleat, only a short distance opposite Kylerhea on Skye (for transport details see page 99). The unclassified single-track road, constructed by 17th-century Hanoverian forces to link the ruin of Bernera Barracks (see below) with Fort Augustus, turns off the A87 and climbs steeply and dramatically through a series of sharp switchbacks to the top of the **Mam Ratagan Pass** (1115 ft). From here the view back across Loch Duich to the Five Sisters of Kintail is simply amazing, and the all-time classic calendar shot.

The road then drops down through Glen More to Glenelg, the main settlement on the peninsula. Known until the 18th century as Kirkton (it's believed a church stood here as far back as the 13th century), Glenelg lies on the old drovers' route that ran from Skye to the cattle markets in the south. This little-known corner of the Western Highlands is Gavin Maxwell country and was featured in *Ring of Bright Water*, his much-loved novel about otters. He disguised the identity of this beautiful, unspoiled stretch of coastline, calling it Camusfearna, and today it remains a quiet backwater.

You can see the famous otters at **Sandaig**, on the road running from Glenelg, where Gavin Maxwell lived. The site of his cottage is now marked with a cairn. As well as otters, you can see numerous seabirds, seals and porpoises in the Sound of Sleat, and around the peninsula you may be lucky enough to catch a glimpse of wildcats, pine martens, golden eagles and the recently reintroduced sea eagles. The village itself consists of a row of whitewashed cottages surrounded by trees and overlooked by the ruins of the 18th-century **Bernera Barracks**. Just before the village the road forks. The right turning leads to the Glenelg-Kylerhea ferry, which makes the 10-minute crossing to Skye, see page 99.

A road runs south from Glenelg to Arnisdale. About 1.5 miles along this road, a branch left leads to the **Glenelg Brochs** – Dun Telve and Dun Dun Troddan – two of the best-preserved Iron Age buildings in the country. Dun Telve, excavated in 1914, stands to a height of over 30 ft and the internal passages are almost intact. The road south from Glenelg continues past Sandaig Bay and runs along the north shore of unearthly Loch Hourn, with great views across the mountains of Knoydart. The road ends at little fishing hamlet of **Arnisdale**, from where you can take a boat across the loch to Barrisdale on the Knoydart Peninsula. For details, see page 88. A bit further along the coast, the road ends at the even tinier hamlet of **Corran**.

Eilean Donan Castle → *Phone code 01599.*

ⓘ *T01599-555202, www.eileandonancastle.com, Mar-Nov 1000-1800, £5, concessions £4.50. Citylink buses between Fort William and Inverness and Skye stop by the castle.*

Some 10 miles west of Shiel Bridge on the A87 is the little village of Dornie, home to the one of Scotland's most-photographed sights, the stunningly located Eilean Donan Castle. It stands on a tiny islet at the confluence of Loch Duich and Loch Alsh, joined to the shore by a narrow stone bridge and backed by high mountains. This great calendar favourite and tourist honeypot has also featured in several movies, including *Highlander*, which starred Sean Connery.

The original castle dates from 1230 when Alexander III had it built to protect the area from marauding Vikings. It was destroyed by King George in 1719 during its occupation by Spanish Jacobite forces sent to help the 'Old Pretender', James Stuart. It then lay in ruins, until one of the Macraes had it rebuilt between 1912 and 1932. Inside, the Banqueting

Hall with its Pipers' Gallery is most impressive, and there's an exhibition of military regalia and interesting displays of the castle's history. The views from the battlements are also worthwhile. However, to escape the tourist hordes, don't forget about that fantastic winding road to Glenelg across the mountains to the south.

Kyle of Lochalsh → *Phone code 01599.*

Before the coming of the controversial Skye Bridge a mile to the north, the little town of Kyle, as it is known, was the main ferry crossing to Skye and consequently a place which attracted a busy tourist trade. Now though, the tourist traffic bypasses Kyle, which notwithstanding tremendous views to Skye, suffers from a workaday feel. There are a couple of banks with ATMs, two small supermarkets and a post office in the village. The TIC ① *T01599-534276, Apr-late Oct Mon-Fri 0930-1700, Sat-Sun 1000-1630*, is at the main seafront car park. There are also toilets here (daily 0800-2100).

Plockton → *Phone code 01599.*

If there were a poll taken of visitors' favourite Highland villages, then you can bet your sporran that Plockton would come top with most folk. If you look for a definition of picturesque in your dictionary, it'll say 'see Plockton'. Well, maybe not – but it should. Actually, the name is derived from Am Ploc that roughly translates as blunt promontory.

Plockton's neat little painted cottages, built in the early 18th century by the landowner to provide fishing employment after clearing traditional crofting lands for sheep, are ranged around the curve of a wooded bay, with flowering gardens and palm trees. Yachts bob up and down in the harbour and there are views across the island-studded waters of Loch Carron to the hills beyond. Even on the telly Plockton's charms proved irresistible, and millions of viewers tuned in each week to watch the TV series *Hamish Macbeth*, which featured Robert Carlyle as the local bobby. Plockton's a popular place with artists who are drawn by the village's setting and the wonderful light. A good place to find some of their work, as well as other souvenirs, is **The Studio Craft Shop**, on the corner of the seafront and the road leading out of town.

There are lots of good walks around the village. One of the best ways to appreciate it is to head up to **Frithard Hill**, from where there are great views of the bay. Another good walk is along the beach, starting from the High School playing fields at the top of the village. The craft shop (and newsagent) sells a booklet (£3) of local walks.

Great Glen to Kyle of Lochalsh listings

For hotel and restaurant price codes and other relevant information, see pages 13-20.

⊙ Where to stay

Glen Shiel *p94*

£££-££ Cluanie Inn, Glenmoriston, some 9 miles east of Shiel Bridge, T01320-340238, www.cluanieinn.com. 10 en suite rooms including 2 with jacuzzi and 1 with a 4-poster bed. Also offers more modest Clubhouse (£35 per person) accommodation. This is one of the Highlands' classic hotels. It's a firm favourite with hikers and climbers and it's easy to see why. After a hard day's ridge walking, what could be better than jumping into the jacuzzi, then having a hot dinner, bar meal and a good real ale or malt beside a log fire. Recommended.

£££-££ Grants at Craigellachie, Ratagan, T01599-511331, www.housebytheloch. co.uk. Open all year. About 1 mile along the road to Glenelg/Kylrerhea ferry is the turn-off to tiny Ratagan and this genuine hidden gem of a place. 4 en suite rooms, 2 in the main house and 2 in the Butt and Ben. Hosts Tony and Liz Taylor have created a little haven of peace, comfort and fine cuisine. It's a restaurant with rooms and the rave reviews for the former (**£££**) are matched by the style and comfort – and superb views – of the latter. The rooms in the But and Ben can be booked on a self-catering basis. Recommended.

££ Glomach House, Aullt-Na-Chruinn, T01599-511222, www.glomach.co.uk. Open all year. 3 en suite rooms. Tidy and comfortable B&B on the shores of Loch Duich at Shiel Bridge. Self-catering cottage also available for rent, comprising 2 double bedrooms. No pets.

££-£ Kintail Lodge Hotel, T01599-511275, www.kintaillodgehotel.co.uk. Open all year. 12 rooms. Small, cosy hotel beautifully located by the shores of Loch Duich, dinner also available. Wee Bunkhouse attached with 12 beds. You can also hire bikes.

£ Ratagan Youth Hostel, just past Shiel Bridge, T01599-511243. Open Feb-Dec. One of the great hikers' hostels.

Camping

Morvich Caravan Club Site, 1.5 miles past Shiel Bridge in direction of Kyle, T01599-511354. Open late Mar-late Oct. Large site with full facilities.

Shiel Shop and campsite, Shiel Bridge, T01599-511221. Small pub/restaurant, with groceries and fuel all close at hand.

Glenelg and around *p95*

£££-££ Glenelg Inn, Glenelg, T01599-522273, www.glenelg-inn.com. Open all year. It's worth stopping in Glenelg, if you've got the time, to experience a night in this wonderfully cosy place. Even if you can't spend the night, at least spend an hour or 2 enjoying the atmosphere, good ale and superb food, either in the dining room (**£££**) or the bar (**££**). If you're really lucky, you may even chance upon an impromptu folk jam. Rooms are spacious and inviting. Warmly recommended.

£ Mrs Chisholm, Glenelg, T01599-522287. Open all year. Cheaper B&B option in the village.

Eilean Donan Castle *p95*

There are several places to stay in the nearby village of Dornie.

£££ Conchra House Hotel, Ardelve, T01599-555233, www.conchrahouse.co.uk. Open all year. 5 en suite rooms. To get here, cross the bridge in Dornie and turn right for Killilan, a tiny hamlet at the head of Loch Long, the hotel is 0.75 mile up this road. This historic 18th-century hunting lodge is peaceful, has lovely views and a reputation for good food.

££ Dornie Hotel, Dornie, T01599-555205, www.dornie-hotel.co.uk. Open all year. 12 rooms, many en suite. A good option and serves very good food (**££**).

££ Loch Duich Hotel, across the bridge from Dornie Hotel, T01599-555213, www.lochduichhotelco.uk. Open all year. 11 en suite rooms. Offers comfortable accommodation, meals (seafood restaurant and bar meals) and live music in the bar on a Sun evening. Wide selection of malt whiskies.

£ Caberfeidh House, Ardelve, by Dornie, T01599-555293, www.caberfeidh.plus.com. Open all year. 5 rooms, 4 with views of the castle. Friendly and comfortable guesthouse. Very good value.

£ Silver Fir Bunkhouse, Carndubh, T01599-555264. A 6-bed bunkhouse.

£ Whitefalls Retreats, near Cochra House Hotel, at Camasluinie, T01599-588205, www.holidayhighlands.co.uk. A 10-bed independent hostel. 1 room sleeps 6 and 1 room sleeps 4.

Kyle of Lochalsh *p96*

It's a good idea to get the TIC to book a room for you, as there's not much choice in Kyle itself.

£££-££ Tingle Creek Hotel, Erbusaig, T01599-534430, www.tinglecreek-hotel.co.uk. Open all year. Small hotel with a big, friendly welcome. Lovely setting and great views. Good food in restaurant and guests can enjoy a drink in the Galleon bar before dinner.

££ Kyle Hotel, Main St, T01599-534204, www.kylehotel.co.uk. Open all year. 31 en suite rooms. Reasonable food (**££**) in restaurant and adjacent Nor-West Café (**£**).

£ Cuchulainn's, Station Rd, T01599-534492. Cheap hostel accommodation and standard restaurant fare (**£**).

Camping

Reraig Caravan Site, 4 miles east of Kyle, at Balmacara, T01599-566215.

Plockton *p96*

£££ The Haven Hotel, Innes St, T01599-544223, www.havenhotelplockton.co.uk. Open all year. 15 en suite rooms. Serves good Scottish food in the restaurant (**££**). Dogs welcome.

£££ Plockton Hotel, Harbour St, T01599-544 274, www.plocktonhotel.co.uk. Open all year. 11 en suite rooms. Comfortable and tastefully furnished rooms above a perenially busy wee bar. All have views across the bay. There area few places along the waterfront and this is among the best. If you eat in the front restaurant (**£££-££**) you'll enjoy views out over the bay. Recommended.

£££ Plockton Inn, Innes St, T01599-544222, www.plocktoninn.co.uk. Open all year. 14 rooms. Small hotel with 7 bedrooms added in an annexe across the road. Very good seafood in restaurant or in lively bar where you can also hear live folk music twice a week (usually Tue and Thu). Open log fires and there's also a great little beer garden at the front where you can sit and enjoy a drink on a balmy summer evening.

££ An Caladh, beside the shore T01599-544356. This is a lovely option right by the shore from where the owner occasionally goes out fishing in the bay.

££ Plockton Gallery@the Manse, Innes St, T01599-544442. Open all year. 3 en suite rooms. Part gallery, part guesthouse, this place offers something different. A bit more expensive than the average but worth it for the quality and service. Veggie options available with a bit of notice, disabled access and parking. Recommended.

££-£ Heron's Flight, Cooper St, T01599-544220, www.heronsflight.org. Open Mar-Oct. 3 rooms. Friendly and welcoming B&B run by Ann Mackenzie and her dog, Ruah. Veggie and continental options for breakfast, no cards accepted. No single occupancy or single night bookings.

£ Nessun Dorma, Burnside, T01599-544235. Bunkhouse 1 mile out of Plockton at the railway station, run by Mick and Gill Coe. Cheapest option. Packed lunches available on request.

£ Shieling, Harbour St, T01599-544282. At the far end of the harbour. There are lots of B&Bs to choose from on the seafront and this is one of the nicest.

🍴 Restaurants

Eilean Donan Castle *p95*
Aside from the hotels listed above, there are a couple of places in Dornie serving decent food, the best of which is probably the **Clachan Pub** where you can enjoy a good-value 3-course evening meal (**££**).

Kyle of Lochalsh *p96*
££ The Waverley Restaurant, Main St, T01599-534337. Daily 1730-2130. Daily specials including vegetarian dishes. Good value.

Plockton *p96*
There are several good eateries in Plockton with the **Plockton Inn**, **Haven Hotel** and **Plockton Hotel**, all serving memorable seafood dishes including huge bowls of mussels. Also try:
££ Plockton Shores, Harbour St, T01599-544263. Open all year. Fabulous choice of scallops, locally sourced beef and vegetarian options. Recommended.
£ Grumpy's, Innes St, right by the harbour. Open all year. A fantastic chippy with a difference, where you'll find the local catch of the day and prawns among the bargain bites for those on a budget.

🎯 What to do

Kyle of Lochalsh *p96*
Boat trips
There are a couple of interesting boat trips from Kyle.
Seaprobe Atlantis, T0800-9804846, www.seaprobeatlantis.com. The *Seaprobe Atlantis*, is a unique sailing craft fitted with underwater windows, providing an amazing view of seals, kelp forests and even a Second World War wreck. A 60-min trip is £9.50, children £4.75.

Plockton *p96*
Boat trips
Calum's Plockton Seal Trips, 32 Harbour St, T01599-544306, www.calums-sealtrips.com. Run 1-hr seal-spotting trips from the harbour, £8, children £5. In addition to seals you may spot otters and rare birdlife. The operator even offers your money back if you don't spot any seals.

🚆 Transport

Glen Shiel *p94*
Bus Citylink buses between **Fort William**, **Inverness** and **Skye** pass through Glen Shiel several times daily.

Glenelg and around *p95*
Ferry The community owned **Glenelg** to **Kylerhea** ferry provides the most scenic connection to **Skye**, www.skyeferry.com. 10-min crossing Easter-Oct daily 1000-1800; Jun-end Aug until 1900. Per car with up to 4 passengers, £12, day return £16.
A more scenic route would be to take the passenger ferry from **Arnisdale** to **Kinlochhourn**, year-round, daily by arrangement, T01599-522247. Expect to pay from £15 per single trip, www.arnisdaleferryservice.com.

Kyle of Lochalsh *p96*
Bus Scottish Citylink buses, T0990-505050, run from Kyle to **Inverness**, 3 daily, 2 hrs; to **Glasgow** via **Fort William**, 4 daily, 5 hrs; and to **Edinburgh** via **Fort William**, 1 daily, 6½ hrs. Scottish Citylink buses run to **Portree**, 1 hr, and **Uig**, 1½ hrs, for ferries to **Tarbert** on Harris and **Lochmaddy** on North Uist. There's also a regular shuttle service across the bridge to **Kyleakin**, every 30 mins.
Train The train journey to **Inverness** from Kyle, though not as spectacular as the West Highland line, is very scenic. It runs 3-4 times Mon-Sat, 2½ hrs, and once or twice on Sun from May-Sep. There's also an observation car and dining car in the summer.

Plockton *p96*
Cycle hire Gordon Mackenzie, T01599-544255. Hires bikes for £15 per day.

Wester Ross

From Loch Carron north to Ullapool, is the region of Wester Ross, an area of dramatic mountain massifs, fjord-like sea lochs and remote coastal villages. Here lies some of Europe's most spectacular scenery, from the isolated peninsula of Applecross to Tolkien-esque peaks of Torridon, which offer some of Scotland's best climbing and hillwalking. There are also gentler attractions such as the vast, sprawling gardens at Inverewe and the beguiling pink sands of Gruinard Bay.

Loch Carron and around → *For listings, see pages 107-111.*

Arriving in Loch Carron
Getting there and around There's a postbus service (Monday to Saturday) from Shieldaig to Kishorn and Lochcarron. The first bus leaves Shieldaig at 0900 and the second at 1020. It's possible to reach Applecross by public transport, but only just. If you catch the 1130 from Shieldaig you can reach Applecross by 1300, via the beautiful and winding coast road. You can also use the railway to enter the region by catching the train to Lochcarron (excluding Sunday). Another option is to catch the Skyeways (No WR87) bus from Inverness to Applecross at 1500 (Monday and Wednesday) and 1600 on a Saturday, which stops at Lochcarron en route.

Along Loch Carron
East of Plockton, just before the road meets the A890 at **Achmore**, is the **West Highland Dairy** ① *T01599-577203*, where you can pick up some good local cheese for a picnic – weather permitting of course. The road passes the turn-off for Stromeferry and continues along the east shore of Loch Carron to **Strathcarron** at its northeastern end, on the Inverness to Kyle of Lochalsh rail line.

Lochcarron village → *Phone code 01520. Population 870.*
Lochcarron village consists of little more than a main street along the shore of the loch, but it has more facilities and services than most other places in these parts. Here you should take the opportunity to withdraw cash at the Bank of Scotland ATM, fill up with petrol and buy some supplies at the small self-service store. The **TIC** ① *within the local post office/grocers, T01520-722357*, is very friendly and has details of some excellent walks in the surrounding hills.

Two miles south of the village on the road to the 15th-century ruins of **Strome Castle** is Lochcarron Weavers, where you can see tartan being made and also buy from a vast range of woven goods.

Loch Kishorn to Applecross
There are many scenic routes in the Highlands but the road from Kishorn, west of Lochcarron to Applecross beats them all. The **Bealach na Ba** ('Pass of the Cattle') is the

highest road in Scotland and is often closed during the winter snows. It climbs relentlessly and dramatically through a series of tortuous switchbacks – both spectacular and terrifying in equal measure. The high plateau, at 2053 ft, is cold and desolate, but from here you have the most amazing views: from Ardnamurchan Peninsula to Loch Torridon, taking in Eigg, Rùm, the Cuillins of Skye, the Old Man of Storr and the Quirang.

The narrow, single-track road then begins its gradual descent to the isolated little village of **Applecross**, site of one Scotland's first Christian monasteries, founded in AD 673. The village consists of a row of whitewashed fishermen's cottages looking across to the island of Raasay and backed by wooded slopes. It's a beautifully tranquil place where you can explore beaches and rock pools or enjoy a stroll along sylvan lanes – and then of course there's the very wonderful **Applecross Inn**, see Where to stay, page 107.

Torridon and around → *For listings, see pages 107-111. Phone code 01445.*

Torridon is perhaps the most striking skyline in the Scottish Highlands. The multi-peaked mountains of **Beinn Alligin**, **Liathach** (pronounced *Lee-ahakh*) and **Beinn Eighe** (*Ben-eay*) form a massive fortress of turrets, spires and pinnacles that provides an awesome backdrop to Loch Torridon, as well as the most exhilarating walking and climbing on the Scottish mainland. The straggly little village of Torridon makes the ideal base from which to tackle these mountains.

Arriving in Torridon
Torridon may offer some of the best walking on the Scottish mainland but it also presents some of the most serious challenges. You need to be fit, experienced and well prepared and also be aware of the notoriously unpredictable weather. You should have a compass and the relevant map. OS Outdoor Leisure series No 8 covers the area. For recommended mountain guides, see page 110.

Around Loch Torridon
The coast road from Applecross meets the A896 from Lochcarron at the lovely little village of **Shieldaig** on the southern shore of Loch Torridon. There's a shop, a post office, a campsite and a couple of B&Bs. Several miles east, a side road turns off the A896 by **Torridon village** and winds its way along the northern shore of the loch, then climbs through dramatic scenery before dropping to the beautiful little village of **Diabaig** (pronounced *Jee-a-beg*), 10 miles from Torridon village. It's a worthwhile side trip, as the views across to the Applecross peninsula and Raasay are fantastic. There's also a great 7-mile coastal walk from Diabaig to Redpoint (see below).

Much of the Torridon massif is in the care of the National Trust for Scotland, and just before Torridon village is the **NTS Countryside Centre** ⓘ *T01445-791221*, where you can get information and advice on walks in the area, as well as books and maps. About 400 yds past the centre is the **Deer Museum**, which has a small display describing the management of red deer in the Highlands as well as some live specimens outside.

Beinn Alligin
Beinn Alligin (3232 ft) is the most westerly of the Torridon peaks and probably the least demanding. The **Allt a'Bhealaich Walk** is a steep but short walk of about two hours. It starts from the car park just beyond the stone bridge that crosses the Abhainn Coire Mhic Nobuil. Follow the path that runs beside the river gorge until you reach the first bridge, cross it and follow the east bank of the Allt a' Bhealaich burn. Higher up, cross the second

bridge and continue to follow the track up to the 380-m contour line, then turn back retracing your steps. This walk doesn't include the ascent of the peak but the views are magnificent. Those who wish to climb the three **Horns of Beinn Alligin** can continue from the 380-m contour line above the second bridge. The track that follows their ridge is exposed and requires rock scrambling experience.

Liathach

Seven-peaked Liathach (3460 ft) stretches over 5 miles, and the magnificent ridge walk is considered by many to be the most impressive in Britain. This walk requires a high level of stamina and will take at least seven to eight hours. It also helps if you have a car waiting at the end.

A good place to start this long and strenuous challenge is about half a mile or so east of Glen Cottage, which is just over 2 miles east of the Countryside Centre. A steep climb takes you to a point just west of **Stuc a'Choire Dhuibh Bhig** (3000 ft). Then retrace your route to climb the twin tops of **Bidein Toll a'Mhuic** (3200 ft), linked by a narrow ridge. The path from here descends to the head of a deep ravine and keeps to the crest of the ridge around the rim of **Coireag Dubh Beag** which plunges steeply to the north. The ridge then rises across a field of huge and unstable boulders to the highest peak – **Spidean a'Choire Leith**. The view from this point is stunning, with Coire na Caime before you, surrounded by 2000-ft sheer cliffs. From here, the path follows a narrow exposed ridge for over a mile towards **Mullach an Rathain** (3358 ft). Unless you are an experienced scrambler with a good head for heights, the best way from here is to take the path to the south, below the sharp pinnacles. Beyond the pinnacles the climb to Mullach an Rathain is straightforward. The track from here to **Sgorr a'Chadail** is a long but fairly easy walk and ends on the path in Coire Mhic Nobuil, see Beinn Alligin, above.

Coire Walk

A less difficult walk, but still requiring a fair degree of fitness and taking most of the day, is the Coire Walk. It follows the River Coire Mhic Nobuil to its watershed and down again by the **Allt a'Choire Dhuibh Mhoir** to the main road in Glen Torridon. Again, two cars will shorten the distance considerably.

The walk starts at the same point as the Beinn Alligin walk (see above). It follows the path up to the first bridge then branches east and continues on the path that runs north of the river, all the way to its source in the pass between Liathach and Beinn Dearg. Here the ground is boggy between the string of pools and lochans and the path is less distinct, but it becomes clear again in the upper reaches of the Coire Dubh Mor, a huge gully that separates Liathach from Beinn Eighe. A little further on, the track joins a stalkers' path which curves round Sail Mhor to the famous **Coire Mhic Fhearchair**, considered to be the most spectacular corrie in Scotland (see Beinn Eighe, below). The Coire path leads to a ford, which is crossed by stepping stones, then descends following the west side of the burn down to the car park on the Torridon road, from where it's about 4.5 miles to Torridon village.

Diabaig to Red Point Walk → *OS Landranger No 19.*

An excellent low-level coastal walk is from Diabaig to Red Point. It is far less strenuous or daunting than the others described above and there is a clear path. It starts at the wooden gate to the right of the post office in Diabaig and ends at Red Point Farm, 7 miles away.

After 4 miles the coastal path reaches the derelict croft houses in the Craig Valley. There are two possible routes from here. You can follow the footpath above the coastline, or leave the footpath after crossing the wooden bridge over the Craig river and climb through an area of woodland. Take a reference from your OS map and you'll reach the highest point, **Meall na h-Uamha**, from where there are superb views. You can then descend to rejoin the coastal path and continue until you reach the glorious golden sands of Red Point, with wonderful views across to Skye and Raasay. Keep to the path through the farm until you reach the car park. Unless you've arranged your own transport here, you'll have to walk back the way you came, or catch the schoolbus to Gairloch, see page 104.

Beinn Eighe National Nature Reserve

While most of the Torridon massif is managed by the National Trust of Scotland, Beinn Eighe (which means 'File Peak' in Gaelic) is under the control of Scottish Natural Heritage. It is Britain's oldest National Nature Reserve, set up in 1951 to protect the ancient Caledonian pine forest west of Kinlochewe. It has since been designated an International Biosphere Reserve and extended to cover 30 square miles. The reserve is the home of a great variety of rare Highland wildlife, including pine martens, wildcats, buzzards, Scottish crossbills and golden eagles. There's also a wide range of flora which can best be appreciated on the excellent mountain trail described below which climbs from the ancient pine woods through alpine vegetation to the tundra-like upper slopes.

About half a mile northwest of Kinlochewe on the A832, is the Beinn Eighe visitor centre, which has excellent interactive audio visual displays about the flora and fauna in the reserve and sells pamphlets on the trails described below.

Beinn Eighe (3309 ft) has nine peaks and is the largest of the Torridon Mountains. To traverse its ridge is a mighty undertaking and can take two days. A much shorter and easier walk around the base of the mountain is described here. The mountain and woodland trails both start and end in the car park at the side of Loch Maree, about 2 miles beyond the visitor centre. The woodland trail heads west along the lochside then crosses the road and climbs for about a mile up to the Conservation cabin before descending back to the starting point. It should take about an hour and is easy to follow, though quite steep in parts, and you'll need a good pair of walking boots. The mountain trail is 4 miles long and rough and steep in parts. You should be well equipped with good walking boots, waterproofs, food and warm clothing. It should take three to four hours. The route is well marked with cairns and you should not stray from the path. The trail heads south from the car park and begins a gentle ascent through woodland to a boggy area and then begins to zigzag up a very steep and rugged section, climbing to over 1000 ft in less than half a mile. This is the steepest section of the trail, but the views back across Loch Maree to Slioch are fabulous. The summit of the mountain trail is **Conservation cairn** (1800 ft) from where you can see the tops of 31 Munros on a clear day and enjoy a close-up view of the impressive Beinn Eighe ridge a few miles to the south. The trail now begins to descend as it heads northwest towards **An t-Allt** (1000 ft), turns northwards down to a small enclosure, then heads east to the deep Allt na h-Airidhe gorge. From here the trail continues down to the treeline and runs through woodland to join up with the top of the Woodland Trail. Follow the path to the right to get back to the car park.

Kinlochewe and Loch Maree → *Phone code 01445.*

On the north side of the Torridon Mountains is the sprawling village of Kinlochewe, at the southeastern end of beautiful Loch Maree. It's a good base for walking in and around Loch

Maree, and has a hotel, post office within the village shop/café and one of the area's scarce **petrol stations** ① *Apr-Oct Mon-Sat 0830-1800, Sun 0900-1700.* The loch is dotted with islands and bordered by the mass of Slioch (3215 ft) to the north and ancient Caledonian pine forest to the south. Running along its northern shore, from **Slioch** almost as far as **Poolewe**, is the remote **Letterewe Estate**, one of Scotland's great deer forests. The A832 skirts the south shore of the loch, running northwest from Kinlochewe, and passes the **Victoria Falls**, a mile or so beyond Talladale. The falls commemorate Queen Victoria's visit in 1877. To find them, look for the Hydro Power signs.

Gairloch and around → *For listings, see pages 107-111. Phone code 01445.*

Gairloch consists of a string of tiny crofting townships scattered around the northeastern shore of the loch of the same name. It's a beautiful place, attracting a large number of visitors who come for the many sandy beaches, excellent walks, golf and fishing, and the chance of seeing seals, porpoises, dolphins and whales in the surrounding waters.

Arriving in Gairloch
Getting there and around There are buses from Inverness three times a week, also buses to Kinlochewe and a local postbus service. From June to October a daily **Scotbus** ① *T01463-224410*, leaves Inverness for Gairloch at 0800, and travels via Kinlochewe to arrive in Gairloch at 0954. The bus continues to Inverewe Garden. ▸▸ *See Transport page 111.*

Tourist information There is a **TIC** ① *T01445-712130, Apr-Sep Mon-Sat 0930-1700, Sun 1100-1500, Oct Mon-Sat 1000-1600*, at the car park in Auchtercairn, where the road branches to Strath. They book accommodation and sell books and maps. There are shops and takeaways in Strath and Auchtercairn, a petrol station in Auchtercairn, and a bank near the harbour at Charleston.

Gairloch Heritage Museum
① *T01445-712287, Apr-Oct Mon-Sat 1000-1700, Oct 1000-1330, £4, concessions £3, children £1.*
If you are interested in local history, or the weather is bad – not unknown – then this museum may entertain for a hour or so. Included are archaeological finds, a mock-up of a crofthouse room, schoolroom and shop, the interior of the local lighthouse and an archive of old photographs. It is found beside the tourist office on the A832 to Poolewe, a few yards beyond the turn-off to Strath.

Big Sand, Melvaig and Midtown
The beach by the golf course at Gairloch is nice, but the beach at Big Sand, a few miles northwest of Strath, is better, and quieter. Further north is Melvaig, from where you can walk to **Rubha Reidh Lighthouse**, see Where to stay, page 109. Around the headland from the lighthouse is the beautiful, secluded beach at **Camas Mor**. This is a good place for spotting sea birds, and there's a great walk from here on a marked footpath to Midtown, 4 miles northwest of Poolewe. You'll have to walk or hitch from here or try and catch a ride with the community ring and ride bus.

The waters around Gairloch are home to a wide variety of marine mammals such as seals, otters, porpoises, dolphins, minke whales and even killer whales. For details of wildlife cruises, see page 111.

Destitution Road

Many of the roads in the area were built during the Potato Famine of 1840 in order to give men work, with funds supplied by Dowager Lady Mackenzie of Gairloch. These became know as the 'Destitution Roads', and one of these is the narrow B8056 which runs west for 9 miles to Red Point from the junction 3 miles south of Gairloch, at Kerrysdale. This is a lovely little side trip and well worth it, especially on a clear evening to enjoy the magnificent sunsets at **Red Point beach**. The beach itself is extremely seductive, backed by steep dunes and looking across to the Trotternish Peninsula on Skye. So romantic is this spot that some people (naming no names) have been known to plight their troth here. Red Point is also the start or finish point for the excellent coastal walk to or from Diabaig, see page 101. On the road to Red Point is the picturesque little hamlet of **Badachro**, tucked away in a wooded, sheltered bay with fishing boats moored in its natural harbour. It's worth stopping off here on the way back from Red Point for a wee dram at the **Badachro Inn**.

There are many other good walks in the area, including to **Flowerdale Falls**, the **Fairy Lochs** and the **USAAF Liberator**. The TIC has a selection of walking guides and OS maps.

Poolewe → *Phone code 01445.*

Five miles east of Gairloch on the other side of the peninsula is the neat little village of Poolewe, straddling the mouth of the River Ewe, where it cascades into sheltered Loch Ewe. There are some good walks around Poolewe, including the one around Loch Kernsary described below. There's also a nice little drive up the side road running along the west shore of Loch Ewe to Cove. You can walk from Midtown, midway along the road, to Rubha Reidh, north of Gairloch (see above).

Loch Kernsary → *OS Landranger Map No 19.*

This straightforward but rewarding walk covers 6 miles and should take around 2½ to three hours. The track is very boggy underfoot in places, especially after rain, so you'll need good boots.

Start in Poolewe, from the car park by the school near the bridge over the Ewe. Head up the single-track road with the river on your right. Go through the gate, then the track heads away from the river and up into woodland. At the Letterewe Estate gate cross the stile and continue to the next fork. Turn left here to Kernsary Estate, with views of Loch Maree and Beinn Eighe to the south. Follow the track to the next gate, go through and cross the wooden bridge. Continue along the track and you'll see Loch Kernsary on your left. At the next fork, turn left over the bridge and pass Kernsary Cottage on the right. Beyond the cottage, go through the gate and immediately head left down towards the burn, where the ground may be boggy. There's no path here, but cross the wooden footbridge and continue straight on, past the piles of stones on your left. Cross the stile, and the path follows the length of Loch Kernsary. At the head of the loch, the path climbs to give you views down to Poolewe. Follow the path down until it eventually takes you to the main road. Turn left and follow the road back to the car park.

Inverewe Garden

ⓘ *T0844-493 2225. Garden open Jan-Mar and Nov-Dec daily 1000-1500; Apr-Oct daily 1000-1600. Visitor Centre and restaurant Apr-Oct daily 1000-1600 (restaurant 1100-1600). £9, concessions £6.50, family £22.*

The reason most people come this way is to visit Inverewe Garden where you'll find an astonishing collection of exotic subtropical plants growing on the same latitude as Siberia, thanks to the mild climate created by the North Atlantic Drift. This wonderful 50-acre oasis of colour is a mecca for garden lovers, but even those who flinch at the mere sight of a lawn-mower will be bowled over by the sheer scale and diversity of plants and flowers on view. The garden was created from a treeless wilderness by Osgood Mackenzie, starting in 1862. By the time of his death in 1922 he had produced an internationally renowned walled and woodland garden. His work was continued by his daughter, who then gave the garden to the National Trust for Scotland in 1952. Since then, the plant collection has diversified even more and an intricate maze of paths leads you through ever-changing displays of Himalayan rhododendrons, Tasmanian eucalyptus, many Chilean and South African species, together with a large collection of New Zealand plants.

The garden is well worth visiting in any weather and at any time of the year, but especially from the end of April through the summer when the rhododendrons are in bloom. You should allow at least a couple of hours to do it justice. The garden is about a mile north of Poolewe on the main A832. There's a visitor centre and gift shop and a good restaurant, which serves snacks and hot meals.

Gruinard Bay → *Phone code 01445.*

North of Poolewe the A832 passes Aultbea on its way to Laide, where it then skirts the shores of Gruinard Bay, with its lovely coves of pink sand. From Laide Post Office a side road branches north to **Mellon Udrigle** and **Opinan**, both with great beaches. It's worthwhile following the signs left to the hamlet of **Mellon Charles**. Here you'll find the fabulous **Perfume Factory** ① *T01445-731618, Apr-Oct daily 1000-1700 (closed on Mon), Nov-Dec Thu-Sat 1100-1600*, with its abundance of natural fragrances derived from the likes of wildflowers. There's also a very good café with lovely views over Loch Ewe. Between Laide and Mellon Udrigle, at **Achgarve**, a road branches left for about mile. From the end of this road you can walk all the way to **Slaggan**, a ruined village on the other side of the peninsula. It's a nice spot for a picnic but don't be tempted to swim in the sea as the tidal race makes it dangerous.

Gruinard Bay is a very beautiful part of the northwest coast but will always be synonymous with **Gruinard Island**, standing ominously in the middle of the bay. The island was used as a testing ground for biological warfare during the Second World War and was contaminated with anthrax spores. The Ministry of Defence finally agreed to decontaminate it in 1990 and it has now been declared 'safe'.

Wester Ross listings

For hotel and restaurant price codes and other relevant information, see pages 13-20.

🛏 Where to stay

Loch Carron and around *p100*
£££ Applecross Inn, Applecross, T01520-744262, www.applecross.uk.com. 7 rooms. There are, sadly, too few authentic Highland hostelries where you could quite happily while away a few hours, or even days, but if you have to be holed up somewhere to escape the rotten weather, then this place is as good as any and better than most. Owner Judith Fish ensures you receive a warm welcome, the atmosphere is friendly and the seafood is so fresh you can almost see it swimming past as you order. Bar food served 1200-2100, children welcome until 2030, ceilidhs on Fri evening. Sit outside in the beer garden on a summer's eve. The rooms upstairs have been refurbished to a high standard and downstairs now includes a bedroom adapted for guests with a disability. Excellent value and highly recommended.
££ Clisham Guest House, Main St, T01520-722995, www.clishamguesthouse.co.uk. Open all year. 3 en suite rooms. Friendly and comfortable accommodation, tea room out front serves home-baked cakes.
££ Little Hill of my Heart, Applecross, T01520-744432. Open all year. 3 rooms. Lovely wee B&B overlooking Camursterrach Bay. Rooms tastefully furnished and breakfasts are a bit out of the ordinary with kedgeree, smoked haddock and salmon fishcakes alongside more familiar staples.
££ The Old Manse, Lochcarron, T01520-722208, www.theoldmanselochcarron.com. 5 rooms. Comfortable, old world style guesthouse with views across the loch.
££ Rockvilla Hotel, Main St, T01520-722379, www.rockvilla-hotel.co.uk. Open all year. 4 rooms. Small, family-run hotel offering very good food (**££**).

Self-catering
Callakille, 8 miles north of Applecross, T01456-486358, www.wildernesscottages.co.uk. A beautifully converted 2-bedroom croft house that's tastefully furnished and an idyllic bolt-hole from the stresses of urban life. Unwind by the roaring fire and enjoy the panoramic views over the Inner Sound of Raasay. In addition to fantastic walking and wildlife spotting opportunities, there's also good trout and sea fishing in the area. From £420 per week. Highly recommended.

Camping
Applecross Campsite, 1 mile from the village, T01520-744268. Open Mar-Oct. Decent facilities, upgraded in 2006. Family friendly and lots to do, with its own café on site (see Restaurants, below).

Torridon and around *p101*
££££-£££ The Torridon, 1 mile south of the turn-off to Torridon village, T01445-791242, www.thetorridon.com. Whatever your budget, this is an excellent option. The 12 tastefully refurbished en suite rooms at the Inn (**£££-££**) form part of this fairytale Gothic pile on the lochside. There's also the Boathouse self-catering option with it own private jetty and beautifully appointed bedrooms (£820 per week). However, it's the dining experience for which The Torridon is renowned (**£££-££**), with the option to fine dine on the freshest locally sourced seafood and game.
£££ The Old Mill Highland Lodge, on Loch Maree at Talladale, halfway between Kinlochewe and Gairloch, T01445-760271, www.theoldmillhighlandlodge.co.uk. Open Mar-Oct. 6 rooms. The best accommodation around here, this converted mill is set in its own gardens. It's friendly and comfortable, offers great food (price includes dinner), seclusion and views.
£££ Tigh-an-Eilean Hotel, Shieldaig, Loch Torridon, T01520-755251. End Mar-Nov.

11 rooms. Great wee, upmarket hotel overlooking the loch, so views are wonderful. Terrific food in the restaurant and also occasional impromptu bursts of folk music. Recommended.

££ Ferroch, Achnasheen, T01445-791451. Open all year. 3 en suite rooms. Superior B&B in former crofthouse. Beautiful location (**£££** including dinner).

££ Hillhaven B&B, Hillhaven, Kinlochewe, T01445-760204, www.kinlochewe.info. Open all year. 3 en suite rooms. Good-value B&B catering for walkers and cyclists.

££ Kinlochewe Hotel, Kinlochewe, T01445-760253, www.kinlochewehotel.co.uk. Open all year. 9 rooms. Offers B&B as well as 12 cheaper (£10 per person per night) bunkhouse beds and cheap bar meals.

££ The Rivendell Guesthouse, Shieldaig, T01520-755250, A relative newcomer to the scene, close to the **Tigh an Eilean Hotel** and with views across to Shieldaig Island.

£ SYHA hostel, on the easternmost fringe of Torridon village, T01445-791284. This 44 bed hostel is ideal for exploring the surrounding Torridon hills. It's about a 20- to 25-min walk from here to the **Torridon Inn** and a well earned pint. Note that at the time of writing, the village store remains closed, a sad reflection perhaps of the areas increasing number of absent landlords – an issue that also affects the likes of Ardnamurchan further south.

Camping

There is a basic campsite at **Taangan Farm**, at the head of Loch Maree.

Gairloch and around *p104*

There are numerous B&Bs scattered through-out the area. Most of the owners will provide maps and information on local walks.

££££ Pool House Hotel, Poolewe, T01445-781272, www.poolhouse.co.uk. Open all year. 7 en suite rooms, all with Royal Navy names reflecting the former use of the house as the Royal Naval headquarters for directing Second World War North Atlantic convoys. On the Cove Rd by the lochside, this former home of Osgood Mackenzie (who designed the nearby gardens) has been transformed into one of the very best hotels in the country (witness the numerous awards and accolades on their website). A stay here does not come cheap, but if you've got the money then look no further, for there is, quite simply, no better place to stay in this category. The dishes created by chef Daniel Hall on the **North by Northwest** dining room are worthy of such luxurious surroundings (**£££**). Very highly recommended.

£££-££ The Creel Restaurant & Charleston House, Gairloch, T01445-712497. Open Mar-Dec. 4 en suite rooms. Guesthouse/restaurant with a reputation for high-quality food (**££**), especially local seafood. Also delicious home-made bread and ice cream. **£££** including dinner.

£££-££ The Old Inn, Gairloch, T01445-712068, www.theoldinn.net. Open all year. 17 rooms. This venerable old pub/restaurant with rooms is constantly winning awards for its fine ales and superb seafood (**££**). Located by the harbour, it makes an excellent base for exploring the area and staying here gives the advantage of not having to move far after enjoying the best pint of real ale for miles around. Recommended for those who don't turn in too early.

££ Burnside B&B, 48 Mellon Charles, 3 miles west of Aultbea, T01445-731270. This small, 3-bedroom guesthouse is a real gem. Very welcoming host with a fund of stories, large breakfast and lovely views. Recommended.

££ Dry Island, Badachro, T01445-741263. Open all year. 1 en suite room, 2-night minimum stay May-Sep. Here's a chance to stay in a B&B on a private island, accessed from the mainland by a floating bridge or on foot at low tide. Beautiful surroundings and all the peace and tranquility you can handle. Also nice touches such as dressing gowns and slippers. For couples there's the chance to get away from it all by hiring the Old Curing Station (built 1785), from £200 per week.

££ Gairloch View Guest House, Auchtercairn, Gairloch, T01445-712666, www.gairlochview.com. A pleasant 2-bedroom option close to all amenities.

££ Kerrysdale House, Gairloch, T01445-712292, www.kerrysdalehouse.co.uk. Open all year. 3 rooms. Charming B&B in a building that dates back to 1793, with the added benefit of a garden to enjoy in summer.

££ Myrtle Bank Hotel, Gairloch, T01445-712004, www.myrtlebankhotel.co.uk. 12 rooms. Modern hotel in the centre of Gairloch overlooking the loch, very good food and service in the restaurant (**£££-££**).

££ Old Smiddy Guest House, in Laide, near Gruinard Bay, T01445-731696, www.oldsmiddy.co.uk. Mar-Oct. 3 rooms. Superior guesthouse in great location, with lavish breakfasts and an excellent restaurant (**£££** for 4-course dinner, BYOB), which is open to non-residents, but book well in advance. Highly recommended.

££-£ Rubha Reidh Lighthouse, 11 miles north of Gairloch, at the end of the road, T01445-771263, www.ruareidh.co.uk. Open all year. This comfortable B&B and hostel has 5 double, twin or family rooms (4 are en suite) and 2 dorms with 4-6 beds (**£** per person). Rooms are fairly plain but it's the wonderful setting you're paying for, and the history (it was built in 1910 by RL Stevenson's cousin). Breakfast is £6 extra and dinner is £13.50 and served at 1900. It's essential to book well ahead in the high season. The whole lighthouse can also be rented on a self-catering basis for parties of 20+ (£1100 for 3 nights in high season). To get here without your own transport, try cycling, hiking or give the Westerbus community bus service (T01445-712255) a call in advance and expect to pay around £2.50 for the journey.

£ Carn Dearg Youth Hostel, 3 miles beyond Gairloch, on the road to Melvaig, T01445-712219. Open 15 May-3 Oct.

£ Duisary, Gairloch, T01445-712252, www.duisary.freeserve.co.uk. Apr-Oct. 3 rooms. Cosy B&B run by Isabel Mackenzie. This modernized crofthouse is on the road that turns off to the right by the **Millcroft Hotel**, beyond the fire station.

£ Mrs A MacIver, Charleston, by the harbour, T01445-712388. Mar-Nov. 3 en suite rooms. Friendly, comfortable B&B.

£ Sail Mhor Croft Independent Hostel, south of Ullapool in Camusnagaul by Dundonnell, T01854-633224, www.sailmhor.co.uk. 16 beds, clean and cosy. Try and call ahead to say you're coming.

£ Stratford House, Strath, Gairloch, T01445-712183, www.stratfordhouse.btinternet.co.uk A very welcoming 2-bedroom option that also offers the chance to enjoy some lovely home-baking in the lounge.

Camping

Badrallach Bothy & Camp Site, near Gruinard Bay, T01445-633281, www.badrallach.com This campsite is situated in the tiny, remote hamlet of Badrallach. A few miles east of Dundonnell, take a side road which branches left and runs for 7 miles. The bothy (it's a lovely backpackers) has a peat fire and 12 beds.

Big Sands Holiday Centre, Big Sand, about a mile beyond Strath, T01445-712152. Open Easter-Oct. Fabulous facilities and truly gobsmacking views.

Camping and Caravan Club Site, between Poolewe Village and Inverewe Garden, T01445-781249. An excellent site.

Gairloch Caravan & Camping Park, Strath, T01445-712373. With full facilities and close to all amenities.

Gruinard Bay Caravan Park, in Laide near Gruinard Bay, T01445-731225. Open Apr-Oct.

❷ Restaurants

Loch Carron and around *p100*
£££-££ Walled Garden Restaurant, Applecross, T01520-744440. Open Mar-Nov. This rustic option prides itself on locally

sourced produce, including the use of vegetables grown and picked from the garden. It's quite an informal place to eat but the food is exquisite. Definitely worth booking ahead at weekends.

££ Applecross Inn, see Where to stay, above. The food here is fantastic, with starters that can include seafood chowder and locally collected oysters. For mains there's the likes of locally reared venison and Applecross Bay prawns.

££ Carron Restaurant, about 5 mins' drive from the village, across the loch on the A890, T01520-722488. Open Apr-Nov Mon-Sat 1030-2100. An excellent option.

££-£ Kishorn Seafood Bar, on the road to Lochcarron from Applecross, after the Bealach na Ba Pass, T01520-733240. Open Apr-Oct. This oasis of culinary excellence must not be missed. The seafood is very fresh and at around £4 for half a dozen Queen Scallops (you read that correctly) is there anywhere in the UK offering such amazing value? More standard fare also on offer for those unfortunate souls who can't eat seafood. Highly recommended.

£ Flower Tunnel, at Applecross campsite (see Where to stay, above). Mar-Nov daily from 0900, meals from 1200. Serves pizza, steak pie, fish and chips, etc, in a large flower-filled plastic tunnel.

Gairloch and around *p104*
Hotels are often the best options for eating out, see Where to stay, above. Of particular note are the **Old Inn**, the **Creel Restaurant** and the **Myrtle Bank Hotel**.

£££-££ Badachro Inn, Badachro, T01445-741255, www.badachroinn.com. Good food in this handily placed hotel on the road to Red Point. Nice views from the dining room and beloved by the yachtie fraternity. A great place for a pint and seafood.

££-£ Blueprint Café, on main road through Gairloch, opposite **Mountain Lodge**, T01445-712397. Open Mar-Nov until 1600 for lunch and snacks and later for dinner. Food is fairly standard but good value nonetheless.

££-£ Inverewe Garden, Poolewe, T01445-781200. Mar-May and Sep daily 1000-1700, May-Aug daily 1000-1730, Oct daily 1000-1600. The best place to eat cheaply around Poolewe.

££-£ Melvaig Inn, Melvich, on road north of Gairloch towards lighthouse, T01445-771212, www.melvaig-inn.co.uk. Open all year 1200-2300. This café-bar/restaurant leans heavily towards meat and chicken though there's also local seafood. All mains are under a tenner, so very good value and there are lovely comfy sofas to enjoy the views over the sea. In truth, with the pool table and juke box, it's more the sort of place you'd expect to find in a city centre – not amidst the splendid solitude of Rua Reidh.

££-£ Mountain Lodge, Strath Sq, Gairloch, T01445-712316. Open Mar-Nov until 1800, later in Jul-Aug. Good veggie options in this very friendly restaurant with outside terrace overlooking Gair Loch and mountains beyond. It is run by mountaineers and also has an adjacent bookshop. Little pricey for its home-baking but can't deny the views are fantastic.

○ What to do

Torridon and around *p101*
Climbing and hillwalking
For those who are not experienced hillwalkers, there's a Ranger Service for visitors. Jul-Aug the ranger takes guided walks up into the mountains 3 times a week. For more details, call T01445-791221.
Island Horizons, Kirkton Rd, T01520-722238. For guided walks around Lochcarron.
Martin Moran, T01520-722361.
A recommended local mountain guide.

Quad biking
Highland Trails, book at The Anchorage post office/craft shop at the harbour or at Flowerdale Estate office, T01445-712378. Quad bike tour of the Flowerdale Deer Forest.

Gairloch and around *p104*
Fishing
For information on sea-angling trips, contact the chandlery shop at the harbour, T01445-712458.

Wildlife cruises
Gairloch Marine Wildlife Centre, by the pier, T01445-712636. You can take excellent wildlife-spotting boat trips aboard, *MV Starquest* that leaves from the Charleston Pier, Mar-Oct, book at the Wildlife Centre. 2-hr cruise, 1000, 1230 and 1500, £20 (subject to weather conditions). You may spot minke whales, seals, porpoise and even killer whales as you explore the coastline.

⊖ Transport

Loch Carron and around *p100*
Bus There's a postbus service to **Shieldaig** from **Kishorn** and **Lochcarron**, Mon-Sat. It's possible to leave **Applecross** by public transport, but only just. A **postbus** service leaves **Applecross** at 0920 to arrive in **Shieldaig** at 1015.

Another option is to catch the Skyeways (No WR87) from **Applecross** post office (Wed and Sat, 0800; call to request on T01599-555477) to arrive in **Shieldaig** at 0900, **Lochcarron** at 0930 and **Achnasheen station** at 1015. If you stay on the bus you'll reach **Inverness** by 1125.

Train Don't forget you can also use the railway to leave the region by catching the train from Lochcarron (Mon-Sat).

Torridon and around *p101*
Bus A postbus journey leaves **Shieldaig** at 1025 and arrives in **Torridon** at 1045 (Mon-Sat only). A postbus service leaves **Shieldaig** for **Applecross**.

For buses between **Gairloch** and **Shieldaig**, **Lochcarron Garage** (No 705) run a service on schooldays that leaves **Shieldaig** at 1400, reaches **Torridon** at 1415, **Kinlochewe** post office at 1435 and **Gairloch** at 1515.

Gairloch and around *p104*
Bus From Jun-Oct there's a daily bus to **Inverness** with Scotbus, T01463-224410. The bus leaves **Inverewe** daily at 1020, 1430 and 1750 respectively, with the first 2 buses terminating at **Achnasheen station** in time to connect with the FirstScotRail train from **Inverness** to **Kyle of Lochalsh**.

Westerbus, T01445-712255, also run a service from **Gairloch** (0745) to **Inverness** (1025), Mon, Wed and Sat via **Mellon Charles/Aultbea** (0820), **Laide** (0835), **Dundonnell** (0850), **Braemore Junction** (for connections to **Ullapool**), and **Strathpeffer** (0952). The same bus company also run a service, Tue, Thu and Fri, between **Laide** (0745) and **Inverness** (1025) with stops including **Poolewe** (0805) and **Loch Maree**.

Ullapool and around

The attractive little fishing port of Ullapool, on the shores of Loch Broom, is the largest settlement in Wester Ross. The grid-pattern village, created in 1788 at the height of the herring boom by the British Fisheries Society, is still an important fishing centre as well as being the major tourist centre in the northwest of Scotland and one of the main ferry terminals for the Outer Hebrides. At the height of the busy summer season the town is swamped by visitors passing through on their way to or from Stornoway on Lewis, heading north into the wilds, or south to Inverness. It has excellent tourist amenities and services, and relatively good transport links, making it the ideal base for those exploring the northwest coast and a good place to be if the weather is bad.

North of Ullapool you enter a different world. The landscape becomes ever more dramatic and unreal – a huge emptiness of bleak moorland punctuated by isolated peaks and shimmering lochs. A narrow and tortuously twisting road winds its way up the coast, past deserted beaches of sparkling white sand washed by turquoise seas. There's not much tourist traffic this far north and once you get off the main A835 and on to the backroads, you can enjoy the wonderful sensation of having all this astonishingly beautiful scenery to yourself.

Arriving in Ullapool

Getting there and around
Ullapool is the mainland terminal for ferries to Stornoway (Lewis). **Scottish Citylink** ① *T08705-505050*, buses from Inverness (twice daily Monday to Saturday, just under 1½ hours, £13.10 return) connect with the ferry to Stornoway. The local **CalMac office** ① *Shore St, opposite the pier, T01854-612358*, also has details. There are buses to places further north, and south along the coast, they stop at the pier near the ferry dock. Monday to Friday the first bus from Ullapool to Achiltibuie leaves at 1040 and if requested by the passenger will stop in Reiff and Altandhu (1130) before continuing to Achiltibuie and Badenscallie. There's a **Tim Dearman Coach** ① *T01349-883585*, service once a day Monday to Saturday (April to the end of September) from Inverness bus station via Ullapool, Lochinver and Kylesku to Scourie. ▸▸ *See Transport page 124.*

Tourist information
The **TIC** ① *6 Argyle St, T01854-612135, Easter-Oct daily, Nov-Easter Mon-Fri 1300-1630*, is well run, helpful and provides an accommodation booking service as well as information on local walks and trips. It also has a good stock of books and maps. To find out what's on, tune in to Loch Broom FM (102.2 and 96.8) or pick up a copy of the *Ullapool News* on Fridays.

Places in Ullapool → *For listings, see pages 119-125. Phone code 01854. Population 1800.*

Ullapool's attractions are very much of the outdoor variety and include the Falls of Measach, Achiltibuie and Stac Pollaidh. However, whilst in town it's worth taking a stroll around the harbour to watch the comings and goings of the fishing fleet, and you might even see the occasional seal or otter swimming close to the shore. The only real 'sight' as such is the **Ullapool Museum and Visitor Centre** ① *T01854-612987, www.ullapoolmuseum.co.uk, Apr-Oct Mon-Sat 1000-1700, Nov-Mar by prior arrangement only, £3, concessions £2, children 50p*, in a converted church in West Argyle Street. It has some interesting displays on local history, including the story of those who set sail from here in 1773 on board *The Hector*, the first ship to carry emigrants from the Highlands to Nova Scotia in Canada.

Walks → *All routes are covered by OS Maps Nos 15, 19 and 20.*
There are several good walking trails which start in Ullapool. One of these is to the top of **Ullapool Hill**, or **Meall Mhor** (886 ft). Starting from the tourist office, head to the end of Argyle Street, turn left on to North Road. Walk down the lane between Broom Court and the Hydro sub-station and then follow the path which zigzags up the hillside. There's a good cairned path up to the top of the hill. The views from the top over Glen Achall, and on a clear day, the mountains of Sutherland, are superb. You can return by traversing the hillside to the top of the Braes, or take a track leading to Loch Achall and follow the Ullapool river through the quarry road back to the village. The return trip takes one to two hours.

A relatively easy, but much longer walk, of five to six hours, is to **Rhidorroch Estate**. Take the A835 north out of Ullapool. Opposite the petrol station and before the bridge, take the road on the right signed 'Quarry'. Go through the quarry keeping to the left, and follow the Ullapool river until you see Loch Achall. Continue along the north bank of the loch for another 6 miles. East Rhidorroch Lodge is on the right; cross the bridge to get there, then skirt the lodge fences and cross to the track which leads up the southwestern hill. This brings you out to Leckmelm, about 4 miles south of Ullapool on the A835. This last section offers wonderful views across Loch Broom to An Teallach. From Leckmelm you can also climb **Beinn Eilideach** (1837 ft).

A good coastal walk is to **Rhue Lighthouse** and back. From the north end of Quay Street go down the steps to the river. Cross the bridges and head left by the football field. Follow the path to the left by the duck pond and cross in front of the bungalow. Then follow the shoreline north for about 2 miles, climbing up the hillside when the tide is high. Follow the path until you reach the little white lighthouse at Rhue Point. To return, take the single-track road out of Rhue back to the main road and up over the hill to Ullapool. It's about 6 miles in total.

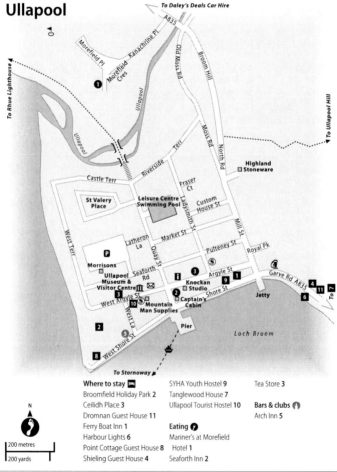

Ullapool

To Daley's Deals Car Hire

To Rhue Lighthouse

To Ullapool Hill

Highland Stoneware

Castle Terr

Riverside

St Valery Place

Leisure Centre Swimming Pool

Fraser Ct

Custom House St

Market St

Latheron La

Pulteney St

Royal Pk

Quay St

Mill St

Morrisons

Seaforth Rd

Argyle St

Garve Rd A835

Ullapool Museum & Visitor Centre

Knockan Studio

Shore St

Jetty

West Argyle St

Captain's Cabin

Mountain Man Supplies

West Terr

West Shore St

Pier

Loch Broom

To Stornoway

Where to stay 🛏
Broomfield Holiday Park **2**
Ceilidh Place **3**
Dromnan Guest House **11**
Ferry Boat Inn **1**
Harbour Lights **6**
Point Cottage Guest House **8**
Shieling Guest House **4**

SYHA Youth Hostel **9**
Tanglewood House **7**
Ullapool Tourist Hostel **10**

Eating 🍴
Mariner's at Morefield Hotel **1**
Seaforth Inn **2**

Tea Store **3**

Bars & clubs 🍸
Arch Inn **5**

N

200 metres
200 yards

There are many more strenuous hiking routes around Ullapool. The A835 south of town gives access to **Beinn Dearg** (3556 ft) and the **Fannichs**, a range of hills on the southern side of Dirrie More. There's also **An Teallach**, a favourite with Scottish climbers, see below. North of Ullapool are the mountains within the Inverpolly National Nature Reserve (see below).

All routes require hillwalking experience and you should be well prepared for the unpredictable weather conditions. A good guidebook is *The Northern Highlands*, SMC *District Guide*, by Tom Strang. ▸▸ *For details of tour operators offering trips, see What to do, page 123.*

South of Ullapool → *For listings, see pages 119-125.*

On the southern shore of Little Loch Broom is the village of **Dundonnell**, from where there are spectacular views of awesome **An Teallach** (3483 ft), a mountain of almost mythical status amongst Scottish climbers and spoken of in hushed, reverential tones. The path to the highest of its summits is clear and begins southeast of the **Dundonell Hotel**. It will take a full day and you'll need to be well prepared (OS map No 19) and heed the usual advice.

The A832 coastal road meets the A835 Ullapool to Inverness main road at Braemore junction, 12 miles south of Ullapool. Before heading on to Ullapool it's worth stopping at the very impressive **Falls of Measach**, just by the junction. The falls plunge 150 ft into the spectacular **Corrieshalloch Gorge** (or 'ugly/fearsome gorge' in Gaelic) and can be crossed by a distinctly wobbly suspension bridge (not for vertigo sufferers). The falls can be reached from the A835, but the most dramatic approach is from the A832 Gairloch road.

North of Ullapool → *For listings, see pages 119-125.*

The region immediately north of Ullapool is called Assynt, and is heaven for serious hillwalkers and climbers. Though most are not Munros, they offer a stiff climb. The views from the summits are truly breathtaking, including across to Skye but it's vital you dress for the mountains and prepare for harsh weather conditions that can materialize at a moments notice from the Atlantic. Amongst the most spectacular of Assynt's distinctive 'island peaks' are **Suilven** (2398 ft), **Ben More Assynt** (3275 ft), **Quinag** (2650 ft) and **Canisp** (2775 ft). Much of this region is protected in the Inverpolly and Inchnadamph National Nature Reserves, home to an extremely rich and diverse wildlife.

Inverpolly National Nature Reserve → *Phone code 01854. OS Landranger No 15.*
About 12 miles north of Ullapool on the main A835 is the exceptional **SNH Visitor Centre** ⓘ *T01854-666234, open all year 24 hrs a day*, at Knockan Crag. It's an interactive display of the geology, flora and fauna of an area that marks some of the world's oldest geological rock formations (www.northwest-highlands-geopark.org.uk). From the visitor centre there's a marked trail which leads up to the **Crag**, and the views from the clifftop are excellent, across to Inverpolly's 'island' peaks of Cul Mór, Cul Beag and Stac Pollaidh.

A few miles north of here is the village of **Knockan**. Nearby, at **Elphin**, is the **Highland and Rare Breeds Farm** ⓘ *mid-May to Sep daily 1000-1700*. Elphin has a great tea room offering fabulous home-baking, it's on the left as you drive towards Ullapool. Beyond Elphin is **Ledmore**, where the A837 branches east towards Lairg and Bonar Bridge. There's a good craft shop at Ledmore where you can buy hand-knitted jumpers.

Between Ullapool and Knockan Crag is the turn-off west (left) to the distinctive craggy peak of **Stac Pollaidh**. A path has been established by the John Muir Trust, which takes you on a circular walk around the peak from the car park. Take the right-hand path and go round at the same level, or climb up the rear to the top, go around the summit and descend by the same path. You'll need a head for heights to reach the summit, as much of the route is exposed, but the stunning views are worth it. Be careful not to stray from the path; it's been put there because of the damage inflicted by tens of thousands of pairs of boots each year, resulting in serious erosion on the south face. It's a fairly easy 2½-hour walk.

Achiltibuie → *Phone code 01854.*
The unclassified single-track road winds its way west past Stac Pollaidh to the turn-off for Achiltibuie. This old crofting village, with whitewashed cottages set back from the sea with views across to the beautiful Summer Isles, is home to a small grocers, post office (excellent for checking out the latest community events on the go) and one of the northwest's best dining options and hotels, the **Summer Isles Hotel**. Look directly south from here and you'll clearly spot the low lying Summer Isles over a mile offshore and a popular destination for experienced sea kayakers.

Another worthwhile attraction is the **Smokehouse** ① *T01854-622353, www.summerislesfoods.co.uk, May-Sep Mon-Sat 0930-1700, free*, at Altandhu, 5 miles north of Achiltibuie. Here you can watch the salmon, herring, trout and other fish being cured before buying some afterwards. Close by is the good value **Am Fuaran Bar** ① *Altandhu, T01854-622339*, where you can get a a sandwich, an evening meal or just a pint and game of pool. A few miles further down the road in Polbain, is the **Coigach Craft and Gift Shop** ① *T01854-622346*, a good place for a cuppa and the chance to buy some local crafts or a fishing permit.

Lochinver and around → *Phone code 01571.*
The road from Achiltibuie north to Lochinver is known locally as the 'wee mad road', and you'd be mad to miss this thrilling route which twists and winds its way through some the northwest's most stunning scenery. A mile south of the village is the magnificent **Achins Bookshop**, a friendly place packed with second-hand books. The village of Lochinver is a working fishing port and the last sizeable village before Thurso. It has a good tourist office, lots of accommodation, a bank with ATM, post office, petrol station and several good eating options. Pick up fishing permits at the post office or Assynt Visitor Centre.

The best place to start is the **Assynt Visitor Centre** ① *T01854-844654, Apr-Oct Mon-Fri 1000-1700, Sun 1000-1600*, which houses the TIC. It has displays on the local geology, history and wildlife and there's also a ranger service with guided walks throughout the summer. Those looking for high quality hand-crafted, earthenware gifts should head for **Highland Stoneware**, see page 123.

A few miles south of Lochinver, beyond Inverkirkaig, is the trail along the river to the **Kirkaig Falls**. The path starts near the Achins Bookshop. Follow the path for about 2 miles until it branches right to the falls in the gorge below. Continue along the main path for about another ¾ mile until you reach Fionn Loch, with superb views of mighty Suilven. The walk up to the falls and back should take around 1½ hours. This is one of the main approaches to the foot of the mountain.

Loch Assynt and Inchnadamph → *Phone code 01571.*
The area east of Lochinver is a remote wilderness of mountains and moorland dotted with lochs and lochans. As well as being a favourite haunt of hardy climbers and walkers

(ask at the Lochinver TIC for the leaflet about local walks), Assynt is a paradise for anglers. Most of the lochs are teeming with brown trout, and fishing permits are readily available throughout the area from the TIC in Lochinver or at local hotels, guesthouses and B&Bs. There's also salmon fishing on the River Kirkaig, available through the **Inver Lodge Hotel** and on Loch Assynt through the **Inchnadamph Lodge**, see Where to stay, page 119.

The A837 Lochinver to Lairg road meets the A894 to Durness 10 miles east of Lochinver at Skiag Bridge by Loch Assynt. Half a mile south of here, by the loch, are the ruins of **Ardvreck Castle**. The castle dates from 1597 and was the stronghold of the Macleods of Assynt until a siege in 1691, when it was taken by the Seaforth Mackenzies. Before that, the Marquess of Montrose had been imprisoned here following his defeat at Carbisdale in 1650. Access to the castle is free, but the ruins are in a dangerous state and should be approached with care.

To the east of the road lies the **Inchnadamph National Nature Reserve**, dominated by the massive peaks of Ben More Assynt and Conival, which should only be attempted by experienced hillwalkers. A few miles south of the village of Inchnadamph, at the fish farm, is a steep, but well-marked footpath up to the **Bone Caves**. This is one of Scotland's oldest historical sites, where the bones of humans and animals such as lynx and bear were found together with sawn-off deer antlers dating from over 8000 years ago.

Lochinver to Kylesku → *Phone code 01571.*
The quickest way north from Lochinver is the A837 east to the junction with the A894 which heads to Kylesku. But by far the most scenic route is the B869 coast road that passes moorland, lochs and beautiful sandy bays. It's best travelled from north to south, giving you the most fantastic views of the whale-backed hump of **Suilven**, rocky talisman of the great poet, Norman MacCaig. Untypically, most of the land in this part of Assynt is owned by local crofters who, under the aegis of the Assynt Crofters' Trust, bought 21,000 acres of the North Assynt Estate, thus setting a precedent for change in the history of land ownership in the Highlands.

The trust now owns the fishing rights to the area and sells permits through local post offices and the tourist office in Lochinver. It has also undertaken a number of conservation projects, including one at **Achmelvich**, a few miles north of Lochinver, at the end of a side road which branches off the coast road. It's worth a detour to see one of the loveliest beaches on the west coast, with sparkling white sand and clear turquoise waters straight out of a Caribbean tourist brochure. A terrific place for a family picnic. There's a great youth hostel here, though the caravan site jars with the beauty of the surrounding landscape.

From the beach car park below the hostel a path leads northwest along the coast. Bear left off the sandy path shortly after the white cottage on the hill ahead comes into view, and follow the footpath until the road is reached at Alltan na Bradhan, where there are the remains of an old meal mill. Continue north from here along the coast for about a mile until you reach a small bay just before Clachtoll and its **campsite** ① *T01575-855373, www.clachtollbeachcampsite.co.uk*, the **Split Rock**. Close by are the remains of an Iron Age broch, but don't cause further damage by clambering over the ruins. Return to the beach by the same path. The walk there and back should take about 1½ hours.

Old Man of Stoer
① *Check access locally during the deer-stalking season which runs from mid-Aug to mid-Oct.*
A side road turns left off the B869 north of Stoer and runs out to **Stoer lighthouse**. From here you can walk across the Stoer Peninsula to the **Old Man of Stoer**, a dramatic rock

pillar standing offshore, surrounded by sheer cliffs. Allow about three hours for the circular walk which starts and ends in the lighthouse car park. There is no public transport to the lighthouse, but the Lochinver to Drumbeg postbus runs to Raffin, 1 mile away. A clear path runs from the car park to the cliffs then follows the line of the cliffs northwards. The path heads inland for a short distance as it bypasses a deep gully then meets the clifftop again, and after a mile or so you can see the Old Man tucked away in a shallow bay, battered by huge waves. Beyond the Old Man the path continues to the headland, the **Point of Stoer**, from where it turns back on itself and climbs **Sidhean Mór** (532 ft). The views from here are fantastic, across to Harris and Lewis and south to the mountains of Assynt. From here, follow the faint path south, back towards the lighthouse, passing a small loch below Sidhean Beag on your left and an obvious cairn on your right. Then you pass a radio mast and follow the clear track back to the lighthouse car park. OS Landranger Map No 15 covers the route. Nine miles further on, in beautiful **Eddrachillis Bay**, is **Drumbeg**, a popular place for anglers who come to fish in the many lochs of North Assynt.

Kylesku → *Phone code 01971.*

The road runs east from Drumbeg, under the shadow of towering **Quinag** (2654 ft), to meet the A894 heading north to Kylesku, site of the sweeping modern road bridge over Loch a'Cháirn Bháin. From Kylesku you can visit Britain's highest waterfall, the 650-ft high **Eas a'Chùal Aluinn**, near the head of Loch Glencoul. Cruises leave from the old ferry jetty below the **Kylesku Hotel** to the falls, see What to do, page 124.

There's also a trail to the top of the falls. It starts at the south end of Loch na Gainmhich, about 3 miles north of Skiag Bridge. Skirting the loch, follow the track in a southeasterly direction up to the head of the Bealach a Bhuirich (the Roaring Pass). Continue until you meet a stream, with several small lochans on your right. Follow this stream until it plunges over the Cliffs of Dubh (the Dark Cliffs). You can get a better view of the falls by walking to the right about 100 yds and descending a heather slope for a short distance. Allow about three to four hours for the round trip.

Scourie and Handa Island → *Phone code 01971.*

Ten miles north of Kylesku is the little crofting community of Scourie, sitting above a sandy bay. Anyone remotely interested in wildlife is strongly advised to make a stop here to visit Handa Island, a sea bird reserve run by the Scottish Wildlife Trust, and one of the best places in the country for bird life. The island is now deserted, except for the warden, but once supported a thriving community of crofters, until the potato famine of 1846 forced them to leave, most emigrating to Canada's Cape Breton. Now it's home to huge colonies of shags, fulmars, razorbills, guillemots and puffins, in season. The best time to visit is during the summer breeding season, from late May to August. There's a footpath right round the island, which is detailed in the free SWT leaflet available at the warden's office when you arrive. You should allow three to four hours. There's a **ferry service** ① *T01971-502077, Mon-Sat 0930-1700, £10 return, children £5,* to the island from Tarbet Beach, 3 miles northwest off the A894, about 2 miles north of Scourie. It sails continuously, depending on demand, from April to September, and the crossing takes 15 minutes. It's no longer possible to take the postbus from Scourie to the jetty for Handa Island so you'll need to walk, cycle, drive or take a taxi. It's worth it though. There is also an excellent wildlife boat trip that leaves from Fanagmore, a mile from Tarbet on the other side of the peninsula. ►► *See What to do, page 124.*

Kinlochbervie and around → *Phone code 01971.*

The road north from Scourie passes Laxford Bridge, where it meets the A838 running southeast to Lairg, see page 138. The A838 also runs north to Durness, on the north coast, see page 126. At Rhiconich, the B801 branches northwest to Kinlochbervie, a small village with a very big fish market. This is one of the west coast's major fishing ports, and huge container lorries thunder along the narrow single-track roads carrying frozen fish and seafood to all corners of Europe. Right by the quayside is the no frills Fisherman's Mission that serves hearty, cheap meals – if they let you in!

A few miles beyond Kinlochbervie is **Oldshoremore**, a tiny crofters' village scattered around a stunning white beach, and a great place to swim. The less hardy can instead explore the hidden rocky coves nearby.

At the end of the road is **Blairmore**, from where a footpath leads to **Sandwood Bay**, one of the west coast's most wonderful beaches and on protected land managed by the John Muir Trust conservation charity. It's a 4-mile walk in each direction but because of its isolation you'll probably have this glorious mile-long stretch of white sand all to yourself. At one end is a spectacular rock pinnacle and it is said to be haunted by the ghost of an ancient shipwrecked mariner. Allow three hours for the walk there and back, plus time at the beach. Romantic souls may wish to take a tent and watch the sunset with a loved one and a bottle of their favourite single malt. Sandwood Bay can also be reached from Cape Wrath, a hard, long day's hike to the north, see page 127.

Ullapool and around listings

For hotel and restaurant price codes and other relevant information, see pages 13-20.

⊖ Where to stay

Ullapool *p113, map p114*
There is no shortage of places to stay in and around Ullapool, ranging from one of the very finest hotels in the UK to guesthouses and B&Bs, a couple of good youth hostels and a campsite. Garve Rd, heading south out of town, has several guesthouses, and there are lots of B&Bs along Seaforth Rd and Pulteney St. Unfortunately the famous **Altnaharrie Inn** has closed, though the ferry from Ullapool to the other side of Loch Broom is running; for details T01854-612656.
£££ The Ceilidh Place, 14 West Argyle Pl, T01854-612103, www.theceilidhplace.com. 13 rooms and each named after a 'famous' visitor who recommended books to be read – and which are left in each of the different, tastefully furnished rooms. Let's face it, this former boat shed that grew from the inspirations of one man is not one

of your run of the mill hotels. It's different and refreshingly so, with a cosy lounge, bookshop, restaurant, bar and café. It also hosts a varied programme of arts events such as live music, plays, poetry readings, exhibitions and ceilidhs. It's a great place to relax and soak up some local culture. Recommended.
£££ Tanglewood House, T01854-612059, www.tanglewoodhouse.co.uk. Open all year. 3 en suite rooms. Chalet-style house in stunning location overlooking Loch Broom, with its own private beach. Part of the **Wolsey Lodge** scheme, so you dine with the hostess, Anne Holloway, who offers superb cooking (4-course dinner £33) in a civilized atmosphere. All rooms have their own balcony and wonderful views across the loch. Highly recommended.
££ Braemore Square Country House, Braemore, T01845-655357, www.braemore square.com. Open all year. 3 rooms. 11 miles south of Ullapool and set in 46 acres of grounds is the former estate house of Victorian engineer Sir John Fowler,

who designed the Forth Rail Bridge. B&B, with comfortable and tastefully furnished rooms, all in splendid isolation. Guests have use of the kitchen. Self-catering also available (£390 per week in summer). Recommended.

££ Dromnan Guest House, Garve Rd, T01854-612333. Open all year. 7 rooms. Very pleasant and friendly guesthouse that also offers free access to the local swimming pool.

££ Ferry Boat Inn, Shore St, T01854-612366, www.ferryboat-inn.com. On the lochside, decent accommodation and food and though cramped, the best pub in town.

££ Harbour Lights Hotel, Garve Rd, on the left, heading into Ullapool on the A835, T01854-612222, www.harbour-lights.co.uk. Open Mar-Oct. 22 rooms. Modern hotel offering good service with comfortable rooms.

££ Point Cottage Guest House, 22 West Shore St, T01854-612494, www.point cottage.co.uk. Open Feb-Nov. 3 en suite rooms. Lovely old fishing cottage at the quieter end of the loch-front.

££ The Shieling Guest House, Garve Rd, T01854-612947. 6 rooms. Purpose built, charming house on the edge of Ullapool and set within an acre of it own grounds with views over the loch and mountains. Even has its own sauna.

£ SYHA youth hostel, Shore St, T01854-612254. Mar-Dec. A very good hostel. You can pick up some information on local walks and it also offers bike hire, internet and laundry facilities. Recommended.

£ Ullapool Tourist Hostel, West House, West Argyle St, T01854-613126. Open all year. This independent hostel has the full range of facilities, including free internet for guests and mountain bike hire. Also runs local bus tours.

Camping
Broomfield Holiday Park, Shore St, T01854-612 0020. Open Easter-Sep. At the west end of the village, this campsite has great views across to the Summer Isles and a laundrette on site.

South of Ullapool *p115*
£££ Dundonnell Hotel, in Dundonnell, south of Ullapool, T01854-633204, www.dundonnellhotel.com. Open Feb-Dec. Good-value hotel and good food, including vegetarian options, in their refurbished **Claymore Restaurant (£££-££)** and **Broombeg Bar**. Worth the stop.

Achiltibuie *p116*
££££ Summer Isles Hotel, T01854-622282, www.summerisleshotel.com. 3 en suite rooms, 2 suites and 1 cottage. Open Easter to mid-Oct. This relaxing, civilized hotel is under the ownership of the Mackays, who also own a hotel on Barra. The hotel enjoys magnificent views across to the Summer Isles and boasts a fabulous restaurant, see Restaurants, below.

£ SYHA Youth Hostel, a few miles south at Achininver, T01854-622254. Mid-May to early Oct. Basic and very cheap.

Lochinver and around *p116*
££££ The Albannach Hotel, Baddidaroch, T01571-844407, www.thealbannach.co.uk. Open Mar-Nov. 6 en suite rooms. This wonderful 18th-century house overlooking Loch Inver is one of the very best places to stay in the northwest and everything a romantic Highland hotel should be. Rooms are tall, dark and handsome and the food in the award-winning restaurant is imaginative and generous, featuring only the freshest of local fish, fowl and game. The price includes dinner. Non-residents are also welcome (£50 for dinner) but booking is essential. Highly recommended.

££££ Inver Lodge Hotel, Iolaire Rd, T01571-844496, www.inverlodgehotel.co.uk. The spacious, luxuriously appointed rooms, each named after a local mountain or loch, look out over the hills and sea whilst head chef Peter Cullen cooks up a storm in the restaurant (**£££-££**). This is a fabulous retreat in the northwest of Scotland. Recommended.

££-£ Veyatie Lochinver, 66 Baddidarroch, T01571-844424, www.veyatie-scotland. co.uk. Open all year. 3 rooms. Superior B&B, welcomes pets and hill walkers.

£ Polcraig, T01571-844429, cathelmac@aol. com. Open all year. 5 en suite rooms. Large modern house offering a friendly welcome and good value B&B.

Loch Assynt and Inchnadamph p55

£££-££ Inchnadamph Hotel, Assynt, T01571-822202, www.inchnadamphhotel. co.uk. An old-fashioned Highland hotel on the shores of Loch Assynt, catering for the hunting and fishing fraternity, see page 116.

££-£ Inchnadamph Lodge, Assynt Field Centre, T01571-822218, www.inch-lodge. co.uk.co.uk. Open all year, but phone ahead Nov-Mar. Great hostel accommodation in bunk rooms, as well as twin, double and family rooms. Continental breakfast is included. It's ideally situated for climbing Ben More Assynt and guides are available.

Lochinver to Kylesku p117

There's not much accommodation around here other than self-catering cottages.

Camping

Clachtoll Beach Campsite, 6 miles north of Lochinver, T01571-855377. May-Sep. Good facilities, friendly owners and in a superb location. Recommended.

Kylesku p118

£££ Kylesku Hotel, T01971-502231, www. kyleskuhotel.co.uk. 6 en suite, tastefully furnished rooms with views across the sea lochs and neighbouring mountains. This is a great place simply to relax, enjoy a malt and dine on great value pub meals and restaurant fare that draws on the best of the region's lamb, beef and seafood. Enjoy.

£££-££ Newton Lodge, T01971-502070, www.newtonlodge.co.uk. Mid-Mar to mid-Oct. 7 en suite rooms. Great views, especially if you use the telescope in the conservatory. Keep an eye out for wildlife, including eagles, and enjoy a chance to really unwind with delicious home-cooking. Another fine example of hospitality that rewards those who make the effort to explore Scotland's landscape beyond Inverness.

Self-catering

Kylesku Lodges, T01971-502003. Beautifully appointed lodges with a patio and delightful wood finishings that overlook sea lochs. Great option for couples and families who wish to escape, fish (wild brown trout), spot wildlife or simply relax. From £395 per week.

Scourie and Handa Island p118

There are lots of options in this area, including the following:

£££-££ Eddrachilles Hotel, Badcall Bay, T01971-502080, www.eddrachilles.com. Mar-Oct. 12 en suite rooms. This charming 200 year-old building stands in 300 acres of grounds overlooking the bay. The food on offer is superb and there's an excellent range of malt whiskies behind the bar.

£££-££ Scourie Hotel, Scourie, T01971-502396, www.scourie-hotel.co.uk. Open Apr-Oct. 20 rooms. A 17th-century former coaching inn popular with anglers, which is also an excellent place to eat (lunch **££**, dinner **£££**).

££ Scourie Lodge, Scourie, T01971-502248. Open Mar-Oct. 3 rooms. There are several B&Bs in the village, but none better than this welcoming lodge. Also does good evening meals and dinner, B&B option from £55.

Camping

There's a campsite on Harbour Rd, T01971-502060.

Kinlochbervie and around p119

£££ Rhiconich Hotel, Rhiconich, T01971-521224, www.rhiconichhotel.co.uk. Open all year. 10 en suite rooms. Modern functional hotel with good facilities and surrounded by superb scenery. Good value lunch and dinner

(1800-2100), whilst you enjoy fine views over Loch Inchard and try to spot the otters, seals and myriad of the wildlife in the area.
££ Old School Hotel, Inshegra, halfway between Kinlochbervie and the A838 at Rhiconich, T01971-521383, www. oldschoolhotel.co.uk. Open Apr-Oct. 6 en suite rooms. This is the best place to stay in the area, with great food served in an intimate former classroom that dates back to the 1800s. Recommended.
£ Benview, T01971-521242. Open Apr-Sep. A friendly B&B.

Camping
There's a small campsite at Oldshoremore, T01971-521281.

Restaurants

Ullapool *p113, map p114*
££ The Ceilidh Place, see Where to stay, above. Open 1100-2300. One of those places that tourists seem to hang around for hours or even days. It exudes a laid-back, cultured ambience. The self-service coffee shop does wholefood all day during the summer, while the restaurant serves more expensive full meals, with an emphasis on vegetarian and seafood at night. There's even outdoor seating. Also hosts live music and various other events, see Bars and clubs, below. Not the cheapest in town but one of the best.
££ Mariner's Restaurant, Morefield Hotel, North Rd, T01854-612161. May-Oct. On the edge of town heading north, in the middle of a housing estate. The setting may be alittle incongruous but the seafood is sensational, which is why people travel from miles around. Good value.
££-£ The Frigate, Shore St, T01854-612969. Open daily 0900-2130. Whether you want porridge for breakfast, a mid-morning bagel, kids meals or steak pie, this bright café bistro caters for all tastes. It's also a good place to stock up on picnic items. Try the ice-cream.
££-£ Seaforth Inn, Quay St, T01854-612122. Popular and award-winning pub serving

delicious seafood, and other staples to suit all pockets. Bar meals downstairs are good value. Their chippy next door is also an award-winning eatery. Gets busy at weekends.
£ Tea Store, 27 Argyll St, T01845-612995. Daily 0800-2000. No-nonsense café serving all day breakfasts, etc, and home-baked goodies. Recommended for a hearty breakfast and to meet the local prawn fishermen.

Achiltibuie *p116*
£££ Summer Isles Hotel, see Where to stay, above. This hotel boasts a great restaurant serving some of the best seafood on the planet. A fine seafood lunch will cost you around £25, whilst a sublime 5-course set dinner will set you back around £52 a head but you can enjoy delicious bar lunches for a fraction of the price. Even if you're not staying or eating here, it's worth stopping to have a drink on the terrace and watch the sun set over the islands. Recommended.

Lochinver and around *p116*
££ Culag Hotel, Lochinver, T01571-844270. Sitting by the harbour, this hotel doesn't impress from the outside but as many locals know this is a great place for a pint, banter and a reasonably priced lunch.
££ Riverside Bistro, Main St, on the way into town on the A837, T01571-844356. Apart from the hotel listed above, the best food is here. Try their famous pies which use the best in local venison, beef, poultry and seafood, and there are also vegetarian and sweet options available. Eat in or takeaway. Not cheap but tasty, with views over the sea.
£ Caberfeidh, Main St, T01571-844321. Near to the bistro, this is the cheap and cheerful option.

Scourie and Handa Island *p118*
££ Old School Hotel & Restaurant, see Where to stay, above. Daily 1200-1400, 1800-2000. Serve really good, home-cooked food to grateful souls who have ventured this far north. The best for miles around.
££ Seafood Restaurant, Tarbet, just above the tiny jetty, T01971-502251, www.seafood

restaurant-tarbet.co.uk. Run by Julian Pearce who also runs Laxford Cruise, see What to do, below. If you're up this way, don't miss a visit to this restaurant which serves the latest catch from the boats. It's a wonderful, if unexpected, place to find, with views across the sea inlets. Recommended.

♪ Bars and clubs

Ullapool *p113, map p114*
Arch Inn, 11 West Shore St, T01854-612454. If you want reasonable bar food, a pool table and a jumping atmosphere as you down your pint, then this is the place to be.
The Ceilidh Place, see Where to stay, above. For something bit more sedate and civilized than the other choices, head here where you can enjoy a quiet drink in the cosy **Parlour Bar** or take advantage of their varied programme of events. There's live music Mon-Sat throughout the summer, and on a Mon in winter there are also ceilidhs and poetry readings. The clubhouse opposite stages plays.
Ferry Boat Inn (or 'FBI' as it's known locally), Shore St. Ullapool's favourite pub though very cramped. It has a Thu night live music session year round, and during the summer you can sit outside on the sea wall and watch the sun go down as you drain your pint of superb real ale.
Seaforth Inn, see Restaurants, above. Gets busy at weekends and has a barn-like feel, but it's a great place to eat and hear live music.

✤ Festivals

Ullapool *p113, map p114*
Sep **Loopallu Festival**, www.loopallu.co.uk. Big music festival held over a weekend in late Sep. Started in 2005 and has seized the imagination of music lovers around the country. Held in various venues around town.

♥ Shopping

Ullapool *p113, map p114*
There's no major supermarket but the town is well supplied with shops.
The Captain's Cabin, on the corner of Quay St and Shore St. Sells books, as wellas crafts and souvenirs.
The Ceilidh Place, see Where to stay, above. Has a good bookshop if you don't plan to head for **Achins** by Lochinver.
Highland Stoneware, Mill St, heading north towards Morefield, T01854-612980, www. highlandstoneware.com. Look no further than here for high quality, hand turned and painted pottery. You can wander round the studios before browsing in their gift shop, which is pricey, but you may have luck in their bargain baskets.
Mountain Man Supplies, opposite the museum, West Argyle St. A good outdoor equipment shop.
On The Rocks, 114 Achmelvich, by Lochinver, T01571-844312. Mon-Sat 1000-1700. Craft shop and gallery, including original paintings of the beautiful sands at Achmelvich.
Unlimited Colour Company, 28 Argyle St, T01854-612844. Mon-Sat 0900-1700. An excellent option for all manner of brightly coloured, hand-dyed natural weaves, scarves, hats, cushions and throws.

Lochinver and around *p116*
Highland Stoneware, above the northern shore of the bay, Lochinver, T01571-844376, Nov-Mar Mon-Fri 0900-1800, Easter-Oct Mon-Fri 0900-1800, Sat 0900-1700, www. highlandstoneware.com. The main 'factory' for this high-quality, hand turned and painted pottery.

✪ What to do

Ullapool *p113, map p114*
Boat tours
Seascape Expeditions, T01854-633708, www.sea-scape.co.uk. 2-hr trips that leave from Ullapool harbour daily in summer

aboard a fast-rib (£28.50 per person). It's an exhilarating 40-mile sea-trip around the Summer Isles with the chance to spot wildlife.
Summer Queen Cruises, 1 Royal Park, T01854-612472, www.summerqueen.co.uk. During the summer, the *MV Summer Queen*, runs 4-hr cruises to the Summer Isles, with a 45-min landing on Tanera Mór with its café and post office. Leave Mon-Sat at 1000 from the pier and costs £26, £13 child. There are also 2-hr wildlife cruises around Loch Broom, Annat Bay and Isle Martin, which leave daily at 1415. Both options offer opportunities to wildlife watch, including possibly seals, dolphins and even minke whales. From £18. Cruises can be booked at the booth by the pier or by calling the number above.

Deer stalking
North Assynt Estate, T01571-855298, www.sportingassynt.co.uk. For deer stalking from late Jul-Oct.

Fishing
With over 150 lochs filled with wild trout and salmon, Assynt is also excellent for fishing. **Assynt Angling Group**, www.assyntangling.co.uk; **Assynt Crofters Trust**, T01571-855298, www.assyntcrofters.co.uk.

Tour operators
Cape Adventure, Ardmore, Rhiconich, T01971-521006, www.capeadventure.co.uk For multi-adventures, including walking weeks and weekends, and sea kayaking, contact this excellentoutdoor operator.

Achiltibuie *p116*
I Macleod, Achiltibuie Post Office, T01854-622200, or at home T018754-622315. For cruises to the Summer Isles from Achiltibuie pier on board the *Hectoria*. Cruises leave Mon-Sat at 1100 and 1430 during Jul and Aug, 1100 only for the rest of year and last approx 3 hrs, with 1 hr ashore on the islands. They cost £22 per person (½-price for children).

Kylesku *p118*
On board the *MV Statesman*, T01971-502345, cruises go to Eas a'Chùal Aluinn waterfall leaving from the old ferry jetty below the Kylesku Hotel. You can also see porpoises, seals and minke whales en route. The 2-hr round trip runs Apr-Oct Mon-Thu and Sun 1100-1500. Costs £15, children £5. You may be able to get closer to the falls by getting off the boat and walking to the bottom, then getting on the next boat.

Scourie and Handa Island *p118*
Laxford Cruises, Seafood Restaurant, Tarbet, T01971-502345. Sail around beautiful Loch Laxford, where you can see lots of birds from nearby Handa Island, as well as seals, porpoises and otters. Trips leave Easter-Sep Sun-Fri 1000, 1200 and 1400. The trips last 1 hr 45 mins and cost £16. For bookings contact Julian Pearce at the restaurant just above the jetty.

⊖ Transport

Ullapool *p113, map p114*
Bus Scottish Citylink buses run Mon-Sat between Ullapool and **Inverness**. There are also buses Mon-Sat to **Inverness** with Rapson's Coaches, T01463-710555, and Spa Coaches, T01997-421311. There are buses Mon-Sat from Inverness to **Lochinver** via Ullapool with **Spa Coaches** and **Tim Dearman Coaches**, T01349-883585. The bus continues to **Achmelvich Youth Hostel**. From Mon-Sat (Sun only in Jul and Aug) there's a daily bus from Inverness via **Ullapool**, **Lochinver**, **Kylesku**, **Scourie** and **Rhiconich** to **Durness** with **Tim Dearman** coaches (carries a bike trailer too). There's a bus Mon, Wed, Thu and Sat to **Gairloch**, operated by **Westerbus**, T01445-712255.

Car hire Daley's Deals, Morefield Industrial Estate, T01854-612848.

Cycle hire Available at hostels (see page 119).

Achiltibuie p116

Bus D&E Coaches, T01463-222444, run Mon-Sat between **Ullapool** and Achiltibuie. There is 1 bus that leaves Achiltibuie on a Sat at 0751, reaching Polbain Stores at 0755, **Altandhu** at 0800, and **Ullapool** at 0900.

Another possibility Mon-Sat is to take the Spa Coaches or Dearman Coach (No 67) from **Ullapool ferry terminal** (1637) to Drumbeg shop via **Elphin** (1656), **Inchnadamph** (1711), **Lochinver** (1730) and **Achmelvich Youth Hostel** before requesting a stop at **Stoer** (1758), **Clashnessie** (1803) or **Drumbeg** (1813).

Lochinver and around p116

Bus There's a postbus service from **Lochinver** to **Lairg**, Mon-Sat, that runs along the main road via **Elphin**. However on its 3rd run from Lochinver post office (1355) it will (on request) detour to **Drumbeg** (1439) via **Clashnessie** (1429) and **Stoer** (1414).

Scourie and Handa Island p118

Bus There's a Tim Dearman Coach service, T01349-883585, once a day Mon-Sat (Apr-Sep) from **Inverness bus station** (0850) via **Ullapool**, **Lochinver** and **Kylesku** to **Scourie** that continues to **Laxford Bridge** (1307), **Kinlochbervie** (1327) and **Rhiconich** (1340) to arrive in **Durness** at 1405.

Kinlochbervie and around p119

Bus George Rapson and IP Mackay, T01971-511343, run Mon-Sat between **Balnakiel Craft Village** (0800) and **Durness** to the train station at **Lairg** (1035) for connections to **Inverness** via **Rhiconich** (0830) and **Kinlochbervie** (0845). On Wed, IP Mackay, T01971-511343, buses travel from **Kinlochbervie Ceilidh Place** (1600) and past the Rhiconich Hotel to **Durness** (35 mins). To travel between **Sheigra** and Kinlochbervie, call Allan Bruce Taxis, T01971-521477.

Directory

Ullapool p113, map p114
Bank Royal Bank of Scotland, Ladysmith St; Bank of Scotland, West Argyle St, with ATM.

North coast

Scotland's rugged north coast is not for the faint hearted: over 100 miles of storm-lashed cliffs, sheer rocky headlands and deserted sandy coves backed by a desolate and eerily silent wilderness of mountain, bog and hill loch; the only place on mainland Britain where arctic flora and fauna come down to sea level. This is Britain's most spectacular and undisturbed coastline, a great place for birdwatching, with vast colonies of seabirds, and there's also a good chance of seeing seals, porpoises and minke whales in the more sheltered estuaries.

Arriving on the north coast

Getting there and around
Getting around the far north without your own transport can be a slow process. Getting to Thurso, the main town, by bus or train is easy, but beyond that things get more difficult. Highland Country Buses run a regular service between Thurso train station and John o'Groats from Monday to Saturday, with at least three daily stopping en route at Gill's Bay. They also run a daily service from Thurso train station to Scrabster (at least three times daily) but it's strongly advised to call ahead (T01463-710555) to confirm times in order not to miss your ferry connection. ▸▸ *See Transport, page 133.*

Tourist information
Durness TIC ① *T01971-511259, Apr-Oct Mon-Sat, Jun-Aug daily*, arranges guided walks and has a small visitor centre with displays on local history, flora and fauna and geology. The **Thurso TIC** ① *Riverside Rd, T01847-893155, Mar-May Mon-Sat 0930-1600, 31 May-4 Jun Mon-Sat 0930-1630, Sun 1000-1600, Jul-5 Sep 0930-1730, Sun 1000-1600, Sep-31 Oct Mon-Sat 0930-1630, Oct-Mar closed*, has a leaflet on local surfing beaches.

Durness and around → *For listings, see pages 131-133. Phone code 01971.*

Durness is not only the most northwesterly village on the British mainland, but also one of the most attractively located, surrounded by sheltered coves of sparkling white sand and machair-covered limestone cliffs. It's worth stopping here for a few days to explore the surrounding area. One of the village's most famous visitors was John Lennon, who used to spend childhood summers here with his Aunt Elizabeth, a local resident. This unlikely relationship was marked in 2002 with the creation of the **John Lennon Memorial Garden**. Beatles fans can now visit this lovely spot which features sculptures by local artist Lotte Glob, as well as standing stones bearing the lyrics to the fab four's classic *In My Life*.

Smoo Cave

A mile east of the village is the vast 200-ft-long Smoo Cave. A path from near the youth hostel leads down to the cave entrance which is hidden away at the end of a steep, narrow inlet. Plunging through the roof of the cathedral-like cavern is an 80-ft waterfall which can be seen from the entrance, but the more adventurous can take a boat trip into the floodlit interior.

A few miles east of the Smoo Cave are a couple of excellent beaches, at **Sangobeg** and **Rispond**, where the road leaves the coast and heads south along the west shore of stunning **Loch Eriboll**. Eriboll is Britain's steepest sea loch and was used by the Royal Navy during the Second World War as a base for protecting Russian convoys.

Balnakeil

About a mile northwest of Durness is the tiny hamlet of Balnakeil, overlooked by a ruined 17th-century church. In the south wall is a grave slab with carved skull-and-crossbones marking the grave of the notorious highwayman Donald MacMurchow. If you're looking for souvenirs, or an escape from the rat race, then head for the **Balnakeil Craft Village** ① *Apr-Oct daily 1000-1800*, an alternative artists' community set up in the 1960s in a former RAF radar station. Here you can buy weavings, pottery, paintings, leatherwork and woodwork in the little prefab huts. The Chocolatier and 'Chocolate Bar' café, **Cocoa Mountain**, is a must visit, specializing in fresh handmade truffles, hot chocolates, coffees and organic teas. You can watch the chocolates being made on the premises. Balnakeil has also become well known in golfing circles. The nine-hole golf course ① *T01971-511364*, is the most northerly in mainland Britain, and its famous ninth hole involves a drive over the Atlantic Ocean. The beach here is glorious, especially in fine weather when the sea turns a brilliant shade of turquoise. Even better, walk north along the bay to Faraid Head, where you can see puffin colonies in early summer. The views across to Cape Wrath in the west and Loch Eriboll in the east, are stupendous.

Cape Wrath

There are several excellent trips around Durness, but the most spectacular is to Cape Wrath, Britain's most northwesterly point. It's a wild place and the name seems entirely appropriate, though it actually derives from the Norse word *hwarf*, meaning 'turning place'. Viking ships used it as a navigation point during their raids on the Scottish west coast. Now a lighthouse stands on the cape, above the 1000 ft-high Clo Mor Cliffs, the highest on the mainland, and breeding ground for huge colonies of seabirds.

You can walk south from here to **Sandwood Bay**, see page 119. It's an exhilarating but long coastal walk, and will take around eight hours. It's safer doing this walk from north to south as the area around the headland is a military firing range and access may be restricted, which could leave you stranded.

To get to Cape Wrath, first take the passenger **ferry** ① *T01971-511343 or 511287, May-Sep daily, £5 return*, across the Kyle of Durness from Keoldale, 2 miles south of Durness. The ferry then connects with a **minibus** ① *T01971-511343, £8*, for the 11 mile journey to the cape (40 minutes).

Tongue to Thurso

The road east from Durness runs around **Loch Eriboll** on its way to the lovely little village of **Tongue**. A causeway crosses the beautiful Kyle of Tongue, but a much more scenic route is the single-track road around its southern side, with great views of **Ben Hope** (3041 ft) looming to the southwest. The village of Tongue is overlooked by the 14th-century ruins of **Varick Castle**, and there's a great beach at **Coldbackie**, 2 miles northeast.

The A836 runs south from Tongue through Altnaharra to Lairg, see page 138. It also continues east to the crofting community of **Bettyhill**, named after the Countess of Sutherland who ruthlessly evicted her tenants from their homes in Strathnaver to make way for more profitable sheep. The whole sorry saga is told in the interesting **Strathnaver Museum** ① *T01641-521418, Apr-Oct Mon-Sat 1000-1300, 1400-1700, £2, concessions £1.50, students, £1, children 50p*, housed in an old church in the village and tells the story of crofting life at the time of the Strathnaver Clearances. There are also Pictish stones in the churchyard behind the museum.

The museum sells a leaflet detailing the many prehistoric sites in the Strathnaver Valley which runs due south from Bettyhill. There are a couple of great beaches around Bettyhill, at **Farr Bay** and at **Torrisdale Bay**, which is the more impressive of the two and forms part of the **Invernaver Nature Reserve**. There's a small **TIC** ① *T01641-521244, Easter-Sep Mon-Sat 1015-1700*, in Bettyhill.

East from Bettyhill the hills of Sutherland begin to give way to the fields of Caithness. The road passes the turn-off to **Strathy Point** before reaching **Melvich**, another small crofting settlement overlooking a lovely sandy bay.

South from Melvich the A897 heads to Helmsdale, see page 141, through the **Flow Country**, a vast expanse of bleak bog of major ecological importance. About 15 miles south of Melvich at Forsinard is an **RSPB Visitor Centre** ① *T01641-571225, www.rspb.co.uk, Easter-Oct daily 0900-1730*, the guided walks through the nature reserve leave from here. These peatlands are a breeding ground for black- and red-throated divers, golden plovers and merlins as well as other species. Otters and roe deer can also be spotted.

Thurso and around → *For listings, see pages 131-133.*

Thurso is the most northerly town on the British mainland and by far the largest settlement on the north coast. In medieval times it was Scotland's chief port for trade with Scandinavia, though most of the town dates from the late 18th century when Sir John Sinclair built the 'new' extension to the old fishing port. The town increased in size to accommodate the workforce of the new nuclear power plant at nearby Dounreay, but the plant's demise has threatened the local economy. Today Thurso is a fairly nondescript place, mostly visited by people catching the ferry to Stromness in Orkney, or the occasional hardcore surfer.

Thurso → *Phone code 01847. Population 9000.*

There's little of real interest in the town centre, but the train station is at the south end of Princes St. Near the harbour are the 17th-century ruins of **Old St Peter's Church**, which stand on the site of the original 13th-century church founded by the Bishop of Caithness. The **Heritage Museum**, which features some Pictish carved stones, now forms part of the **Caithness Horizons** ① *www.caithnesshorizons.co.uk*, development which is situated in the town hall on the High Street. There may be little in the way of activity in the town, but 10 miles west of Thurso there's plenty of radioactivity at the **Dounreay Nuclear Power Station**. Though its fast breeder reactors were decommissioned in 1994, the plant is still a major local employer and now reprocesses spent nuclear fuel. The **Dounreay Visitor Centre**, previously situated at the power station, is now part of the Caithness Horizons development and offers the opportunity to learn more about nuclear power.

Strathmore to Braemore → *OS sheet No 11 covers the route.*

This walk gives a flavour of the bleak but beautiful landscape of the Caithness hinterland. The 16-mile linear route starts from **Strathmore Lodge**. To get there, head south from Thurso on the B874. After a short distance turn on to the B870 and follow it for 10 miles to the little hamlet of Westerdale, which stands on the River Thurso. Turn right here on to an unnumbered road and follow this road for about 5 miles. Just past the white Strathmore Lodge the road splits. Follow the right-hand track which runs through commercial forestry, before emerging on to open moor with Loch More on the left.

Where the forestry begins again on the right, the track swings left across an arm of the loch and heads southwards. At the southern end of the loch a track runs left to **Dalnaha**, but keep going straight ahead, along the valley of the River Thurso. You then reach a cluster of buildings at **Dalnawillan Lodge**. Ignore the track which heads off to the right and carry straight on, past the house at **Dalganachan**, over Rumsdale Water and on to the

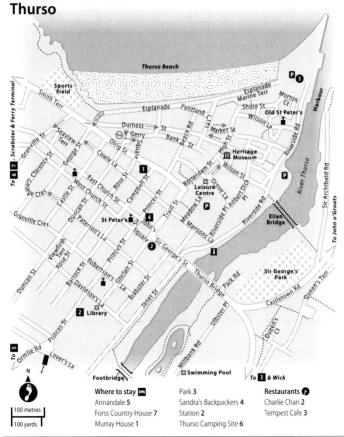

Thurso

Where to stay
Annandale **5**
Forss Country House **7**
Murray House **1**

Park **3**
Sandra's Backpackers **4**
Station **2**
Thurso Camping Site **6**

Restaurants
Charlie Chan **2**
Tempest Cafe **3**

junction before **The Glutt**, which is a series of buildings. Turn left here and follow the track for a further 4 miles until you reach the junction beside Lochan nan Bò Riabach. Continue down the valley of Berriedale Water to Braemore. There is no public transport from here, so you'll have to arrange your own transport if you don't want to retrace your steps.

Dunnet Head ➔ *Phone code 01847.*

About 10 miles northeast of Thurso is the most northerly point on the British mainland. No, not John o'Groats, but Dunnet Head. It's reached by turning off the Thurso to John o'Groats road at Dunnett, at the east end of Dunnett Bay, a 3-mile-long sandy beach that's popular with surfers who come to tackle the gigantic waves of the **Pentland Firth**, the wild and treacherous strait between the mainland and Orkney. Dunnet Bay has an excellent reef break and there's another good reef break at Brims Ness to the west. Further west still, at Strathy Bay, you'll find rollers that can match anything in Hawaii (though the water's obviously a lot colder). Dunnett Head is a much nicer place than John o'Groats, with marvellous views across to Orkney and along the entire north coast (on a clear day). There's a Victorian lighthouse out at the point, and the dramatic seacliffs are teeming with seabirds. There's also a great little café, see Restaurants page 132.

Some 15 miles east of Thurso are the **Castle and Gardens of Mey** ① *T01847-851473, www.castleofmey.org.uk, May-Jul, mid-Aug to Sep daily 1030-1600, £9.50, concessions £8.50, children £4, under 5s free, family £23, visitor centre, tea room and shop open daily 1000-1700.* Built by the 4th Earl of Caithness, the castle's future was under threat until the intervention of the late Queen Mother who bought it in 1952 and who holidayed here every year. The castle still welcomes royal visitors in the shape of Prince Charles who holidays here each summer.

John o'Groats ➔ *Phone code 01955.*

Let's be honest, John o'Groat's isn't the most inspiring place to visit. It's beloved by tourists who think they've reached the northernmost point of the UK mainland (it's actually Dunnet Head) and charity walkers, runners and cyclists who've made the admirable long haul from Land's End over 700 miles to the south. But with the notable exception of the excellent **Northcoast Marine Adventures** fast rib tours at the harbour, there's little here to persuade you to prolong your stay. It gets its name from the Dutchman Jan de Groot, who was commissioned by King James IV to run a ferry service to Orkney in 1496. Ferries still operate from here to Burwick in Orkney, see Transport, page 133. There's a **TIC** ① *T01955-611373, Apr-Oct Mon-Sat,* as well as a post office, craft shops and a chippy.

Two miles east of John o'Groats is **Duncansby Head**, which is far more rewarding. South of the headland a path leads to the spectacular **Duncansby Stacks**, a series of dramatic rock formations. The 200-ft cliffs are home to countless seabirds and you can see the narrow, sheer-sided inlets known locally as *geos*.

North coast listings

For hotel and restaurant price codes and other relevant information, see pages 13-20.

⊖ Where to stay

Durness and around *p126*
£££ Mackays Rooms & Restaurant, Durness, T01971-511202, www.visitmackays.com. Easter-Oct. 7 en suite rooms. The modern, uninspiring exterior hides one of the best hotel experiences in the north of Scotland. Rooms are spacious and tastefully furnished with not a hint of tartan cheesiness on display. Staff are efficient and the food in the restaurant a revelation. Excellent value. Recommended.

£££-££ Tongue Hotel, Tongue, T01847-611206. Open all year (except Christmas week). 19 en suite rooms. This former hunting lodge of the infamous Duke of Sutherland has great views across the Kyle of Tongue and the staff are extremely accommodating. Catering mostly for anglers it can arrange impromptu fishing trips and the restaurant does good food.

££ Ben Loyal Hotel, Tongue, T01847-611216, www.benloyal.co.uk. Open all year. 11 en suite rooms. Friendly, hospitable small hotel and a good choice for the area. Food is recommended and the bar is a good place to while away an evening or 2.

££ Bighouse Lodge, Melvich, T01641-531207, www.bighouseestate.com. Open May-Oct. 12 rooms. 18th-century mansion converted into a small hotel at the mouth of the Halladale river in 4 acres of its own grounds. Mainly aimed at the huntin' shootin' an' fishin' brigade.

££ Farr Bay Inn, Bettyhill, T01641-521230, www.farrbayinn.co.uk. 4 good en suite rooms and decent bar food too. Note that the property is for sale at the time of writing, as a going concern.

££ Glengolly B&B, Durness, T01971-511255, www.glengolly.com. Open all year. 3 rooms, all with en suite or private facilities. Good value B&B in a working croft.

££ Rhian Cottage, Tongue, T01847-611257, www.rhiancottage.co.uk. Open all year. 5 rooms. Good value B&B with comfortable rooms and conservatory. Great breakfasts (cater for vegans) with lovely touches that include filling your thermos flask and preparing a packed lunch (£6.50).

£ Cloisters, Talmine, T01847-601286, www.cloistertal.demon.co.uk. Open all year. 3 en suite rooms, 1 with disabled facilities. B&B in 19th-century converted church.

£ Durness SYHA Youth Hostel, Smoo, to the east of the village, T01971-511264, www.syha.org.uk. Mid-Mar to early Oct. Basic but comfortable, and handy for the beach and Smoo cave.

£ SYHA Youth Hostel, Tongue, T01847-611789, T08701-553255. Mid-Mar to late Oct. Beautifully situated at the east end of the causeway, with views towards Ben Loyal and the sea lochs. Great value.

Camping
Talmine, T01847-601225, 5 miles north of Tongue. By the beach.

Thurso and around *p128, map p129*
Thurso has a wide variety of accommodation, most of it fairly average.

£££ Borgie Lodge Hotel, Skerray, by Thurso, T01641-521332, www.borgie lodgehotel. co.uk. Open all year. 8 rooms (7 en suite). Fine, small country hotel with appeal for gun sports and fishing types but also very fine food.

£££-££ Forss Country House Hotel, 4 miles out of Thurso at Bridge of Forss, T01847-861201, www.forsshousehotel. co.uk. The nicest place to stay by far around Thurso, if not the entire north coast. This small, family-run hotel is set in 20 acres of lovely woodland and has an excellent restaurant (**£££-££**), open to non-residents (but pre-book). Rooms are spacious (the en suite bathrooms are bigger than many other hotel rooms), the attention to detail is impressive and the service is spot on. Nothing is too much trouble for the staff here. Highly recommended.

££ Bencorragh House, Upper Gills in Canisbay, a few miles west of John o'Groats, T01955-611449, www.bencorraghhouse.com. Mar-Oct. Very decent B&B in farmhouse.

££ Murray House, 1 Campbell St, T01847-895759, www.murrayhousebb.com. Open all year. 5 en suite rooms. Friendly and welcoming B&B, dinner also available by prior arrangement. Good value.

££ Park Hotel, Oldfield, at the south end of town, 10 mins' walk from train station, T01847-893251, www.parkhotelthurso.co.uk. Open all year. 21 en suite rooms. Modern and rather functional building but clean, comfortable and extremely hospitable with good food at reasonable prices. Rooms at the front have best views.

££ Sharvedda, Strathy Point, by Thurso, T01641-541311, www.sharvedda.co.uk. 3 rooms. Good quality B&B also offering evening meals by prior arrangement.

££ Station Hotel & Apartments, 54 Princes St, Thurso, T01847-892003, www.stationthurso.co.uk. Open all year. 38 en suite rooms. Central with decent food. Friendly and welcoming, good value.

£ Annandale, 2 Rendel Govan Rd, T01847-893942, thomson@annandale2.freeserve.co.uk. Open all year. 3 rooms. Very good-value B&B.

£ Sandra's Backpackers, 24-26 Princes St, T01847-894575, www.sandras-backpackers.co.uk. Probably the best option at the very cheapest end of the scale and right beside a good chip shop.

Camping

There are a couple of campsites at John o'Groats and further west by the beach at Huna. Ask at the TIC.

Thurso Camping Site, north of town on the road to Scrabster, T01847-892244. The nearest campsite to Thurso.

❼ Restaurants

Durness and around *p126*

££ The Seafood Platter, Durness, T01971-511224. Open Mar-Oct Mon-Sat 1000-1700 (till 2100 peak season), Sun 1200-1700. Fresh, local seafood cooked at its best. Recommended.

£ Cocoa Mountain, Balnakeil Craft Village, Durness, T01971 511233, www.cocoa mountain.co.uk. Easter-Sep 0900-1800, Oct-Easter 1000-1700. Very popular, high-quality chocolatier and café.

Thurso and around *p128, map p129*

The **Forss Country House Hotel** (see Where to stay, above), is the best place to eat in the area; the other hotels listed are good options in town for a decent meal.

£££ The Bower Inn, between Thurso and Wick, turn off the coast road at Castletown and follow the B876 until you see the sign for Gillock, T01955-661292. A close second to the **Forss** for upmarket places to eat in the area.

£££ The Captain's Galley, Scrabster, T01847-894999, www.captainsgalley.co.uk. Open for dinner Tue-Sat 1900-2100. Small restaurant so booking is a must. Top-notch seafood restaurant in unpretentious surroundings, just the freshest of food brought to you within mins of being landed (or so it seems). Best choice hereabouts.

££ Charlie Chan, 2 Sinclair St, T01847-890888. Best of the ubiquitous Chinese restaurants in town.

£ Dunnett Head Tearoom, Dunnett Head, a few miles from the lighthouse, T01847-851774. Apr-Oct daily 1500-2000. Serves snacks and meals to hardy surfers.

£ Tempest Café, by the harbour next to the surf shop of the same name (see What to do, below), T01847-892500, www.tempestsurf.co.uk. Open Tue-Sun 1000-1800. Good, chilled vibe. Menu features typical surfer-type fare (ie loads of carbs).

🎭 Entertainment

Thurso and around *p128, map p129*
Viking Bowl, Ormlie Rd, T01847-895050.
Compex with bowling and cinema.

🎯 What to do

Thurso and around *p128, map p129*
Boat trips
John o'Groats Ferries, Ferry Office, John
o'Groats, T01955-611353, www.jogferry.
co.uk. Operate **Orkney Islands Day Tours**,
which leave daily May-Sep at 0900, return
at 1945 (£46, children £23, under 5s free).
A shorter day tour goes daily from Jun-Sep
at 1030, returns at 1800 (£42, children
£12, under 5s free). There's also a wildlife
cruise Jun-Aug, which departs at 1430 (£15,
children £7.50, under 5s free, family £37.50).
Northcoast Marine Adventures, John
o'Groats harbour, T01955-611797, www.
northcoast-marine-adventures.co.uk. Mar-
Oct daily 1000-1930. Whether you want to
spot seals, explore sea caves or zip across
the huge waves of the Pentland Firth, you'll
have fun aboard this high powered rigid
inflatable boat that leaves every 2nd hour
from the harbour. £20, children £12.

Surfing
The best break in the region, indeed, one
of the best breaks in the world, is Thurso
East. For a detailed description of the wave
and how to access it, see Footprint's *Surfing
Britain*, which describes all the breaks along
this coast. A good surf shop is **Tempest Surf**,
by the harbour in Thurso, T01847-892500,
www.tempestsurf.co.uk. Daily 1000-1800.

🚌 Transport

Durness and around *p126*
Bus On the 2nd and 4th Sat of every
month there's 1 bus from **Durness** post
office, via **Tongue** and **Bettyhill** to **Thurso**
with IP Mackay, T01971-511343. There's a

postbus service from **Tongue** to **Lairg** via
Altnaharra, Mon-Sat, departing Tongue at
0815 Mon-Fri and 0745 on a Sat.
From Mon-Sat (Sun Jul-Aug only) there's
a daily bus from **Durness** to **Inverness**
via **Rhiconich**, **Scourie**, **Kyleskuand**,
Lochinver, **Ullapool** with Tim Dearman
coaches, T01349-883585, it carries a bike
trailer too. On a Wed only, IP Mackay buses,
T01971-511343 (No 807), runs between
Durness (1635), and **Kinlochbervie**.

Thurso and around *p128, map p129*
Bus Citylink buses, T0870-5505050, run
to **Inverness** 4 times daily, 3½ hrs. Those
from Inverness continue to **Scrabster**
to connect with ferries to **Stromness**
in **Orkney**. Citylink buses to **Inverness**
connect with buses to **Edinburgh**.
Highland Country Buses, T01463-710555,
run local services to **Bettyhill**, 3 times
daily Mon-Fri, 1 hr 10 mins, on a route that
includes **Reay**. There are regular daily buses
to **Wick** via **Halkirk** or **Castletown**.

Car hire William Dunnett & Co,
T01847-893101, www.dunnets.co.uk.

Cycle hire The Bike & Camping Shop,
the Arcade, 34 High St, T01847-896124.
Rents mountain bikes for £10 per day.

Ferry Northlink Ferries, www.northlink
ferries.co.uk, to **Stromness** in (Orkney)
leave from **Scrabster**, 2 miles north of
Thurso. John o'Groats Ferries sail to
Burwick (Orkney) twice daily from
May-Sep, 40 mins, £18 one way, £28
return. A connecting bus takes
passengers on to **Kirkwall**, 40 mins,
price included in ferry ticket.

Train 3 trains leave daily from **Inverness**
(3½ hrs), 2 of them connecting with the
ferries from **Scrabster** to **Stromness**
(Orkney). Trains continue to **Wick** (30 mins)
and trains to **Inverness** leave from here.

East coast

The east coast of the Highlands, from Inverness north to Wick, doesn't have the same draw as the west coast and attracts far fewer visitors, but it has its own, gentler appeal, and there are many lovely little seaside towns to explore, especially the singular former sea port of Cromarty. The main attraction in these parts, though, is undoubtedly the resident pod of bottlenose dolphins, which can be seen along the Moray coast between May and September.

The Black Isle → *For listings, see pages 143-147. Phone code 01381.*

Across the Kessock Bridge from Inverness is the Black Isle, which is neither an island nor black. It enjoys long hours of sunshine and low rainfall, and is an attractive landscape of rolling acres of barley and stately woods of oak and beech dropping down to the Moray coast. It also has a compelling atmosphere – a combination perhaps of its soft microclimate, lush vegetation and attractive architecture. Its main attractions are the picturesque town of Cromarty and Chanonry Point, on the southern side near Rosemarkie, which is one of the best dolphin-spotting sites in Europe.

North Kessock to Tore

On the north side of the Kessock Bridge, just north of the village, is the North Kessock **TIC** ① *T0845 2255121, Easter-Oct daily.* Next door is the **Dolphin and Seal Visitor Centre**, which gives details of accredited dolphin cruises. You can see dolphins from the village of North Kessock just to the south.

One of the many sacred wells (and caves) in the area is the unmissable **Clootie Well**, on the verge of the main road between Tore and Munlochy Bay Nature Reserve. It was once blessed by St Curitan (see below) and is thought to cure sick children. Thousands of rags still flutter from the surrounding trees, though well-worshippers are in danger of being mown down by traffic. Despite the presence of cars, it's an eerie place.

Fortrose and Chanonry Point

Further east on this road, beyond Munlochy and Avoch (pronounced *Och*) is the village of Fortrose, on the east shore. The magnificent cathedral at Fortrose is now largely a ruin; rainwashed carved faces of rose-coloured sandstone peer down from roof bosses, and snapped-off stumps of window tracery are a reminder of Reformation vandalism. On the golf course at **Chanonry Point**, overlooking the Moray Firth, a plaque marks the spot where the Brahan Seer was boiled in a barrel of tar. Chanonry Point is also a great place for seeing dolphins. They come close to shore at high tide and there's a good chance of seeing them leaping above the waves.

Rosemarkie

A few miles from Fortrose on the north side of Chanonry Point is the tiny village of Rosemarkie. Celtic saints Curitan and Boniface selected this sheltered spot on the southern shore for their Christian mission in the seventh century. St Boniface is remembered at nearby St Bennet's Well. **Groam House Museum** ① *T01381-620961, www.groamhouse. org.uk, May-Oct Mon-Sat 1000-1700, Sun 1400-1630, Mar, Apr, Nov-early Dec Sat-Sun 1400-1600, free,* houses a huge collection of Pictish sculptured stones found locally, imaginatively displayed alongside contemporary artwork inspired by them. A year-round programme of events and lectures is devoted to the study of Pictish culture. A lovely marked trail leads into Fairy Glen, now a nature reserve, from the top end of the High Street, through a wooded gorge where you may spot woodpeckers and treecreepers. The name obviously derives from the fairies that live here, though the last sighting was in the 1970s.

Cromarty → *Phone code 01381.*

On the northeastern tip of the Black Isle Peninsula, at the mouth of the Cromarty Firth, is the gorgeous wee town of Cromarty, one of the east coast's major attractions. Its neat white-harled houses interspersed with gracious merchants' residences are almost unchanged since the 18th century when it was a sea port thriving on trade as far afield as Russia and the Baltic. Many emigrants bound for the New World embarked here. The town's prosperity, based on textiles and fishing, turned to decline and dereliction. Although restored and fully populated, Cromarty now has the atmosphere of a backwater, though a very attractive one at that, where you feel as if you're stepping back in time, in stark contrast to the numerous oil rigs moored on the opposite shore in Nigg Bay.

For an insight into the history of the area, visit the 18th-century **Cromarty Courthouse** ① *Church St, T01381-600418, www.cromarty-courthouse.org.uk, Apr-Sep daily 1000-1700, Adults £2, includes loan of headset for recorded tour of the town's other historic buildings,* which houses the town's museum. Next to the courthouse is the thatch-roofed **Hugh Miller's Cottage** ① *T08444-932158, www.nts.org.uk, Mar-Sep daily 1300-1700, Oct Sun and Tue only 1300-1700, £5.50, concessions £4.50, family £15,* birthplace of the eminent local geologist and author. Also worth seeing is the elegant 17th-century **East Church**.

There's a good walk along a coastal path from the east end of the village through woodland to the top of the South Sutor headland, one of the two steep headlands guarding the narrow entrance to the Cromarty Firth. There are excellent views from here across the Moray Firth. Leaflets describing this and other local walks are available at the Cromarty Courthouse.

One of Cromarty's main attractions is its dolphins. They can be seen from the shore, or with a boat trip, see What to do, page 146. To the west, the mudflats of **Udale Bay** are an RSPB reserve and a haven for wading birds and wintering duck and geese, which can be viewed from a hide.

Poyntzfield Herb Garden is an organic plant nursery specializing in rare and native medicinal herbs. Worth visiting if only for a glimpse of the house, and the view from the car park over the Cromarty Firth through massive beech trees.

The Cromarty Firth → *For listings, see pages 143-147.*

Dingwall and around → *Phone code 01349.*

Dingwall, at the head of the Cromarty Firth, has two major claims to fame. Not only is it believed to be the birthplace of Macbeth, it was also the home for many years of Neil Gunn (1891-1973), perhaps the Highlands' greatest literary figure, see also page 141. It's a fairly dull, though functional town, with good shops and banks lining its long main street. **Dingwall Museum** ① *T01349-865366, May-Sep Mon-Sat 1000-1630, nominal entry fee payable,* tells the history of this Royal Burgh.

East of Dingwall, before Evanton, is **Storehouse of Foulis** ① *T01349-830038, www. storehouseoffoulis.co.uk, Mon-Sat 0900-1800, Sun 1000-1700, free*, which has history and wildlife exhibitions, and offers the chance to see the local seal population. Standing on a hill above **Evanton** is the **Fyrish Monument**, a replica of the Gate of Negapatam in India, built by local men and funded by local military hero, Sir Hector Munro, to commemorate his capture of the Indian town, in 1781. To get there, turn off the B9176 towards Boath. It's a stiff two-hour climb up to the top.

The Cromarty Firth is a centre for repairing North Sea oil rigs, and many of the villages along its north shore have benefited from the oil industry. One of these is **Invergordon**, just west of Nigg Bay, which has suffered in recent years due to the closure of the local aluminium factory. Beyond Invergordon, a road branches south to Nigg Ferry. The ferry from Cromarty to **Nigg** was once a major thoroughfare, and now a tiny two-car ferry makes the 20-minute crossing in the summer months (every 30 minutes from 0800-1815). From the ferry you get a good view of **Nigg Bay**, a vast natural harbour used in both world wars by the Royal Navy. Its entry is guarded by the dramatic headlands of the Sutors, identified in folklore as friendly giants. The oil rigs ranged along the firth and the oil terminal at Nigg, are a dramatic and not unpleasant contrast with Lilliputian Cromarty.

Strathpeffer and around → *Phone code 01997.*
Just along from the Cromarty Firth is Strathpeffer, which gets busy in the summer with coach parties, but it's a pleasant place and there are some excellent walks in the surrounding hills. The little village gained recognition in 1819 when Doctor Morrison, a physician from Aberdeen, bathed in its sulphur springs and cured himself of rheumatoid arthritis. He quickly spread the word and Strathpeffer became a fashionable spa resort attracting thousands of visitors. Two world wars intervened and the town's popularity declined. Today the only reminder of its past is the **Water Sampling Pavilion** in the square where you can test the waters. There's a seasonal **TIC** ① *main square, T01997-421415.*

Just outside Strathpeffer on the road to Dingwall is the **Highland Museum of Childhood** ① *T01997-421031, Mar-Oct Mon-Sat 1000-1700, Sun 1400-1700, Jul-Aug Mon-Fri 1000-1900, Sat 1000-1700, Sun 1400-1700, £2.50, concessions £2, children £1.50, family £6*, which has historical displays on childhood in the Highlands, as well as collections of dolls, toys and games.

A fine walk is to **Knock Farrel** and the **Touchstone Maze**, site of an Iron Age vitrified fort which lies at the north end of a ridge known locally as the **Cat's Back**. A marked trail starts from Blackmuir Wood car park. Head up the hill from town, turn left up a road immediately before the youth hostel, and the car park is on the left. The walk is 6 miles in total and takes about three hours. Aside from OS Landranger sheet 26, the route is also described in a Forestry Commission leaflet *Forests of Easter Ross*, available from tourist offices.

Another excellent side trip is to **Rogie Falls**, near Contin, which is 3 miles southwest of Strathpeffer on the main A835 Inverness to Ullapool road. The short walk up to the falls starts from the car park 3 miles north of Contin on the A835. There are also some pleasant woodland walks around here. Experienced hikers can tackle magnificent **Ben Wyvis** (3432 ft). The route to the summit starts 4 miles north of Garve, 7 miles northwest of Contin.

Tain and around → *For listings, see pages 143-147.*

Squeezed between the Cromarty Firth to the south and the Dornoch Firth to the north is the Tain Peninsula, whose largest town is Tain, a place with a 1950s time-warp feel. It has an impressive historical portfolio: its backstreets are an intriguing jigsaw of imposing merchants' houses, steep vennels, secret gardens and dormer windows. The town serves a vast hinterland. Among the hills are little-visited backwoods and farm towns, narrow valleys lined with crofts where cattle graze in boggy haughs and, to the west, glens and moorland. Along the seaboard are the windswept fields of the Tarbat Peninsula. Good sea angling is to be had from the harbours of the otherwise dull coastal villages such as Balintore, and at Shandwick is a massive Pictish stone. It is said that unbaptized children were buried near the stone which is now in the Museum of Scotland in Edinburgh.

Tain

The **Collegiate church** is on Castle Brae, just off the High Street, and inside is a 17th-century panel painted with the badges of the trade guilds, a reminder of the town's busy international trade. Another reminder is the imposing 16th-century **Tolbooth** in the High Street. Next to the church is **Tain through Time** ① *T01862-894089, www.tainmuseum. org.uk, Apr-Oct Mon-Sat 1000-1700, £3.50, children over 6 and concessions £2.50, family (up to 2 adults and 4 children) £10*, a museum housed in the Pilgrimage which charts the town's medieval history. One of Tain's main attractions, just off the A9 to the north of town, is the very fine **Glenmorangie whisky distillery** ① *T01862-892477, www.glenmorangie.com, Mon-Fri 0900-1700, Jun-Aug Sat 1000-1600, Sun 1200-1600, tours (45 mins) from 1030-1530, approx £2.50*, where you can see how the world-famous whisky is made and try a sample. Famous for its various wood finishes, Glenmorangie remains Scotland's best-selling single malt whisky. You can now stay here, in some considerable style and comfort, at **Glenmorangie House** (see Where to stay, page 143).

Just to the south of town, off the A9, is the **Aldie Water Mill**, a restored 16th-century mill in working order, with various high-quality craft shops attached. Nearby is the **Tain Pottery** ① *T01862-894112, www.tainpottery.co.uk, Apr-Oct Mon-Fri 0900-1800, Sat-Sun 1000-1700, Nov-Mar Mon-Sat 0900-1730*, which you can also visit.

Portnahomack

The seaside village of Portnahomack, or 'port of Colman', is named after the missionary who was keen as mustard to found a religious settlement here. Archaeological work is revealing the importance of this area in Pictish times. The **Tarbat Discovery Centre** ① *T01862-871351, www.tarbat-discovery.co.uk, Easter-Apr and Oct daily 1400-1700, May-Sep daily 1000-1700, £3.50, under 12s free, concession £2*, in Tarbat Old Church, displays recently discovered Pictish stonecarving. From the harbour, with its 18th-century girnals (grain warehouses) and sheltered sandy beach, you can see a huge stretch of the Sutherland coast, and the great sandbanks – the 'gizzen brigs' – at the mouth of the Dornoch Firth. Boat trips are available from the harbour for sea angling. A worthwhile trip is out to Tarbat Ness lighthouse, about 3 miles north.

Hill of Fearn

South from Portnahomack, just west of the junction of the B9165 and the B9166, is Hill of Fearn. Fearn Abbey was moved here around 1250 from its original site near Edderton, where it was too vulnerable to sea raiders. It later became the parish church, but one Sunday in 1742 lightning struck the roof which fell in, killing 38 worshippers. This tragedy was preceded by a fairy harbinger sighted at nearby Loch Eye. In Hill of Fearn is the excellent **Anta Factory Shop** ① *www.anta.co.uk, Mon-Sat 0930-1730, Sun 1000-1700*, one of the very best places in the country for classy tartan furnishing fabrics, as well as tartan rugs and throws, and pottery.

The Dornoch Firth → *For listings, see pages 143-147.*

Fairies were said to cross the Dornoch Firth on cockle shells and were once seen building a bridge of fairy gold, perhaps a forerunner of the Dornoch Bridge which carries the A9 across the firth just north of Tain. A more pleasant and interesting route is to follow the A836 along the south shore. From The Struie, reached by the B9176 which branches south at Easter Fearn, there's a panoramic view over the Dornoch Firth and the Sutherland hills.

Edderton to the Kyle of Sutherland
In the churches of Edderton and Kincardine are Pictish stones. Another stands in a field northwest of Edderton (but don't disturb the crops or livestock). A quartz boulder at **Ardgay**, the 'Clach Eiteag', commemorates the cattle tryst and fair which once took place locally.

Ten miles from Ardgay, at the end of lovely Strathcarron, is the isolated **Croick church**, one of the most poignant reminders of the infamous Clearances. Here, in 1845, 90 local folk took refuge in the churchyard after they had been evicted from their homes in Glencalvie by the despicable Duke of Sutherland to make way for his sheep flocks. A reporter from *The Times* was there to describe this "wretched spectacle", as men, women and children were carted off, many never to return. His report is there to read, but far more evocative and harrowing are the names and messages the people scratched in spidery copperplate in the window panes.

North of Ardgay is the **Kyle of Sutherland**, where several rivers converge to flood into the sea through lush water meadows. Montrose was defeated here, at Carbisdale, in 1651. Overlooking the Kyle, at **Culrain**, is the 19th-century **Carbisdale Castle**, once home of the exiled King of Norway. It now houses a youth hostel, see Where to stay, page 144. After the Dornoch Ferry disaster of 1809, a bridge was built over the Kyle at **Bonar Bridge**, from where the A949 runs eastwards to join the main A9 just before Dornoch, while the A836 continues north to Lairg (see below). A few miles north of Invershin are the **Falls of Shin**, an excellent place to watch salmon battling upstream on their way to their spawning grounds (best seen June to September). The visitor centre has information about six easy walks in the immediate area; all are under an hour long. It also boasts an excellent café/shop (see Restaurants, page 145) and a shop described as 'Harrods of the north' (Mohammed Al Fayed's estate is close by, which explains the goods on offer).

Lairg → *Phone code 01549.*
Eleven miles north of Bonar Bridge is the uninspiring village of Lairg, the region's main transport hub. Lairg is best known for its annual lamb sale, when young sheep from all over the north of Scotland are bought and sold. It is said that all roads meet at Lairg, and it's certainly a hard place to avoid. From here, the A839 heads east to meet the A9 between Dornoch and Golspie, and west to meet the A837 which runs out to Lochinver. The A836 heads north to Tongue, and south to Bonar Bridge. The A838 meanwhile heads northwest to Laxford Bridge and on to Durness, near Cape Wrath. There's a TIC ① *T01549-402160, Apr-Oct daily.*

There are several interesting walks around the village, some of which lead to prehistoric sites, such as the Neolithic hut circles at nearby **Ord Hill**. These walks, and many others in the region, are described with maps in the Forestry Commission's leaflet *Forests of the Far North*, which is available at the Ferrycroft Countryside Centre and the TIC.

Dornoch and around → *Phone code 01862.*
Dornoch is another architectural delight, with its deep, golden sandstone houses and leafy cathedral square. Bishop Gilbert of Moravia (Moray) built the cathedral circa 1245.

His family's success in gaining a foothold in northeast Scotland against the Norsemen was rewarded with the Earldom of Sutherland. It was trouble with the Jarls which prompted Gilbert to move his power base here from Caithness, mindful that his predecessor had been boiled in butter by the locals (proof that too much of the stuff can kill you). The TIC ① T08452-255121, Oct-May Mon-Fri 0900-1700, Jun and Sep Sat 1000-1600, Jul-Aug Mon-Fri 0900-1700, Sat 1000-1600, Sun 1000-1600, is on Castle Street.

The 13th-century **cathedral** ① Mon-Fri 0730-2000, has volunteers welcoming visitors to the cathedral from 1000-1600 from mid-May to mid-Sep, was badly damaged in 1570, then subjected to an ill-conceived 'restoration' by the Countess of Sutherland in 1835. Among the few surviving features is a series of gargoyles, including a green man, and the effigy of an unknown knight. Opposite the cathedral is the 16th-century Bishop's Palace, now a hotel, see Where to stay, page 144.

Nowadays Dornoch is famous for its links golf course, one of the world's finest and relatively easy to get on. It overlooks miles of dunes and a pristine sandy beach. A stone near the links marks the spot where the last witch in Scotland was burned, in 1722. Folklore recounts a bloody battle against raiding Vikings in 1259 on the beach at Embo, just to the north, in which Sir Richard Murray was killed. The battle is commemorated at the Earl's Cross. Trout fishing is available on Dornoch Lochans; enquire locally.

Straggling crofting townships such as **Rogart** are scattered through the glens and around the coast, all occupied and worked vigorously. The coastal population was swollen in the 19th century by tenants evicted from the inland glens; they were resettled here and encouraged to try fishing at such villages as Embo. Others joined the eager flood of emigrants to the New World already under way. Crofting tenancies still exist, but crofters now enjoy more protection.

North of Dornoch is **Loch Fleet**, a river estuary with a ferocious tidal race at its mouth and an SNH reserve protecting rare birds and plants. The rotting skeletons of the fishing fleet abandoned in the First World War lie in the sand on the south shore west of the car park. Nearby is **Skibo Castle**, where the couple formerly known as "Mr and Mrs Madonna" tied the knot, in relative secrecy. It is home to the very, very exclusive **Carnegie Club** ① www.carnegieclub.co.uk, for envious voyeurs or those with too much money. There are several walks in the forestry plantations in the area.

Far northeast coast → For listings, see pages 143-147.

North of Dornoch, the A9 follows the coast of Sutherland into the neighbouring county of Caithness through a series of straggling villages, still haunted by the memories of the Duke of Sutherland, one of Scotland's most odious landowners. The chief town in these parts is Wick, once the busiest herring port in Europe.

Arriving in the far northeast coast
Getting there and around A few miles north of Wick, is the airport. There are direct flights here from Kirkwall (Orkney), Sumburgh (Shetland) and Aberdeen, Stornoway, Durham, Bristol, Newcastle, Edinburgh and Southampton. For the most up to date information on the taxi, car hire and bus service options available to you on arrival at Wick airport, it's recommended to contact airport information on T01955-602215. The train and bus stations are next to each other behind the hospital. If you don't fancy flying, don't forget there are regular trains from London to Inverness, with **ScotRail** ① T0845-601 5929, www.firstgroup.com/scotrail, trains travelling north to Thurso and Wick.

The light fantastic

Due to the absence of light pollution, Scotland offers some of the best areas of inky dark sky in Europe. Visit www.dark skyscotland.org.uk. A feature of visiting the far north of Scotland in winter is the chance of seeing the Aurora Borealis, or Northern Lights, which decorate the night skies like a gigantic laser show. The best time to see them is between October and March – especially during December and January. Try to get as far north as you can, though there are no guarantees of a sighting as cloud cover can obscure visibility. Any of the north-facing coastal villages are a good bet.

Golspie → *Phone code 01408. Population 1650.*

The picturesque little village of Golspie (around 1800 inhabitants) offers more than just a couple of banks and a supermarket. For half a mile from here are the **Highland Wildcat Trails** ① *www.highlandwildcat.com*, Scotland's most northerly purpose built mountain bike tracks with over 20 miles of trail to suit every level of rider. What's more, after you've hired a bike at Square Wheels in Strathpeffer the forested trails are free to explore.

In Golspie there's also an 18-hole golf course, and the **Orcadian Stone Company** has a large display of fossils and geological specimens from the Highlands and beyond. The town lives in the dark shadow of the Sutherlands: on **Beinn a'Bhraggaidh** (1293 ft), to the southwest, is a huge, 100 ft-high monument to the Duke of Sutherland. Those who make it up to the monument and who know something of the Duke's many despicable acts may find the inscription risible, as it describes him as "a judicious, kind and liberal landlord". There's no reference to the fact that he forcibly evicted 15,000 tenants from his estate. Not surprisingly, locals would like to see this eyesore removed from the landscape, broken into tiny pieces and then scattered far and wide. Unfortunately, and most surprisingly, they have thus far been unsuccessful.

A mile north of the village is the grotesque form of **Dunrobin Castle** ① *T01408-633177, Mar-May, Sep-Oct Mon-Sat 1030-1630, Sun 1200-1630, Jun-Aug Mon-Sat 1030-1730, Sun 1200-1730, £8.50, concessions £7, children £5.* This is the ancient seat of the Dukes of Sutherland, who once owned more land than anyone else in the British Empire. Much enlarged and aggrandized in the 19th century, with fairytale turrets, the enormous 189-room castle, the largest house in the Highlands, is stuffed full of fine furniture, paintings, tapestries and objets d'art. The whole unedifying spectacle is a legacy to obscene wealth and unimaginable greed, on a par with Nicolae Ceausescu's palace in Bucharest. The hideous confection overlooks admittedly beautiful gardens laid out with box hedges, ornamental trees and fountains. The museum is an animal-lover's nightmare and almost a caricature of the aristocracy, with a spectacular Victorian taxidermy collection. There are also local antiquities, some from ancient brochs, and Pictish stonecarvings.

Brora → *Phone code 01408. Population 1860.*

Brora sits at the mouth of the River Brora which, as everywhere on this coast, is the site of a once-lucrative salmon netting industry. At the harbour, the ice house is a relic of the herring boom. Coal mines, opened in the 16th century, salt pans and a brickworks are all defunct. Still very much alive, however, is **Hunter's**, the local weavers of heavyweight traditional tweeds, and a good place to invest in some natty headwear. A mile or so north of town is the interesting **Clynelish distillery** ① *T01408-623000, www.malts.com, Easter-Sep Mon-Fri*

1000-1700, Oct Mon-Fri 1000-1600, Nov-Easter by appointment only. Tour £5. Something of a cult amongst whisky lovers, this malt is distinctive for its briny flavour. **Castle Cole** in lovely Strath Brora, 8 miles northwest, is one of several ruined brochs. Another, **Carn Liath** (signposted), is by the main road, 3 miles south of Brora.

Helmsdale → *Phone code 01431.*

North of Brora is the former herring port of Helmsdale, which gets busy in the summer. The village is most notable for its excellent **Timespan Heritage Centre** ① *T01431-821327, Easter-Oct Mon-Sat 1000-1700, Sun 1200-1700, £4, concessions £3, children £2, Family £10,* which brings the history of the Highlands to life through a series of high-tech displays, sound effects and an audio-visual programme. There's also a café and shop on site. The **TIC** ① *T01431-821402, www.helmsdale.org*, is situated within Strath Ullie Crafts on the harbour next to the river side car park.

North from Helmsdale the A9 climbs spectacularly up the **Ord of Caithness** and over the pass enters a desolate, treeless landscape; an area devastated during the Clearances. To get some idea of the hardships people had to endure, stop at the ruined crofting village of **Badbea**, just beyond Ousdale. At **Berriedale**, a farm track leads west to the Wag, from where you can climb **Morven** (2313 ft), the highest hill in Caithness, with amazing views across the whole county.

Dunbeath → *Phone code 01593.*

The A9 coast road then drops down into Dunbeath, a pleasant little village at the mouth of a small *strath* (or glen). This was the birthplace of one of Scotland's foremost writers, Neil Gunn (1891-1973). His finest works, such as *The Silver Darlings* and *Highland River*, reflect his experiences of growing up in the northeast and are fascinating accounts of life here during the days of the herring boom, though the sleepy harbour of today is barely recognizable as the erstwhile bustling fishing port. The villages of Dunbeath, and Latheron to the north, are included on the **Neil Gunn Trail**, as is the beautiful walk up the glen, described in the leaflet available at the **Dunbeath Heritage Centre** ① *T01593-731233, www.dunbeath-heritage.org. uk, Easter-Oct daily 1000-1700, other times by arrangement, £2, concessions £1, children free.* Here, in Neil Gunn's former school, you can learn all about the life and works of the famous novelist as well as the history of Caithness. Just outside the village is the **Laidhay Croft Museum** ① *T01593-731244, Easter-Oct daily 1000-1700, £2, children 50p*, a restored traditional longhouse with stable, house and byre all under the same roof. It also has a tea room.

Wick and around → *Phone code 01955.*

A century ago Wick was Europe's busiest herring port, its harbour jam-packed with fishing boats and larger ships exporting tons of salted fish to Russia, Scandinavia and the West Indian slave plantations. The fishing industry has long since gone, and the demise of the nearby nuclear power station at Douneray has only added to the tangible sense of ennui. There are, however, some interesting archaeological sites in Caithness, as well as the dramatic landscapes, and Wick makes a useful base for exploring the area. There is a TIC ① *T01955-602547, Sep-Jul Mon-Sat 0900-1730, Aug Mon-Sat 0900-1730, Sun 1100-1600*, in McAllans menswear shop on the High Street.

Wick is actually two towns. On one side of the river is Wick proper and on the other is Pulteneytown, the model town planned by Thomas Telford for the British Fisheries Society in 1806 to house evicted crofters who came to work here. Now it's one great living museum of fishermen's cottages and derelict sheds and stores around the near-

After the goldrush

A short drive from Helmsdale, up the Strath of Kildonan (or Strath Ullie), is Baile an Or (Gaelic for 'goldfield'), site of the great Sutherland Gold Rush of 1869. It all started after local man Robert Gilchrist returned home from the Australian gold fields only to discover gold here, on his doorstep. His success brought others rushing to Kildonan, and soon a shanty town had sprung up to accommodate them.

Within a year the gold rush was over, but small amounts are still found today. Anyone who fancies their luck can try a bit of gold panning in the Kildonan Burn at Baile an Or, about a mile from Kildonan train station. You can rent out gold panning kits at Strath Ullie Crafts & Fishing Tackle, opposite the Timespan Heritage Centre in Helmsdale, for £2.50 per day, and licences are free.

deserted quays. It gives a good idea of the scale of the herring trade during its heyday in the mid-19th century, when over 1000 boats set sail to catch the 'silver darlings'. Here, on Bank Row, is the superb **Wick Heritage Centre** ① *T01955-605393, www.wickheritage.org, Easter-Oct Mon-Sat 1000-1545, £3, children 50p*. The highlight of the centre is its massive photographic collection dating from the late 19th century.

Three miles north of Wick are the impressive 15th-century clifftop ruins of **Sinclair and Girnigoe Castle**. There is a good walk along the rocky shore east of town to The Trinkie, a natural rock pool fed by the sea, and about a mile further on to the Brig o' Trams. Ask for details at the TIC. Before Wick, at Ulbster, is another archaeological site, the **Cairn o' Get**. Opposite the sign are the precipitous **Whaligoe Steps**, which lead to a picturesque harbour.

Archaeological sites around Caithness

Caithness may lack the impressive henges of other parts of the UK but it does boast a number of stone rows: areas covered by large numbers of small stones arranged in geometric patterns. These are thought to date from circa 2000 BC. The best and most easily accessible is the **Hill o' Many Stanes**. To get there, drive 9 miles south of Wick. On the A9 and turn right onto a minor road where you see the signpost. A short way up this road is a signposted gate into the field, on the left-hand side. A path leads to the curious fan-shaped configuration of Bronze Age standing stones; 200 of them in 22 rows. No one yet knows their precise purpose but studies have shown that there were once 600 stones here.

There are also a couple of Pictish Brochs in Caithness. These were almost entirely unique to the north and northwest of Scotland and were windowless, dry-stone towers, between 10 and 45 ft in height, with a circular ground plan. The walls were hollow in places to allow staircases and small chambers. These were built between 2000 BC and AD 200, though they continued in use after that time, and were used for both domestic and defensive purposes. There are remains of a broch at **Nybster**, 7 miles south of John o'Groats on the A9. Look out for the sign for the harbour and broch on the right heading north. Turn onto the minor road which leads down to a small car park. Follow the path along the clifftop to the broch, which stands on a headland surrounded by steep cliffs on three sides. Just to the south of here, at Keiss, are the remains of another broch.

One of the most interesting archaeological sites in the north are the well-preserved **Grey Cairns of Camster**. These chambered cairns, dating from the third and fourth millenia BC, are burial mounds of stone raised around carefully structured circular chambers with narrow entrance passages. To get there, head a mile east of Lybster on the A9, then turn left on to the minor road leading north to Watten. The cairns are 5 miles along this road, on the left-hand side. They comprise two enormous prehistoric burial chambers dating from 2500 BC. They are amazingly complete, with corbelled ceilings, and can be entered on hands and knees through narrow passageways.

East coast listings

For hotel and restaurant price codes and other relevant information, see pages 13-20.

🛏 Where to stay

Cromarty *p135*
For such an appealing place, there's precious little accommodation, so it's advisable to book ahead during the summer months.
££ Royal Hotel, Marine Terr, T01381-600 217, www.royalcromartyhotel.co.uk. Open all year. 10 rooms. The best place to stay, with a good restaurant (**£££-££**), and cheaper meals available in the bar.
££-£ Braelangwell House, Balblair, T01381-610353, www.btinternet.com/braelangwell. Mar-Sep. 3 rooms. Superior standard of B&B in elegant Georgian house. Recommended.

Dingwall and around *p135*
£££ The Dower House, 2 miles north of Muir of Ord on A862 to Dingwall, T01463-870090, www.thedowerhouse.co.uk. Open all year. 3 en suite double rooms and 1 suite. Very comfortable small hotel set in 5 acres of woodland and gardens, excellent food (dinner **££**). Worth the money. It won the Good Hotel Guide 2008 Cesar Award. Recommended.
£££ Kinkell House Hotel, Easter Kinkell, Conan Bridge, by Dingwall, T01349-861270, www.kinkellhousehotel.com. 9 en suite rooms. Lovely country hotel in farmland. Style, comfort and attention to detail, as well as superb cooking.
£££ Tulloch Castle Hotel, Tulloch Castle Dr, T01349-861325, www.tullochcastle.co.uk. Open all year. 19 en suite rooms. This 12th-century castle is the smartest place around, 4-poster bed costs a bit more. No pets. Children under 3 free.

££ Fairfield House, Craig Rd, Dingwall, T01349-864754. Open all year. 4 en suite rooms. Better-than-average B&B.

Strathpeffer and around *p136*
£££-££ Coull House Hotel, Contin, 3 miles southwest of Strathpeffer, T01997-421487, www.coulhousehotel.com. Open all year. 20 rooms. Top of the list is this elegant 19th-century country house offering fine food. Excellent choice.
££-£ White Lodge, the Square, T01997-421730, www.the-white-lodge.co.uk. Open all year. 2 en suite rooms. Another very good B&B. Self-catering cottage available.
£ Brunstane Lodge Hotel, Golf Course Rd, T01997-421261, www.brunstanelodge.com. Open all year. 6 en suite rooms. Good little hotel serving decent cheap bar meals.
£ Craigvar, the Square, Strathpeffer, T01997-421622, www.craigvar.com. Open all year. 3 en suite rooms. Elegant Georgian house offering considerable style and comfort at this price, one of the best B&Bs in the region. Recommended.

Tain *p137*
££££-£££ Glenmorangie House at Cadboll, Fearn, by Tain, T01862-871671, www.theglenmorangiehouse.com. 6 en suite rooms. Owned by the whisky people, this place oozes style. Accommodation in the main house is supplemented by 3 cottages which sleep a total of 6. Price includes a lavish 5-course dinner and afternoon tea as well as breakfast. Recommended.
£££ Morangie House Hotel, Morangie Rd, T01862-892281, www.morangiehotel.com. 26 rooms. Now part of the Swallow chain, this Victorian hotel still serves excellent food in its restaurant. Very good value.

£££-££ Mansfield House Hotel, Scotsburn Rd, T01862-892052. 19th-century baronial splendour and superb cuisine. Restaurant also open to non-residents (**£££**). Highly recommended.
£ Golf View House, 13 Knockbreck Rd, T01862-892856, www.golf-view.co.uk. Open Feb-Nov. 3 en suite rooms and 1 suite. Substantial house offering very fine B&B.

Lairg p138
££ Highland House, 88 Station Rd, T01549-402414, www.lairghighlandhouse.co.uk. Open all year. 3 en suite rooms. Good B&B.
£ Lairg Highland Hotel, Main St, T01549-402243, www.highland-hotel.co.uk. Open all year. 6 en suite rooms. Decent value, also does bar meals.
£ Sleeperzzz.com, Rogart Station, Rogart, T01408-641343, www.sleeperzzz.com. The most interesting place to stay, where you can get cheap hostel accommodation in the 3 old rail carriages that have been converted to sleep 20 people. There's a 10% discount for bike or train users and children under 12 receive a 25% discount.

Edderton to the Kyle of Sutherland p138
£ Carbisdale Castle Youth Hostel, Culrain, T08700-0041109, www.carbisdale.org. Mar-Oct (except the 1st 2 weeks in May). The largest and most sumptuous hostel in Scotland, and possibly anywhere else, is 0.5 miles up a steep hill from the station. Staying here is an amazing experience and will charm any frustrated would-be aristocrat. Available Nov-Feb for exclusive hire.

Dornoch and around p138
There are lots of good B&Bs.
£££ 2 Quail Restaurant and Rooms, Castle St, T01862-811811, www.2quail.com. Open Apr-Oct Tue-Sat for dinner, Nov-Mar Fri-Sat only. 3 rooms above 1 of the very best (and smallest) restaurants in the region, run by Michael and Kerensa Carr. Rooms are not huge but the magnificent set 3-course

menu using Scottish produce (**£££**) more than compensates. Highly recommended.
£££-££ Dornoch Castle Hotel, Castle St, T01862-810216, www.dornochcastlehotel. com. Open Apr-Oct. Formerly the Bishop's Palace, this 16th-century building is full of character and boasts excellent food (**£££**). Good special offers.
££ Auchlea Guest House, Auchlea, T01862-811524, www.auchlea.co.uk. Open all year. 3 en suite rooms in a modern bungalow run by Mrs Garvie. Serves a full, traditional Scottish breakfast with porridge.

Camping
Dornoch Caravan Park, by the golf course and the beach, T01862-810423.

Brora p140
£££ Royal Marine Hotel, Golf Rd, T01408-621252, www.royalmarinebrora.com. Open all year. Early 20th-century country house designed by Robert Lorimer, this fine golf hotel boasts an indoor pool, spa and gym. Has an excellent reputation for its food.
£ Glenaveron, Golf Rd, T01408-621601, www. glenaveron.co.uk. 3 en suite rooms. Among the many B&Bs here, this is an excellent choice and good value. Under 6s free.

Helmsdale p141
££ Navidale House Hotel, Navidale, T01431-821258. Open Feb-Nov. 10 rooms. Most upmarket choice, a good place to eat.
£ Broomhill House, T01431-821259, www.blancebroomhill.com. Open all year. 2 en suite rooms. Good-value B&B with a distinctive turret, run by Sylvia Blance. Evening meals served on request.
£ SYHA Youth Hostel, Stafford St, T01431-821636. Offers 24 beds, some private rooms.
£ Torbuie, Navidale, T01431-821424. Open Apr-Oct. Good value B&B. En suite rooms with sea views.

Wick and around p141
££ The Clachan, 13 Randolph Pl, South Rd, TT01955-605384, www.theclachan.co.uk.

Open all year. 3 en suite rooms. Best B&B in town in our opinion.
££ Portland Arms Hotel, 15 miles south, Lybster, T01593-721721, www.portlandarms. co.uk. Open all year. 22 rooms. Best around, a 19th-century coaching inn, full of character serving great food in both formal and informal settings (**£££-££**).
££-£ Wellington Guest House, 41-43 High St, T01955-603287. Open Mar-Oct. Worthwhile choice if **The Clachan** is full.

❼ Restaurants

Cromarty *p135*
££ Cromarty Arms, opposite Cromarty Courthouse, T01381 600230. Cheap home-made bar food. Also has live music some nights.
££ Sutor Creek, 21 Bank St, T01381-600855, www.sutorcreek.co.uk. Wed-Sun 1100-2100. Cooperative café/restaurant that's famous for its superb wood-fired pizzas, but also other dishes using local ingredients in season. Recommended.
££ Thistle's Restaurant, Church St, T01381-600471. Has an imaginative menu, including interesting vegetarian dishes.
£ Binnie's Tearoom, Church St. A great place for tea and scones.

Portnahomack *p137*
£££-££ The Oyster Catcher, Main St, T01862-871560, www.the-oystercatcher. co.uk. Open Mar-Oct Wed-Sun. A great place to eat out here is this small café/restaurant serving a wide variety of snacks and lunches, and dinner from 1930 (if booked). Crêpes are a speciality, but it also does pasta, soups, seafood and fish.

Edderton to the Kyle of Sutherland *p138*
££-£ Falls of Shin Restaurant, Achany Glen, by Lairg, T01549-402231. Open Jun-Sep from 0930, Oct-May from 1000. A gastronomic oasis housed in the most unlikely of places. Simple food cooked to

perfection, probably better than your mum makes. Good value.

Brora *p140*
£££-££ Il Padrino, Station Sq, T01408-622011. Tue-Sun for lunch and dinner (open from 1100 for coffee, from 1200 for meals). Good italian food, if a bit pricey.

Helmsdale *p141*
££ La Mirage, Dunrobin St, opposite the TIC, T0143-821 615, www.lamirage.org. Daily 1100-2100. Famous tea room whose erstwhile proprietress, the inimitable Nancy Sinclair, modelled herself, and her tea room, on Barbara Cartland, queen of romantic novels. The whole effect is pure kitsch. Good food though, especially the fish and chips.

Wick and around *p141*
The best places to eat are out of town at the **Portland Arms Hotel** (see Where to stay, above) and the **Bower Inn**, see page 132.
££ Bord de L'Eau, Market St, T01955-604400. Open Tue-Sat for lunch and dinner. French bistro-style cooking. Very popular with locals.
££ Queen's Hotel, Francis St, T01955-602992. Probably the next best place in town.
£ Cabrelli's, 134 High St. Great café serving large portions of carbs to locals.

❽ Shopping

Tain *p137*
Bannerman Seafoods, The Burgage, T01862-892322, www.bannerman-seafoods. co.uk. A fish and seafood wholesalers, sells local mussels.
Brown's Gallery, Castle Brae, www.browns art.com. Showcases work by Highland artists.

Dornoch and around *p138*
The Dornoch Bookshop, High St, T01862-810165. The only bookshop in the area and stocks local books.

⚙ What to do

Cromarty p135
Boat trips
Dolphin-spotting boat trips leave from Cromarty, but go with an accredited operator. **EcoVentures**, Harbour Workshop, Victoria Pl, T01381-600323, www.ecoventures.co.uk. ½-day and full-day trips leave from the harbour to see porpoises, seals, dolphins, and perhaps even killer whales further out. Accredited operator.

Mountain biking
The challenging tracks of Learnie Red RockTrails are just 3 miles from Rosemarkie village. See also www.HiMBA.org.uk and www.forestry.gov.uk/mtbscotland.

⊖ Transport

Cromarty p135
Bus Highland Bus & Coach, T01463-233371, runs a service to **Inverness** from **Fortrose** and **Cromarty**, up to 12 times daily Mon-Sat, once on Sun. There is also a once daily Mon and Fri service from **Dingwall**.

Dingwall and around p135
Bus There are hourly buses between **Inverness** and **Invergordon**, via Dingwall. There are also hourly buses between **Inverness** and Dingwall via **Muir of Ord**. There are buses between Dingwall and **Rosemarkie**, Mon and Fri, and between Dingwall and **Cromarty**, Mon and Fri.

Train Dingwall is on the rail line between **Inverness** and **Kyle of Lochalsh** and **Thurso**. There are several trains daily in each direction, 30 mins to Inverness.

Strathpeffer and around p136
Bus There are regular buses between Strathpeffer and **Dingwall**.

Cycle hire **Square Wheels**, the Square, T01997-421000. The place to buy or hire

your mountain bike kit (from £15) for a fantastic day in the hills.

Tain p137
Bus Citylink buses between **Inverness** and **Thurso** pass through Tain Mon-Fri. There are also buses to **Portmahomack**, Mon-Fri; **Balintore**, Mon-Sat; **Lairg** via **Bonar Bridge**, Mon-Sat; and **Dornoch** via **Bonar Bridge**, once a day Mon-Thu with Inverness Traction, T01463-239292, and Rapson's of Brora, T01408-621245.

Train Tain is on the **Inverness** to **Thurso** rail line. There are 3 trains daily in each direction.

Lairg p138
Bus Inverness Traction buses, T01463-239292, run from here to **Ullapool**, with connections to **Lochinver** and **Durness**, from May to early Oct, Mon-Sat. Lairg is also the central point for several **postbus** routes, T01463-256228.

Train Trains between **Inverness** and **Thurso** stop at Lairg and Rogart stations 3 times daily.

Dornoch and around p138
Bus Hourly buses run daily between **Inverness** and **Lairg** stop in **Ardgay** and **Bonar Bridge**. Citylink buses between **Inverness** and **Thurso** also stop in Dornoch up to 8 times daily.

Train Services between **Inverness** and **Thurso** stop at **Ardgay** and **Culrain**.

Helmsdale p141
Bus and train Buses and trains are the same as for Wick (see below). Helmsdale is on the **Inverness** to **Wick/Thurso** rail line.

Wick and around p141
Air Direct flights to **Kirkwall** (Orkney), **Sumburgh** (Shetland) and Mon-Fri to **Aberdeen, Stornoway, Durham, Bristol**

and **Newcastle** with Eastern Airways, T01652-680600. Destinations with **Flybe**, T0871-700 0535, www.flybe.com, include **Edinburgh** and **Southampton**.

Bus Scottish Citylink, T08705-505050, buses between **Inverness** and **Thurso** stop en route in **Wick** (3 daily). There are also regular local buses to **Thurso**, via **Halkirk** or **Castletown**, and buses to **Helmsdale**, daily, and **John o'Groats**, Mon-Sat.

Car and cycle hire Richard's Garage, Francis St, T01955-604123.

Train Trains leave for **Inverness**, daily, 4 hrs, via **Thurso**, **Helmsdale**, **Golspie**, **Lairg** and **Dingwall**.

Contents

Footnotes

Index